LC

S

S

PADEREWSKI

As I Knew Him

PADEREWSKI

AS I KNEW HIM

From the Diary of

ANIELA STRAKACZ

TRANSLATED FROM THE POLISH BY

Halina Chybowska

New Brunswick

RUTGERS UNIVERSITY PRESS

1949

TO A GREAT AMERICAN
AND A LIFELONG FRIEND OF PADEREWSKI

Colonel Rupert Hughes

IN GRATEFUL ACKNOWLEDGMENT OF
THE INVALUABLE HELP HE RENDERED
IN PAYING THIS HUMBLE TRIBUTE
OF ADMIRATION AND LOVE

CONTENTS

Foreword

When, as a young girl in 1917, I resolved to keep a diary, I never thought that it might eventually appear in book form. My diary has no literary pretensions. It is merely a chronicle of events and personal experiences, the significance of which—especially in the first phase—I did not always appreciate.

When I thumb through these yellowed pages of twenty-five years ago, I often smile at the naïveté of certain remarks but more often regret the futility of once-expressed hopes.

However, I have decided to make no major changes nor any additions, because the sole value of my diary lies in its spontaneity and authenticity.

Against the background of the global convulsions of the first half of the twentieth century, and particularly against the background of the uncompromising fight of the Polish nation for its freedom and independence, the life and deeds of Ignacy Jan Paderewski, his thoughts and aspirations, radiate the highest virtues of the man, the citizen, and the patriot. Some day a biographer will utilize the wealth of documentary material to present a comprehensive study of that great figure who, during his lifetime, won the appellation of a "modern immortal." The future historian will record the great influence which Paderewski exercised over his contemporaries as a great artist endowed with the divine spark, who by his art swept millions to the heights of beauty and idealism.

To forestall any possible misunderstanding, I wish to state that my diary does not aspire to fulfill this task. On the contrary, it relates only my personal experiences and the observations I made as the wife of Paderewski's private secretary during the last twenty-three years of his life, and therefore it may serve as a source of firsthand information for some future historian.

I must also make clear that the diary omits many facts and events extremely important and essential for recreating the full personality of Paderewski, simply because I spent only certain periods of each year with him and his family. I am well aware that I did not have the opportunity to meet all of the legion of Paderewski's friends—outstanding national and social leaders—who were drawn into the vortex of his rich life. This is particularly true of numerous Americans of Polish extraction who, having done so much to further the Polish cause, had a special place in Paderewski's affections and were the recipients of his lifelong gratitude.

With these few explanatory notes, I place my diary in the hands of the unprejudiced reader. It was written with deepest respect and love for a man to whom Poland owes much, who lived and died with the thought of his people uppermost in his mind; who entered his country's service undeterred by difficulties or opposition, and even malice, prejudice, and slanderous attacks; who had unswerving faith in the spiritual values of the nation from which he stemmed and from which he drew the strength to fight for her rights, thus becoming to the whole world the living symbol of his heroic land.

Today, when Poland is again under the yoke of foreign domination, and the Polish nation is engaged in the same struggle for freedom, Paderewski's immortal spirit lights the thorny way towards victory.

Let me conclude with Paderewski's own words, spoken in Paris in January 1940 at the inaugural session of the Polish National Council:

"Although we are few in number, although all the provinces of the Republic do not as yet have their representatives among us, we solemnly vow to speak for the whole Nation, for all its strata and all its segments.

"The tragic moments which Poland is experiencing place before us the single solitary aim of all our endeavors—ultimate victory and the liberation of our country from its enemies. This aim will be our constant beacon light, overshadowing, as it does, everything else.

"We are not fighting for a gentry's, a people's, or a workers' Poland. We are not fighting for a Poland of the peasants, for a capitalist or a socialist Poland; we are fighting for an independent Poland, for a Poland that will be a Mother to her faithful children, for a Poland such as our bards have dreamed of and foretold, for a Poland of the Chrobrys and the Jagiellons of old, for a Poland that has been laved by the blood of the defenders of Warsaw, Westerplatte, Hel, Modlin and Lwow, for a Poland for which thousands of nameless heroes have given their lives, for which thousands of others are ready to die at any time!"

My grateful appreciation goes to dear Helena Liibke for letting me use a number of photographs from her collection, as well as to Mr. Stephen Pasternacki of Los Angeles, Calif., for his friendly gesture in preparing the prints for publication.

The signature *S. S.* in bracketed annotations refers to Sylwin Strakacz, my husband.

New York   ANIELA STRAKACZ
July 1, 1949

1

Poland

Close to the Heart of Poland

Warsaw, Square of the Three Crosses, No. 3 — April 9, 1917.
How strange everything was today! My cousin Myszka
came in from the country and I went to see her at Auntie
Ossolinska's. I had no sooner entered the foyer than Aunt
Ossolinska, seeing me, said to the lady who was standing
beside her in the doorway of the dining room: "This is
Aniela Karszo-Siedlewska." [The author's maiden name.]
I curtsied to the strange lady, who took one look at me
and said: "You will be close to the heart of Poland and the
man you are going to marry will be an ambassador. Not an
ordinary ambassador — he will be an ambassador of Polish
souls. You will spend your whole life traveling. You will
hardly ever unpack your trunks. . . ."

"She's the famous Mirta Noel," Myszka whispered to
me when we were in the dining room. The most famous
fortuneteller in Poland! The woman who had been disowned
by her socially prominent family because she took up such a
profession! I couldn't make any sense out of the other things
Myszka told me. It was all so sudden and unexpected that
I was taken aback. I didn't listen to Mirta Noel till she
finished because I was afraid I'd forget the beginning. It's
all so strange I must write these words down again: "You
will be close to the heart of Poland. . . ."

November 11, 1918. Our people are disarming Germans all
over Warsaw. Occasionally there are sounds of gunfire, but
nobody seems afraid to go out — there are greater crowds
than usual in the streets. Even little girls are doing their bit,
and I felt my honor depended upon disarming at least one
German. I was terrified by the boldness of my determination,
as I didn't have the slightest notion how to carry it out.

3

As I was coming home, I saw a German coming toward me. He was armed and in military garb. I was a little afraid at first and then asked him to hand over his spiked helmet. He meekly doffed his headgear and gave it to me. Your belt, please! Off comes the belt. Letting his hands fall to his sides, he stood there waiting. Glancing at his medals, I wanted to tell him to give them to me too, but suddenly I was overcome by a feeling of great shame—I still don't know whether I am ashamed of myself or that German.

All the way home, I saw our people, mostly girls and boys, stopping German soldiers and taking away their weapons and helmets. I was wondering how I could get more booty, because one helmet and one belt would hardly be enough to make a first-class impression at home. Just then a German appeared and, before I could open my mouth, he gave me his helmet, belt, and dagger. I took them all and hurried away. Identical scenes were repeated every few steps. There was no cab in sight and I hurried home with the load getting heavier at every minute.

Our butler, Andrzej, opened the door and when he saw how I was weighted down, he wanted to know what on earth I was bringing home and where was it supposed to be deposited.

"What do you mean," I said, "I'm not just bringing something in. I've been disarming Germans just like everyone else. . . . I can give the things to a museum."

Andrzej shrugged his shoulders. "Who would think of giving those German buckets with larding-pins to a museum? Throw them out instead of cluttering the house up with junk." I certainly will do no such thing. I'm going to save them as a souvenir of the day I disarmed Germans in the streets of Warsaw. But I don't think I want to do any more disarming, I've had my fill of it.

December 31, 1918. Warsaw is all excited. Paderewski is coming. The sole topic of conversation is where to station oneself to get the best view of Paderewski. Everybody is cudgeling his brain for names of friends who live in apartments on the streets where Paderewski is to pass on his way to the Bristol Hotel. I'm so glad Mrs. Zalewska invited me to her home. It'll be a wonderful vantage point, commanding a view of the ride from the station and of the procession up Aleje Jerozolimskie. How kind of her to invite me when her list of guests must be a foot long.

January 1, 1919. Although Paderewski was not due in Warsaw until the evening, Mrs. Zalewska's guests assembled in the morning. Knowing that practically everybody in Warsaw would turn out to welcome him, we were all afraid the crowds would be so dense we'd never be able to get through to our "reserved seats."

Our hostess was most charming. She shortened the period of waiting by serving us, invaders, with a buffet meal throughout the day. She certainly lived up to her reputation of treating her guests to the finest in homemade delicacies.

I was at the best window, but I was so crowded that I was in constant fear of falling over the low third-floor window sill into the street below. Never shall I forget the scene. What crowds! They looked like a gigantic black anthill, illumined by a forest of flaming torches. As far as the eye could reach, the windows fronting the thoroughfare were like pincushions dotted with human heads.

Suddenly a murmur rose from the crowd and grew into a crescendo of cries, "He's here!" The human anthill swayed, the torches flickered more wildly, and a mighty roar went up: "Long live Paderewski! Long live Wilson! Long live America! Long live the Entente!"

Then in the very spot where I imagined Paderewski to be, because the multitude there was thickest, I noticed a great agitation accompanied by a good deal of shouting. My heart stood still. What could have happened? But just at that moment the cry: "Long live Paderewski!" rent the air. The enthusiastic crowd had unharnessed the horses from Paderewski's landau and was pulling the vehicle with

Paderewski standing up in it and bowing in every direction. Seated next to him was Mme. Paderewska, while in front sat an aide in the light blue uniform of the Haller Army.

The man-drawn landau turned the corner slowly, giving me a better opportunity to get a close look at Paderewski's magnificent leonine head and his erect fiery figure. A fleeting glimpse and he was gone—but the crowds cheered on madly.

When we were thanking Mrs. Zalewska for her hospitality, someone came in to tell us that one of the second-floor balconies on Nowy Swiat Street had caved in under the weight of the spectators. One person was reported to have been killed.

February 4, 1919. Today my brother Jan announced that he was leaving the Chief Welfare Council for the Secretariat of the President of the Council of Ministers, Ignacy Paderewski. Jan told Father he got the position through Mr. Sylwin Strakacz, Paderewski's private secretary. Mr. Strakacz? The name arrested my attention. I don't know him personally, but I do know him by sight. He was a classmate of my brother Tadeusz at the Chrzanowski School. For years I used to run into him almost daily on my way home for lunch. He always looked at me so strangely that I had to turn away my head in order not to laugh. He must have liked me. I wonder if that had anything to do with Jan's getting the Paderewski appointment.

February 11, 1919. Today we are giving a farewell reception for Jan's colleagues at the Chief Welfare Council. There will be twelve gentlemen at supper tonight, including Stanislaw Strakacz, the brother of Paderewski's secretary. I'm not going to put in an appearance because it will be a stag party. But I shall put on a pretty dress and take pains with my hair-do just in case.

Later. There were thirteen men because Mr. Strakacz brought his younger brother, Sylwin, the one who is Paderewski's secretary. They all insisted I join them at the table, so Jan came to my room to fetch me. It was a good thing I had done my hair becomingly. The extra guest *was* the same Mr. Strakacz I used to pass in the street when he was a student at the Chrzanowski School—round face, frightfully crumpled cap in the student tradition, from underneath which peeped out a pair of slightly protruding but nice ears. The same Mr. Strakacz who always used to look at me in such a way that I felt the urge to laugh. When I saw him tonight, I felt like laughing all over again.

Protocol was certainly disregarded in seating the guests. Mr. Sylwin Strakacz, the youngest of the whole company, sat down at my right. The traditional cup of *barszcz* was already standing in front of each guest. Andrzej was serving meat dumplings, the culinary forte of our cook. I did not feel at all self-conscious at being the only woman among so many elderly and dignified gentlemen. I felt sure of myself, I was well dressed and supper would be first-rate, so there was nothing to be afraid of. But the secretary of Mr. Paderewski didn't say a word to me; he just kept looking at me the way he used to years ago, in his student days. I wanted to be gracious, so I took a dumpling from the dish with the intention of putting it on my staring neighbor's plate. In the process, my hand brushed against my cup, upsetting it and spilling the *barszcz* all over the table and my neighbor. I was angry with myself, but not too embarrassed, because Mr. Strakacz seemed to be enchanted with everything, even with having *barszcz* spilled all over him!

February 12, 1919. Mr. Sylwin Strakacz sent me flowers today, probably to thank me for yesterday's reception. Could it be that he intends to court me? That *would* be a problem, because I have no intention of getting married yet, and he is too busy. He told me only yesterday that work goes on day and night around Paderewski. He never has a free moment and it was a miracle he could come over to our house at all. Indeed, soon after supper he excused himself and went back to the Bristol Hotel.

March 26, 1919. Sylwin Strakacz comes over every day, sometimes twice a day. His calls can hardly be called visits — he drops in only for a minute because he never has any time, but he always brings me flowers and candy. How does he know I am fond of chocolates? He probably can tell by the fact that each box is gone when he comes again. How does he know when he can find me at home and when to wait for me at the gate of the Ujazdowski Hospital where I'm a volunteer nurse?

April 21, 1919. A funny meeting occurred in the street today. I usually come off duty at the hospital promptly at 6 P.M. Being a military hospital, no one can get in without a pass. To my surprise, I found three young men waiting for me at the gate. Mr. Strakacz had left the Parliament Building, whither he had accompanied the President, to see me for a few minutes. Count D., in uniform (we always laugh at him because his sword rattles against the pavement when he walks), was standing near him, while a little further on was Mr. Z., the mayor of Lublin, who had come to Warsaw for several days. Mr. Z. had called on me at home and not having found me in, had come to the hospital. None of the three were acquainted, so I introduced them to one another. As we walked home down Wiejska Street, I wondered how to get rid of the young men somewhere along the way. I knew Mr. Strakacz would go back to the Parliament, just a few steps away. But what could I do with the other two? We were already coming upon the Square of the Three Crosses when, at the last house on Wiejska Street, I suddenly stopped and bade my escorts good-bye. I explained I was invited here to my girl friend's, and extending my hand, which was tenderly pressed by both gentlemen, I disappeared inside the gate, waited long enough to permit my friends to go their separate ways, and then hurried home.

Andrzej must have blabbed again as to where they could find me, and this in spite of my repeated requests to him to say merely: "The young lady isn't in and I don't know when she'll be back." I don't want any suitors around. It's very boring. They go into raptures about everything and I don't know what to say to them.

May 18, 1919. I had a truly wonderful surprise today. Around noon a magnificent Cadillac pulled up in front of Pavilion IX [the Ujazdowski Hospital]. Everybody knew it was the automobile of the President of the Council of Ministers — there isn't another like it in Warsaw. Could it be someone to see me? The chauffeur handed me a small envelope with a calling card inside: "SYLWIN STRAKACZ. We returned from Paris last night. Gifts from the White Cross for Pavilion IX to be distributed by you. I shall take the liberty of calling on you at ten this evening." The limousine was loaded with packages. Heavens, what joy! Our hospital is so poor, we need literally everything, our wounded and sick soldiers have so few comforts. Within ten minutes my Pavilion IX became not only well equipped but downright rich. How sweet and kind of Mr. Strakacz to remember my poor soldiers.

May 21, 1919. The President and his entire secretarial staff are soon leaving for Paris again, to attend the peace conference. This time they'll be gone longer than before. I, too, am going away for the whole summer to practice horticulture at the Froelich estate in Sleszyn. Just as soon as things get green, I long for the country with all my heart, even though I couldn't live without Warsaw. I think Sylwin would like us to become engaged before he leaves. I don't want to, I can't make up my mind. What will my darling father do, all alone without me?

If I do get married, it will be only because of Andrzej. He's so impossible, sometimes I can't bear it. He's always making me cry and he starts rows with all the servants. He simply won't listen to me and acts as if he were the lady of the house. When he goes out, he locks the front door; twice I couldn't get into the house. I had to ask the superintendent to bring a ladder and by climbing to the balcony I got in through a window that luckily was open. Otherwise I should have had to wait until Andrzej deigned to return.

Father will never reprimand Andrzej. He doesn't interfere in domestic affairs, leaving everything to me. He thinks Andrzej is a saint, nothing can be changed in the house, everything must be exactly as it was when Mother was alive. Only Andrzej wasn't so unruly then.

I suppose I'll have to get married ultimately. But not yet. I must postpone it until September.

"Please Come to Warsaw"

Sleszyn, Kujawy — July 19, 1919. I received a large package from the post office today. It was from Paris. What can it be, I wondered as I opened one of the boxes inside the parcel. It was stationery, light blue with my monogram. How lovely it was. Another box — more stationery, white. A third with green stationery, a fourth, a fifth, a sixth — that was a little too much. I'm rather disappointed and slightly ashamed of myself. Sylwin writes me such beautiful long letters every day. I hardly ever answer, I don't know what to say to him any more. I've already informed him that I graft roses, that it's a terribly boring occupation, that I pick cucumbers and tomatoes, but I can't tell him that I'm having a wonderful time dancing at the neighbors until four or five in the morning. Or that Mr. F. locks me up in my room so that I should get enough sleep because, he says, I'm so conscientious that I'm apt to go straight to work in the garden after a sleepless night. Horticulture students must be up by six, so I climb out the window at dawn to work in the garden and climb back two hours later ready for breakfast, making it appear as if I'd just gotten up.

The F.'s are very kind to me. They're always asking me

what Warsaw would have to say if Aniela returned from Sleszyn looking worn out. Meanwhile, I've gained ten pounds despite my outrageous flirting.

July 24, 1919. What shall I do? There isn't a soul I can turn to for advice. Mrs. F. has gone to Ciechocinek Spa, Mr. F. has left for an inspection tour of the Agricultural Circles. Only the children and their French governess have remained behind. Here's what happened this afternoon: I was working in the garden when I suddenly recognized Bolek's familiar figure coming down the road. I couldn't believe my eyes. What would the newsboy, who sells papers in front of the Bristol Hotel, be doing here? This good-looking lad always calls out the names of the papers in French and in English, he must have been taught to do so by the foreigners who stay at the Bristol. He attracted the President's notice, who told Sylwin to look after him. Sylwin sends him on errands whenever he needs an intelligent messenger. But why on earth should he have come here, I kept asking myself.

Bolek soon explained: "Mr. Strakacz sent me with this letter, Miss. He wants you to please come to Warsaw for three days." It seems that the President and Sylwin returned from Paris yesterday, and Sylwin's note pleaded that I come to Warsaw for the weekend. My first reaction was that I couldn't possibly go for there is no one on the estate and the garden was left in my charge. But there must be some important reason for Sylwin's asking me. Maybe I can go to Warsaw and explain to the F.'s on my return. I'd see Father, and I know he'd be glad to see me, but what would I tell him if he should ask me why I came. I wanted to keep Bolek for supper, but he was in a hurry and took the next train back to Warsaw. He'll tell Sylwin that I shall take the 4:20 tomorrow afternoon.

So I Said Yes!

Warsaw—July 25, 1919. I had hoped Sylwin wouldn't be at the station. I looked frightful with a red nose, shiny cheeks, and those horrible freckles. I couldn't get my hair to look presentable, and my hat only made it worse. I prayed I shouldn't meet anyone I know before I'd had a chance to get home. That's why I rode third class. The train was awfully crowded and I had to stand in the corridor during the whole trip. It was absolutely out of the question to get a seat in a compartment.

When the train pulled into Milanowek [a small town twenty-five miles from Warsaw], there was Sylwin waiting on the platform. Was I surprised! He boarded the train and elbowed his way through the crowded car to my side. We stood all the rest of the way to Warsaw.

There was no one in when we got here. Father usually doesn't come home from the Lourse Cafe until late at night and Andrzej is, of course, never here. A surprised Antoniowa [the cook] opened the door for me. All the furniture was swathed in slip covers, the rugs were rolled up and reeked of moth balls. I asked Sylwin up to my room and opened the door onto the balcony to let the air in. Sylwin wore a very solemn expression. What was he going to say? Maybe he would propose to me just like that, right after a train trip. What answer should I give him if he did?

"I have a passport for you," he said. "Would you like to see it?"

"What passport?"

"To go abroad with. If you consent to marry me, the passport is all ready for you. We could go to Paris after our wedding and then to Biarritz."

Half dazed, I looked at the photograph which I had once given him, or rather which he simply took. Sure enough, the inscription read: "Diplomatic Passport, Aniela Strakacz." I was dumbfounded.

"Do you agree?"

"Yes," I replied mechanically as if in a trance.

"We'll get married on Thursday, August 7th, because I've reserved two Pullman tickets to Paris for that date."

"I prefer to wait until September," I ventured timidly.

"It would be difficult to wait that long," Sylwin answered. "One doesn't know how things will shape up by then, and it may be more difficult for us to go abroad."

. . . So I have said Yes. The die is cast; I cannot turn back. Sylwin said he would come tonight at ten to ask Father for my hand. I don't envy him.

Later. I went with Sylwin to face Father. After all, one must not be a coward. I had no idea what Father would say to him, but in any case I felt I had to stand by my fiance.

"Do you earn enough to support my daughter? Because I can't give her anything," Father's even voice responded to Sylwin's proposal.

"I am now earning two thousand marks a month. I should think that ought to assure us a decent livelihood," Sylwin replied.

That's not very much, the thought flashed through my head.

"Besides, I'm not quite certain whether I shall remain with President Paderewski. I've been offered the post of secretary in the Polish Legation at Tokyo."

I began to feel a little faint. What if I should find out I didn't care for Sylwin as a husband? I'd be afraid to come home alone from such a distance. . . . Here I was already thinking of *divorce*. A feeling of uncertainty overcame me. And then suddenly my father turned to me and gently said: "Do what you think is best, it is your life."

What terrifies me most is the thought that as Sylwin's fiancée I shall have to call on the Paderewskis. The time has been set for 6 P.M. tomorrow. I agreed to go on the condition that Sylwin give me his word of honor that we shan't stay there more than a few minutes, just long enough to introduce me to them.

I'm so afraid of the meeting. How will they receive me? What shall I talk about with such a Great Man? Dear God, it's too late already. Why did I become engaged?

July 26, 1919, Saturday. Sylwin came for me at six. On the way to the Royal Castle, where the Paderewskis are now permanently established, I kept praying that they would like me and that the visit would be a short one.

Sylwin escorted me into a room in which the President and his wife were standing, engaged in conversation with several other guests. I went up to President Paderewski. He looked at me, took me by both hands and exclaimed: "What a sweet child!" Just then Mme. Paderewska came up, shook my hand, and removed my hat, saying, "You'll stay for supper. . . ."

I got in at midnight. I felt thoroughly at home with the Paderewskis.

Good-bye Freedom

Back in Sleszyn, Kujawy — August 3, 1919, Sunday. I'm going to be married next Thursday, only four days from now. I've already packed all my things and have explained to Mr. F., in Mrs. F.'s absence, that I shall be compelled to break off my horticulture training because of my wedding.

My last day of freedom. I confided to Stanislaw Froelich that I'd like to take a farewell ride on horseback. As a special treat, he had the bay mare saddled for me and the dappled stallion for himself — the best two horses in the neighborhood.

We started off at a brisk trot across the yard into a side

road lined with chestnut trees. The mare was high spirited and carried me ahead of Stanislaw. We flew over the stubble-field like the wind. What ecstasy it is to ride like this! My mare falls into a gallop. Since she has no bridle bit today, I can't force her back into a trot, but there's no harm racing over the stubble.

Suddenly she makes a sharp turn, and before I know it, I've jumped over a narrow ditch and am being borne back to Sleszyn at a full gallop along the rough, rocky road. Having lost control over the horse, I give her free rein, hoping she will tire and stop of her own accord. Because I've lost my beret and all my combs, my hair has become undone and gets in my eyes. Meanwhile my mare is racing on and on. By now I'm thinking with despair that she'll ruin her legs on this rocky road, that not only is she not my horse, but the best horse for miles around. What a responsibility!

Now I see my own doom. We're approaching the courtyard gate, I can already see the stable. If she doesn't stop, she'll gallop into the stable, killing herself and me. I'll never see Father again, I won't see Sylwin and there will be no wedding. . . .

I'm taking mental leave of everyone, convinced my end is near, when I suddenly see before me the face of my mother. Mother! Then I no longer see anything, but bounce up and down like a ball on the mare's head, her tail, and back again in the saddle. The horse's hoofs dig into the ground, she flexes her heaving body and comes to a complete halt—ten feet away from the gate. . . . It will be a long time before I forget this farewell ride. "The bay carried you three miles!" Stanislaw said.

Nothing can harm me. Mother always watches over me and God will never abandon me. That's what I believe.

Everybody has been so kind to me. They all wish me well, only the gardener is indignant because I'm interrupting my training just to get married.

Good-bye, freedom. I'm off for Warsaw!

Paderewski Sent Champagne

Warsaw—August 4, 1919, Monday. We're getting married Thursday at four o'clock. We've got to invite a lot of people to the wedding and we don't have enough time to prepare an elaborate lunch so we're having just an afternoon reception. Only, what will we serve our guests? Pastry shops aren't allowed to bake cakes, let alone a wedding cake; whipped cream doesn't exist and there's no sweet cream either, because of the restrictions due to old-time war regulations.

Sylwin consoles me that he received special permission to have the necessary food prepared and has already ordered everything. He says on Thursday noon the Ziemianska Cafe will send over a wedding cake, pastry, and a bowl of whipped cream. Sylwin loves whipped cream.

The President has already sent us large cases of champagne. I guess there's no use worrying. Andrzej will take care of the rest.

We'll have to put up the curtains, lay out the rugs. There'll probably be a lot of guests, but nobody seems to know exactly how many. We don't even know who's coming. Everyone's away for the summer and we didn't have enough time to send out formal invitations to our friends.

August 7, 1919—My Wedding Day. Dear Mr. Jozef, my faithful hairdresser, came the first thing this morning to dress my hair for the wedding. He said it would be quieter that early. He'll come again at three to pin on my veil.

Funny, I don't feel it's the day of my wedding. The hairdresser did right to come so early. No sooner had he left than the doorbell rang and—a pleasant surprise—there was my cousin Natalka back from the front, wearing a uniform, her arm in a sling. We hadn't seen each other since the start of hostilities at the Eastern Front. My nursing instinct came to life at the sight of her bandaged arm and I asked whether her wound needed dressing and how she got it. But Natalka wouldn't answer, she just kept eying the table in the dining room and exclaiming: "Good heavens! Is that real whipped cream? And all those cakes!"

"Yes, I'm getting married at 4 o'clock today."

"Well, what about me," Natalka demands. "I'm not going to be left alone, I'm going to get married too."

August 9, 1919. How hectic my wedding day was! I must put down my impressions while I still remember it all.

At four o'clock I was in my wedding gown and veil, ready to leave for the church. I went out on my balcony and my whole beloved Square of the Three Crosses turned out to look at me. All the huckstresses from the market place ran out into the street and gathered under my balcony. Loudly blowing their noses, they commented mournfully: "To think such a child is getting married. But you'll stay here with us, won't you, dearie?" The policeman saluted me smartly, the cab drivers at the cabstand bowed.

The telephone rang. The distressed voice of Sylwin's father came over the wire: "My child, can you suggest something? It's four o'clock and Sylwin is in the bathtub! You're going to be late and to think that the Bishop and the Paderewskis are waiting."

"If Sylwin is in the tub, you can help him better than I can. It's all the same with me. I'm in no hurry to get married."

I waited, uncommonly calm, even indifferent, as if my person wasn't the one involved. Up to now I hadn't even had a moment's time to think about myself. Perhaps it was better so. Guided by my instinct, I had faith in my future, that's why I could be so unruffled. Suddenly I recalled a remark repeated to me by Sylwin's cousin: "That's the little girl," pointing to me, "I will one day marry," said Sylwin when he was but fourteen and I nine! I suppose that means he'll always love me. Anyway, I believe in providence.

I was very sorry that my brothers were not at home for

the wedding. Jan is in Paris, Tadeusz at the front. He was recently decorated with the *Virtuti Militari* medal by Pilsudski.

At long last Sylwin appeared, apologizing for the delay. He'd been on duty with the President up to the very last minute. It was just his luck that the morning's diplomatic mail had come in from Paris, creating plenty of urgent work.

We rode to the Cathedral—Father, Aunt Lossow, Natalka, and we. There were such crowds in front of the Cathedral that it was difficult for our carriage to get through. People stood on the sidewalks and overflowed into the street. They weren't waiting for us, they were all eager to catch a glimpse of Paderewski. It was almost impossible to get inside the church through that sea of people.

We *were* late! The Bishop had waited a full hour for us. So had the Paderewskis. It was scandalous to be that late, but at least the crowd got a chance to see the President. I wrapped my veil around my arm about a dozen times and we pushed our way toward the altar.

From church we rode home for the reception. Our drawing room was chock-full of high-ranking government officials. This one was a Minister, that one a Vice Minister, each more important than the next. I didn't know a soul and couldn't get rid of the strange feeling that this wasn't my home. Suddenly there was a commotion at the door and everyone rose to his feet. The Paderewskis with Major and Mrs. Iwanowski had arrived. I couldn't even greet them because the President was immediately surrounded by such a host of dignitaries that I couldn't get near him.

In a little while the crowd around him thinned. No wonder—he was talking with my millionaire aunt from Lublin. When you see *her* coming you run. Everybody's afraid of Auntie. I'm not, but I steer clear of her. She's too rich, that's the trouble with her.

But now I was getting nervous because Auntie was talking the President's ear off. After all, she wasn't supposed to monopolize all of his time! I was worried because I did not know what she was talking to him about and I didn't dare go up to them. I felt I should rescue the President. The bright idea of bringing him some whipped cream occurred to me. "Andrzej, where's the cream?" Andrzej shrugged his shoulders and mumbled something about there not being any. I stared at him, disbelieving. So he calmly explained that when Mr. Strakacz dropped in for a minute at noon and saw there was only one bowl of whipped cream, he said it wouldn't be enough for so many guests anyway, and together with Miss Natalka, he cleaned out the bowl.

Just then Sylwin came up to remind Andrzej that it was time to serve the champagne. Where was it? Andrzej maintained a discreet silence. This, it developed, was another story. It seems that while we were away at church, Andrzej, who alone was glad and proud that I was getting married, was so thrilled about the whole thing that he distributed the two big cases of champagne, which had been a gift from the President, among the cab drivers, the huckstresses in the Square, and the proprietors and salesmen of our neighborhood stores. He had offered champagne to everyone he met on the Square of the Three Crosses saying: "Remember the wedding of our Young Lady!" And so the two cases of Veuve-Cliquot were gone. We laughed. There was nothing we could do about it anyway. To tell the truth, we didn't have the heart to begrudge a little champagne to the good people who had known me from childhood and among whom I had grown up.

Fortunately, the situation wasn't altogether hopeless. Father had mead brought up from the wine cellar. The bottles were so moss-covered that they aroused wonder among our guests, who thought they were at least a hundred years old. Screwing up my courage, I walked up to the President with a glass of mead and boldly asked him if my Aunt had worn him out. The President smiled, bent over my ear and replied in a very gentle and soft voice: "Not too much, but if I should meet your Auntie at either the North or the South Pole, I'd recognize her at once!" Such was my first real conversation with President Paderewski.

The guests left. Sylwin went to his home on Chlodna Street to pick up his luggage, as we were leaving for Paris shortly after seven. I started packing. Unopened wedding presents were still lying around my room: a magnificent manicuring set from my mother-in-law, a suitcase from Sylwin's brother Wladek and his wife, a traveling bag from Aunt Grodzinska and another suitcase. What should I put into them? My wedding gown will come in handy — thank heavens it's short and without a train. I'll take my wedding shoes too. What next? My housecoat! Oh, but I left it in Sleszyn. My good dress has a tomato stain on it. I brought my lingerie from the country, but no one had time to launder it. I quickly locked the suitcases before anyone might notice they were empty.

When it was time to go to the station, I said good-bye to Father. He couldn't keep back his tears. I saw him cry like that only once before — when Mother died. Had I known it would hit him so badly, I would never have gotten married. I felt very sad.

There were more crowds at the railroad station. How kind of the Paderewskis to see us off. It seems to me that they love Sylwin almost as if he were their own son. There were so many people around that you'd think it was the Paderewskis and not we who were going away, but then there always are crowds around Paderewski.

When we arrived at the station, we noticed the horrified expressions on everybody's face. We had come too late. The train for Paris had just left! I broke into hearty laughter. They all gathered around me, exclaiming "My, what a sweet disposition! You don't get angry, you're always laughing!" Secretly I was glad I could go back home. Father would be overjoyed to see me. (Father never sees people off, never attends funerals, never talks over the telephone and never writes letters. That's probably why he's always so nice and good-humored. I'd like to be like him.) But Sylwin wouldn't hear of going back. There wouldn't be another diplomatic train for Paris until a week later, so Sylwin quickly changed our plans and made it possible for us to board a train for Cracow.

We're Never Alone

Warsaw, Square of the Three Crosses, No. 3 — September 12, 1919. We're back from our honeymoon in Paris and Biarritz. We had a wonderful trip, greatly enhanced by the generous check which the President gave Sylwin just before we left Warsaw. I'm so deeply grateful to him not only for his kind heart, but for his treating Sylwin like a son.

The President probably sensed I'm an only daughter, atrociously spoiled by everyone, who was expected to marry a fairy tale prince. Nobody approved of my marrying Sylwin and I've had many unpleasant moments because of it, but since Father, Jan, and Tadeusz are on my side, I don't care what the others say. I'm going to show Warsaw — I'm going to show all of Poland — that even if I did marry "only" Mr. Strakacz, I shall live like a queen!

Meanwhile, on our return to Warsaw we had just fifteen francs to our name. Undaunted, we decided we were going to live at the Bristol — surely they would have to find a room for Paderewski's secretary. But there was Andrzej waiting for us at the station. Greeting us happily, he informed us that Father had prepared the whole house for us. We swallowed our pride and rode home to Father, who retained only the smallest room in the house for himself.

October 1919. Now that I'm a married woman, I have two homes. I sleep in our house on the Square and try to be there when Father is around. But I really spend my days at the Castle to be with Sylwin, only I seldom see him even there, he's so busy with the President. I don't do anything for days at a time, but time passes quickly. The Castle's reception room is filled from morning till night with people having business with the President or waiting to see Mme. Paderewska. The Paderewskis are so hospitable that they invite virtually everybody to lunch or supper. Their two main meals of the day are really large-scale receptions. The entire secretarial staff of both the President and Mme. Paderewska are permanent guests at the dining table twice a day. So am I.

November 1919. A lot of people feel offended because Sylwin and I haven't called on them; they refuse to believe that we're never alone and that Sylwin is with the President day and night. Around midnight he takes me home and returns to the Castle for more work. They work all night and at about six in the morning, after they've finished their work and before they retire, they play cards for twenty minutes. That's the President's habit—to relax I suppose. How they can stand it is beyond me! I don't do anything and am always tired. During the card games, Sylwin at least yawns and is sometimes only semiconscious.

Mme. Paderewska works as hard as her husband. She sees visitors during the day and works with her secretaries just as late into the night as the President. Mme. Paderewska really does a man's job. There are those who hold it against her. They say she butts into everything, even into politics. How ridiculous! After all, she has her tremendous work as the head of the White Cross, through which Polish American organizations send wonderful gifts for Polish soldiers, for the poor, and for Poland's hungry children.

Just suppose Mme. Paderewska did not interfere with the Castle routine—so many people would surely drive the President to his death: everybody wants to see him, everybody wants to offer him advice, and there are plenty of individuals milling around whom I'd never allow inside the Castle, let alone to see the President. Mme. Paderewska is very energetic. When she sees someone is taking too much of the President's time, she walks into his office and says

Minister so-and-so is waiting, something that Sylwin doesn't
dare do. That's why they're so hostile to her. Nobody under-
stands her just because we in Poland don't observe the
foreign custom of a wife's being her husband's secretary or
of a daughter's being her father's assistant. I'd like to help
too, but I'm so afraid somebody might say something about
my meddling that I merely roam around the Castle answering
all questions with an "I don't know."

November 4, 1919. We've just received an invitation to dine
at the American Legation tonight. We are to accompany the
Paderewskis. I am a little surprised at our attending this
dinner because the President spends only a few days at a
time in Warsaw, and the rest in Paris where the present
negotiations require his almost constant presence. But the
President couldn't refuse Minister Hugh Gibson's invitation
because he regards him as a truly sincere and devoted personal friend and a friend of the Polish cause.

I'm terrified at the thought of going tonight. I don't
know a word of English, but I'm a little reassured by the
news that the American Minister speaks excellent French.
This will be my first appearance among the Warsaw diplomatic corps. I can't help being glad that my debut will take
place in the cordial atmosphere of friendship between President Paderewski and Minister Gibson.

The American Legation in Warsaw is housed in the
"Blue Palace," the town house of the head of one of the
oldest and worthiest Polish families, Ordynat Maurycy
Zamoyski. Count Z. placed his palace at the disposal of the
American Legation until suitable and permanent quarters are
found or built in Warsaw. Several other aristocratic families
have made the same gesture, facilitating the settling in reborn
Poland of representatives of friendly countries.

Later. We arrived at the Legation with the Paderewskis. Of
course, after our host had greeted me graciously, he devoted
his attention to them, which gave me a chance to overcome

my shyness and to take a quick look at the magnificent works
of art accumulated by generations of Zamoyskis.

Soon I was feeling completely at ease, thanks to the
social grace and pleasant directness of Mr. Maurice Pate, a
young American attached to the Hoover Relief Mission.
Sensing my discomfiture and discovering that I don't know
English, he came to my rescue. At length we were asked to
sit down to dinner. The dining room was somber in style and
all the woodwork was dark. The huge mahogany table was
not covered with a tablecloth, but in front of each guest was
a large lace doilie, on which stood the famous Zamoyski
service. The crystal on the table reflected all the colors of the
rainbow, and the Venetian goblets of paper-thin glass with a
coat of arms engraved on them seemed to me so fragile that
I picked them up with anxiety. The thought occurred to me
that if these wonderful things belonged to me, I'd never let
strangers use them.

As the conversation alternated between English and
French, I could follow at least half of it. The President threw
me a side glance every once in a while. He probably sensed
my shyness. Mme. Paderewska paid no attention to me at
all, probably so as not to embarrass me.

To climax our visit we drank a glass of ancient Tokay, of
which Minister Gibson managed to get a few bottles from
the famous Fukier wine cellar.

On the way back to the Castle the Paderewskis commented
upon the open-hearted hospitality of Minister Gibson. Mr.
Pate and the Legation's secretary, Mr. Bliss Lane, impressed
the President as very congenial and capable young diplomats.
The President added: "It is touching to see Maurice Pate so
friendly toward Poland."

November 11, 1919. I'm terribly indignant and Sylwin is upset. Fine thing, politics. The political parties are starting to
quarrel in earnest. The Socialists want for president Jozef
Pilsudski, who is now Chief of State; the National Democrats
are for Dmowski; the Peasant Party recognizes no one but

Witos; and they all want to get rid of Paderewski, who belongs to no party. He's strong only through the might of his spirit, through his greatness and purity of heart. He's the most popular man in the world. Nobody dares to say anything bad about Paderewski—nobody would believe it anyway—so they attempt to discredit those nearest and dearest to him. Sylwin comes in for his share, but to think that Mme. Paderewska must be so unfairly attacked is revolting.

[While Paderewski was busy at the Paris Peace Conference trying to secure for Poland the most favourable conditions for her future development, his opponents in Poland were preparing to oust him as the head of the government. They knew only too well that Paderewski's personal prestige, the almost reverential admiration in which he was held by the masses, would void any attempt to attack him directly. Therefore a plan was conceived to reach him through an attack on his beloved wife. Immediately a whispering campaign was started, accusing Mme. Paderewska of interference in affairs of State and charging that she dictated her husband's political activities as she had managed his artistic career. In spite of their obvious absurdity, these rumours were widely circulated and the campaign of vilification was extended to include other members of Paderewski's immediate staff. When these rumours finally reached Paderewski, he considered it beneath his dignity to undertake any counter-measures. *S. S.*]

December, 1919. The President gave a magnificent reception at the Castle for American newspapermen. Dinner for half a hundred and then dancing to the music of the best orchestra.

For the first time in my life I wore a black evening dress and I was quite scared I'd be a wallflower. I was afraid there would be so many important and beautiful women from the diplomatic corps no one would ask me for a dance.

Several hundred more people were invited for after dinner. Our ballroom at the Castle is beautiful and the floor is mirror-like. The President and Sylwin had not appeared as yet. I felt very foolish all alone and abandoned. I might as well be single, for Sylwin is always with the President. Even when I am with them, I am in the background alone.

I saw Mr. Stanislaw O. come in and felt relieved. He doesn't dance but at least I thought he might come up and talk to me. Instead he stopped to converse with the lovely wife of the Spanish envoy.

Utterly miserable, I became aware that my new slippers were tight and uncomfortable. Sitting down in a corner I quickly removed one shoe and hid it under my chair. No sooner had I done this than Mr. O. came up and introduced Prince R. to me. A low bow and I was asked to dance. In no time the shoe was back on my foot. What a dancer! When the music stopped the Prince said, "You dance divinely, Madame!" My spirits rose and my shoes no longer hurt.

The President wished to show his foreign guests some Polish dances. A search was on for a couple that would do the *oberek* and the *kujawiak* best. Mr. S., a cabinet member, turned to Paderewski: "Mr. President, with your permission I shall dance the oberek with Mrs. Strakacz." The President smiled with pleasure at having found a volunteer couple for the exhibition dance. I was delighted — but not for long. After a second or two I realized we were not dancing in time with the music. I tried to follow my partner rather than the music. I found myself involved in a series of jumping, kneeling, and stamping steps executed in such a peculiar tempo and so unexpectedly that if I weren't such a controlled dancer, we'd surely both have sprawled out on that slippery parquet floor. I was so terrified by my partner's un-co-ordinated movements that I took hold of his collar and hung on for dear life to maintain my equilibrium and to create at least an illusion of a harmoniously dancing couple. Those foreigners must have thought our *oberek* some kind of a wild dance.

A Few Politicians

February 6, 1920. Tomorrow we leave for Switzerland. After his resignation from office, Paderewski decided to go to his estate at Riond Bosson near Morges. Sylwin obtained a six months leave of absence from the Ministry of Foreign Affairs. All this happened so quickly that I have hardly had time to adjust myself to the new turn of events. When, after having re-established Poland as a free and sovereign country, Paderewski returned triumphant, his opponents decided that they had no further use for him and led an all-out attack against him in the Parliament. Paderewski won a vote of confidence by a slim margin, but he resigned as Prime Minister and a new Cabinet was formed.

[Paderewski belonged to no political party and served no separate group or faction, but the interest of his country in general. He was acclaimed as a providential leader during a national emergency, but when conditions became more or less normal, leaders of the Polish left-wing parties decided that the time had come to get rid of Paderewski and his middle-of-the-road program, and to try to apply their respective formulas for shaping the future of Poland. When the Polish Peasant Party, under the leadership of Wincenty Witos, finally opposed Paderewski and joined the left-wing group, although a vote of non-confidence in the Paderewski Government failed to pass in the House, Paderewski decided to resign from office. He explained that his decision was prompted by the fact that the Polish Peasant Party, though in the minority in the House, represented about 60 per cent of the entire population of Poland, consisting of farmers and rural workers. As a true believer in the principles of democracy, Paderewski would not stay in office knowing that he was supported by the minority against the wishes of the majority. *S. S.*]

What a tragedy it must be for a great patriot to see his work undone, his plans for social reforms shattered on the verge of realization, his vision of a happy Poland gone—all because of the meanness of a few politicians!

I guess Paderewski feels the tragedy of the situation more than anybody else. Sylwin says the President would have forgiven gladly any injustice dealt him personally, but he is terribly worried about the future of his beloved country. At this stage of its newly regained statehood, he would have known how to lead and rehabilitate Poland, yet was prevented from doing so.

The President must be a saint. He's suffered so much unpleasantness, so much injustice and slander, yet you never hear him complain or criticize. But often now in his eyes there is an expression I've never seen before, thoughtful and sad. Whatever happens, Sylwin and I will never leave the President.

2

Exile

So Many Guests

On the Train—February 7, 1920. When we arrived at the
station this morning, we found a great crowd before the
President's private car. People were getting on and off, running around and shouting. It was a real bedlam. I could
hardly get through the throng. In the process I lost Sylwin
and my things. I couldn't see the Paderewskis anywhere in
that mob. No one of the strange faces all around paid the
slightest attention to me. I didn't know what to do. As I was
wondering whether I should turn back, someone gave me a
hard push, crying that the train was about to leave. Hastily I
jumped aboard. The corridor of the car was jammed with
humanity. At last the train left and I was suddenly all alone
in the corridor. The doors to all the compartments were
closed and I didn't dare to knock at any of them.

Finally, hearing no voices issuing from one compartment,
I cautiously opened the door and saw a mountain of suitcases.
In the corner something moved—I looked again and recognized Mr. Walter, the aged American correspondent who
covers all of Paderewski's trips. Mr. Walter likes me a lot
and always observes me benignly through his enormous
glasses. He invariably talks at great length to me even
though I don't understand a word of his English. So I merely
nod my head and say Yes every once in a while, which seems
to satisfy him completely.

Mr. Walter tried to make room for me so gracefully that
the pyramid of luggage came tumbling down, making an un-
holy racket. This was followed by a ghastly human screech.
Wheeling around in terror, I saw the parrot which had been
given Mme. Paderewska by someone in Warsaw. I hate
parrots and I simply can't understand how anyone can take
birds in a cage on a trip! But Mme. Paderewska is the kind
of person who insists on saving the ugliest and lowliest

presents. She won't allow anything to be thrown away. Besides, I hear she's quite fond of parrots. She already has several at Riond Bosson.

Mr. Walter talked on and on. Suddenly I heard the word "dinner," and I realized how hungry I was. We made our way to the dining car. The Paderewskis and Major and Mrs. Iwanowski were seated at one of the tables. When the President saw us, he smiled cordially and said to me, "I'm glad you've come, because I've been quite worried that our little girl wasn't traveling with us." Mme. Paderewska waved Mr. Walter and me to a near-by table, adding that Sylwin would join us shortly with Capt. K.

February 9, 1920. As we approached the Swiss border I became quite uneasy about being examined by customs officials. It's against the war regulations to take jewelry or gold from one country into another, and Father had given me all of Mother's jewelry which I now had in my possession.

After a three-hour stop at Buchs on the Swiss frontier, we moved on. I couldn't understand what had happened. Why hadn't we been examined, why had no one asked us questions? Capt. K. explained that it was like this at every frontier all over the world. Paderewski's personal belongings as well as the belongings of all members of his party are never inspected. It is a tribute and courtesy paid to Paderewski by every country.

Later at Riond Bosson. Two hired cars were waiting for us at the Morges station. Morges is a small but trim town picturesquely located on the very shore of Lake Geneva. A wide road connects it with Paderewski's residence, Riond Bosson. A short ride and we had arrived at our destination. A sizable crowd, ranging from old men and women to infants, stood in front of the house—the servants were out in full force to greet their returned masters. The Paderewskis shook hands all around, exchanging a few words with everyone.

Entering the foyer, I paused, stunned by the sheer beauty

of what I saw. I hardly knew what to gaze at first—the fabulous interior about which I had heard so much or the enchanting view afforded through the French door and the enormous windows in the drawing room of azure Lake Geneva nestling among the snow-covered bluish mountains. So clear was the air that I could see plain as day the majesty of Mont Blanc, eternally snow capped, rosy in the sunshine. Nothing that I had been told about the spectacular loveliness of Riond Bosson's view of Mont Blanc had prepared me for this breath-taking sight!

The foyer is sumptuously furnished. A huge billiard table dominates the center. All the walls are lined with showcases and shelves with colorful Chinese cloisonné and porcelain. A gigantic silk Chinese rug hangs from the balustrade of the second floor, the mighty dragon stark white against a bright red background. It must be very ancient and very precious.

Two Steinway grand pianos stand back to back in the drawing room. Covered with white tapestries, they are graced by an array of autographed photographs in magnificent frames, among them a picture of Queen Victoria. The walls are literally alive with paintings. There are many portraits and sculptures of Paderewski as a younger man. And flowers, flowers everywhere. Enormous bunches of chrysanthemums and pompons in every vase. Seeing all this for the first time I could only marvel that so much splendor could be assembled under one roof.

When I came into the dining room, the first thing that caught my eye was the immense triptych painted by Jacek Malczewski. I think it's his most beautiful work. The center part shows a life-size Christ surrounded by a halo. To one side sits a pensive Polish peasant in his long peasant coat, to the other a soldier in Russian uniform. I had no time to think about the allegory because I saw Mme. Paderewska kissing a short roly-poly lady with glowing pink cheeks. "How are you, dear Antosieczka!" from both the Paderewskis. It was Mrs. Wilkonska, Paderewski's sister.

"You see, Helenka," [Mme. Paderewska's first name]
Mrs. Wilkonska rejoined, "even Mont Blanc is welcoming
Ignace [Mr. Paderewski] today. It's visible for the first
time in weeks. All it does here is rain and rain. This Switzerland can make you forget what the sun looks like."

Then Mrs. Wilkonska, who resides here permanently and
has charge of the entire household, greeted the rest of us
with obvious reserve. I guess she wasn't too happy to see so
many new guests barging in on her domain.

Our room is on the third floor. The corner room is Mrs.
Wilkonska's, the rest are guest rooms. Sylwin says there
usually aren't enough of them to go round, so that the Hotel
Mont Blanc in Morges regularly has a few rooms reserved
for Paderewski. That's where Mr. Walter is staying.

Our room, like the whole house, is crammed with furniture and a variety of objects that have sentimental rather than
practical value. Each room has two or three clocks, oil paintings, watercolors, and etchings. Each item comes from a
different country and period and there is a story connected
with each. It's all very interesting but living in such a museum
is quite a problem. I don't even know where to put my things.

Riond Bosson—February 15, 1920. The first days of our stay
here were utterly ruined by the missing chauffeur and cook.

When we were leaving Warsaw, Paderewski wanted to
take his Cadillac, presented to him by Mr. Hoover, so it was
decided to load the Cadillac on an open freight car attached
to our train. When we reached the Czech border it developed
that because of the increased speed of the train it would be
dangerous to leave the open freight car attached to the express train. The stationmaster conferred with Sylwin and,
as it was late in the night, he had to make the decision to
detach the freight car and accept the promise that it would
follow on the next freight train leaving for Switzerland.
However, in view of the troublesome times and being warned
that a Cadillac without an escort could too easily disappear on
its way, the chauffeur and the cook, whom Mr. Paderewski

was taking to Switzerland, agreed to stay with the car. The next morning when the Paderewskis were informed of the incident, Sylwin was bitterly reproached for exposing the two men to a dangerous ride in wintertime. Mme. Paderewska's imagination went further by suggesting that the two men might be attacked by robbers attempting to steal the car. Upon our arrival in Riond Bosson, Mme. Paderewska continued to worry and heckle Sylwin with reproaches steadily increasing in intensity. Mrs. Wilkonska joined her sister-in-law in bewailing their fate. Sylwin and I were made responsible for anything that might happen to them. We pretended to be nonchalant, but we were really getting pretty worried ourselves.

At long last, this afternoon at four, the Morges railroad station telephoned that the freight car with the Cadillac and its two passengers had arrived. There was general rejoicing as Sylwin rushed down to the station.

March 2, 1920. We never keep the same seat at the table. Only the Paderewskis and Mrs. Wilkonska have their regular places. The seating arrangement depends on who the guests are, and there hasn't been a single lunch or dinner so far at which visitors have not been present.

Paderewski seats all the guests himself, which is no mean feat when you're dealing with important people who don't always speak the same languages. The President solves these riddles without giving them a second thought. Nobody ever feels slighted. On the contrary, everyone is convinced he is being singled out for special attention.

Paderewski has a wonderful gift of entertaining his guests. He can talk with anyone about a subject of interest to that person and his conversation is full of facts, sparkling, and witty. When he converses in English, he immediately translates his remarks into French or Polish for the benefit of those who don't understand English. I just sit quietly, taking it all in. I wouldn't dream of saying anything myself, even in Polish. It seems strange to me that the President never dis-

cusses music or politics at luncheons or dinners. And I have
yet to hear him speak disparagingly of anyone.

April 5, 1920. Around noon a telephone call came through
from the Morges station. General Rozwadowski had arrived
with his aide, Lieutenant Romaniszyn. Mrs. Wilkonska's
usual lamentation turned into despair: "*Boze! Boze!* [God!
Oh God!] So many guests. And they've come all the way
from Poland, so they must intend to stay a while. Poor
Ignace, they're going to harass him again."

Lunch was a great success. Paderewski was in excellent
spirits and the guests almost forgot to eat, listening to him.
Lieutenant Romaniszyn is a native of Zakopane, a real
mountaineer who speaks a beautiful highlander dialect and
has a limitless repertoire of regional folk anecdotes. He related one at the table, moving Paderewski to hearty laughter.
The non-Poles in our company of course understood nothing.
But a moment later, to the Lieutenant's amazement, his host
was translating the untranslatable story (the joke lay in a
play upon words and in the special mountaineer pronunci-
ation) into English, apparently with such skill that the
American newspapermen present were howling with delight.
Lieutenant Romaniszyn told another mountain tale. Paderewski repeated his previous exploit. The Americans listened
appreciatively. A real contest ensued. The Lieutenant told
anecdote after anecdote, each more difficult than the preceding
one. In each case it seemed to us that *this* anecdote simply
could not be translated. But the President translated them all
with equal ease and wit. Our foreign friends alternated between guffaws and exclamations of undisguised admiration.
Tears streaming down his face, my neighbor sighed, "The
man's a genius."

April 30, 1920. For several days Mme. Paderewska has
vainly tried to talk her husband into going for a walk in the
park. For some strange reason, the President hardly ever
leaves the house. I can't understand his lack of interest in the

gorgeous park and the orchard to which he himself has added numerous trees brought from all parts of the world.

To each invitation of his wife, he replies in a gentle unruffled voice, "Later" or "I'll go tomorrow." Mrs. Wilkonska keeps sputtering: How can anybody live without fresh air. Mme. Paderewska seconds her: Of course it's all Sylwin's fault—he's to blame because he's always bringing guests over, or finding something important to take care of when the time comes for Ignace to take a walk.

But today, after his five o'clock tea, Paderewski suddenly arrived at a decision. Without a word to anyone, he went into the foyer and started looking for his hat and coat. In a trice his old valet, Marcel, who knows the President's habits better than any of us, appeared out of nowhere and helped him with his coat, scarf, gloves, and hat. Then Paderewski walked down the steps of the terrace and into the park, followed at a discreet distance by Sylwin and Marcel, and at an even greater distance by Mme. Paderewska and her secretary Andzia.

Meanwhile, Mrs. Wilkonska pattered into the drawing room and back again into the dining room, glanced through the window, and murmured with satisfaction: "They've finally gone."

Then she hastened into the drawing room, made sure the doors and windows were closed, and sat down at the Steinway. Noticing my surprise, she exclaimed:

"When Ignace is home, I can't do any playing. It's the one thing I love to do."

She played beautifully—from memory. Even though her tiny hands could hardly take in an octave, she managed to perform the most difficult compositions. I listened to her with wonder and admiration.

Come to think of it, I've never heard Paderewski play in all the time I've known him. I used to think that when Paderewski devoted himself to political activity, he merely stopped giving concerts, but I see now that he doesn't touch the piano even in private.

May 4, 1920. Guests, guests, and more guests. There is a never-ending procession of pilgrims to Riond Bosson from all the corners of the earth. The guests have to be entertained. I never have any time left for my English lesson nor for reading. I'm so exhausted by this perpetual social whirl that I have to overcome my sleepiness to make even a short entry in my diary.

Among our guests today was Wronski, a young Polish American tenor from Milan's La Scala. After dinner we had our coffee in the drawing room. Mrs. Wilkonska poured while Andzia and I served. An American asked Wronski to sing something in Polish. He tactfully declined—he would have gladly sung but he couldn't be his own accompanist and nobody would dare to sit down at the piano in Paderewski's presence. Suddenly Wronski blanched, speechless with emotion: Paderewski was at the piano, idly running his fingers along the keyboard and inviting Wronski to sing. The poor tenor later confessed he had feared he wouldn't be able to find his voice, so moved was he by the unexpected honor. But Paderewski was already playing: *Umarl Maciek Umarl* [a Polish folk song].

Wronski has a beautiful velvety voice and Paderewski was discreet in his accompaniment, trying not to draw attention away from the young singer. I caught Mr. Walter in the act of furtively wiping away his tears under the pretext of polishing his tremendous steamed-over goggles.

I hoped Paderewski would play for many minutes. There were tears in everybody's eyes and no one seemed ashamed of them. A lump came up in my throat. But Paderewski, as if embarrassed by his departure from his custom of not playing, had risen from the piano. "How about some bridge, Sylwin?" And he went into the card room with those whose good fortune it was to be chosen his bridge partners for the evening.

June 6, 1920. Sylwin and I are leaving for Warsaw tomorrow morning. We've taken leave of Paderewski tonight because he's invisible mornings. Only his valet can see him before

noon. Sylwin himself breaks this rule only in truly exceptional cases because the President devotes the morning
hours to reading and writing and doesn't like to be disturbed.

On the Train — June 7, 1920. At eleven o'clock this morning
we were about to get into the car when Mme. Paderewska
came to ask us upstairs: "Ignace wants to say good-bye."

We felt more than honored by this exceptional summons.
Dashing up the private staircase, we came upon the President
waiting for us on the landing. He was wearing a navy blue
silk dressing gown (our present from Paris, we noted
proudly) and looked like someone out of this world in the
magnificent halo of gray hair, with a slightly golden cast,
that fell into deep waves. Extending his hands to us, he
apologized for coming out to us in such informal attire. We
wished to kiss his hands, but he wouldn't hear of it. He
kissed me on both cheeks. "Good-bye, dear children, give
my regards to your parents, and come back in good health."

He radiated so much goodness that it was hard for me to
leave him. But it was getting late, so we hurried down and
were soon speeding toward the railroad station.

Warsaw — June 15, 1920. A telegram came from Morges
today. Something urgent has turned up and Paderewski wants
Sylwin to come back to Switzerland immediately. We've been
here only a week and now Sylwin has to leave tomorrow.
Sylwin wants me to go back with him but the news from the
front is so bad I'd rather stay with Father. He might need me.

[The front is that of the Polish-Soviet War, which culminated in
the invasion of Poland by the Red Armies and in the Polish victory
in the Battle of Warsaw of August 15, 1920. The peace was restored by the Treaty of Riga of March 18, 1921, between Poland,
Russia, and the Ukraine. *S. S.*]

We've decided that I shall remain here a little longer and
then go on to Switzerland alone. I'm afraid to travel by my-

self. These days traveling to Switzerland isn't so easy—it's
a roundabout route via Buchs—but I'm ashamed to admit my
fears.

I don't believe there's anything terribly urgent at Riond
Bosson. Paderewski must miss Sylwin, and Mme. Paderewska probably sent the telegram to make her husband happy.
Too bad, I'll just have to travel alone. The President is the
most important person in the world to us and there is no
sacrifice I wouldn't make for him.

Riond Bosson—June 23, 1920. Here I am back in Morges.
My first trip abroad on my own is over, thank heavens. It
wasn't so easy. There was endless red tape at every frontier.
I had the greatest trouble with my jewelry. How could I explain that I never part with it and that I'm not transporting
it for commercial reasons?

At the Swiss frontier, at Buchs, we all had to get off the
train for inspection. Then the thunderbolt struck. After
checking my passport, the customs official pointed to a bar-
racks a few hundred feet away from the station and said:
"Since you're coming from Russia, you must undergo de-
lousing treatment and stay in quarantine for two weeks."

I grew weak from fright and indignation. Two weeks in
quarantine! What would they think in Riond Bosson if I
didn't even have the chance to notify them where I had
disappeared to? I launched into an eloquent speech, explaining
that I had a Polish diplomatic passport, that I wasn't coming
from Russia and that I had no intention of being deloused.
The official remained adamant, turning a deaf ear to my
arguments. I could no longer control my rage. "Would you
really want me to bring lice from your quarantine to Paderewski's home in Morges?" I exploded.

In a flash the official was all attention. "What did you
say? Paderewski in Morges?"

I told him I was the wife of Paderewski's private secretary and that I was on my way to Riond Bosson. The metamorphosis was immediate and complete. He grabbed my

suitcases and made a dash for the train that was getting ready to start. Pushing me into a compartment, he bade me bon voyage. I didn't know whether to remain indignant or to laugh the incident off. It is heart-warming to know that Paderewski's name acts like a magic wand.

The Swiss are apparently trying to ward off infiltration of disease by quarantine, but they don't seem to understand that lice are innocent playthings as compared with the moral plague that is crossing frontiers not in the rags of wretched human beings but in the briefcases of some diplomats traveling in first-class compartments.

Political Triumph

July 20, 1920. Yesterday there was a long-distance telephone call from Warsaw. The Minister of Foreign Affairs was on the wire. Paderewski never talks over the phone, so Sylwin spoke for him. It was very important. When a conference of the foreign ministers of France, England, and Poland was suggested, Lloyd George announced that he would not participate unless Poland was represented by Paderewski. The new Polish Cabinet has humbled itself and requested Paderewski to be Poland's delegate.

Paderewski has agreed. After his Cabinet fell, he became a private person, but in the present difficult political and military situation confronting his country, he has not refused to represent a government of whose policy he disapproves. He must be totally incapable of bearing a personal grudge. Even though he is far from his land, in voluntary exile, Poland's welfare is always uppermost in his mind.

I'm elated at Paderewski's political triumph and also at the thought that I shall go with him to Paris and Aix-les-Bains. Maybe I'll even see and get to know Lloyd George and Clemenceau.

Paris—July 22, 1920. We're staying at the Ritz. The entire second floor has been reserved for Paderewski. The hotel people refer to it as the suite of the Queen of Rumania because she usually stops here when in Paris.

Upon our arrival we were taken on a tour of the second floor. We were shown the President's suite, our rooms, and the rooms for the secretarial staff. In the private drawing room we came upon a throng of guests, personal friends of the Paderewskis who had gathered there to welcome them. I met so many new people that I can't possibly remember all their names. I was quite impressed by Miss Mariotka Mickiewicz, the granddaughter of Adam Mickiewicz [Poland's greatest bard and poet].

We had no time to unpack or to change after the trip. Our guests literally kidnapped us and we had to devote all our attention to them. Dinner was a natural way out of our predicament. But it was served in the dining room on our floor and everybody stayed until late in the evening.

I had thought it was only at Riond Bosson that company took up so much time, but I see things are much more complicated in Paris.

August 15, 1920. Paris is enchanting in the summer but we practically never see it. It's true that all social life gravitates around the Ritz, but I would so love to stroll along the boulevards and window-shop. Sometimes we don't go out of the hotel for three days at a time.

The telephone starts ringing early in the morning. Hundreds of people want to see the Paderewskis and all calls are directed to us. Sylwin, Miss Helena Liibke (Mme. Paderewska's secretary), and I take turns answering the phone. We try to satisfy everybody but we occasionally have to resort to subterfuges to get rid of some people whom we know for certain Paderewski does not wish to see. People do not realize that it is physically impossible for him to receive all those who wish to see him and they put all the blame on us. Sylwin makes a note of every phone call and asks the

President if he'd care to see the person. Often he says No, and then we have to rack our brains for an excuse to refuse the appointment without creating bad feeling.

Another delicate problem is presented by a group of elderly ladies, old friends of the Paderewskis. Some of them are secretly in love with the President and cluster around Mme. Paderewska in the hope that they will catch a glimpse of her husband or that they will be invited to stay for lunch or dinner. Both Paderewskis reciprocate real friendship. Still, they'd like to relax and have some privacy once in a while. They don't always manage to get it because the strategy of the determined elderly ladies generally wins out. Mme. Paderewska frequently even lends them her discreet assistance in the belief that the President will be entertained.

The only breaks in Paderewski's heavy schedule are the daily one-hour walks in the Bois de Boulogne. Each afternoon the four of us—really five, because Mme. Paderewska invariably takes along her beloved Pekinese, Ping—ride to a deserted section of the park and pile out into the fresh air. Ping waddles behind Mme. Paderewska, the very picture of dignity. Sometimes Paderewski races with me. I always come off second best. This surprises me because I consider myself a good sprinter and then I *am* forty years younger. Sylwin says Paderewski does setting-up exercises every morning for twenty minutes. That must account for his excellent physical condition.

During our outing yesterday Mme. Paderewska informed me that my hat was hideous. This didn't bother me too much because when it comes to clothes, I prefer to be guided by male opinion. But I didn't notice any approbation in the glance Paderewski bestowed upon my hat either. Back in the hotel, Mme. Paderewska discreetly pressed two hundred francs into my hand, saying: "Please do me a favor and buy yourself a pretty hat as a gift from me." It was an embarrassing situation to say the least. Somehow I didn't feel right about accepting money to buy a gift for myself. Besides, I've always prided myself on my good taste in selecting clothes, so that it hurt my vanity to be told I needed a new hat. But I was afraid I might offend the Paderewskis if I refused the money. I kept it and slipped out of the hotel, fully intending to buy at least three hats for such an extravagant sum.

I was rather taken aback to discover that hats which fell to my liking started at two hundred francs. Accordingly, I lowered my requirements to a single hat. I finally found a black velvet number which I thought very becoming. I hurried back to the Ritz, anticipating the sensation my chic headgear would create. Just as I was entering the drawing room, the Paderewskis came in through the other door to greet their dinner guests. Mme. Paderewska looked at me, then at the chapeau, and opined: "That hat makes you look *comme une pompe funèbre!*" Paderewski threw me a quick glance and proceeded to greet the guests.

How was I supposed to know Paderewski hates black dresses, black hats, and any kind of black attire? So that's why Mme. Paderewska's extensive wardrobe doesn't include a single black dress! I still feel like crying for having added fifty francs of my own to a present which I shall never in my life wear again.

Aix-les-Bains, France—August 17, 1920. We've arrived in Aix-les-Bains today and we're stopping at the Hotel Mirabeau, which stands in a huge park. From every window all you see is mountains. I feel lost in the labyrinths of long corridors that are constantly filled with reporters and cameramen.

News from home has raised our spirits. The Battle of Warsaw is drawing to a close, the Bolshevik horde is in retreat, Poland is finally being liberated from the Asiatic invader.

August 25, 1920. The Conference has been on now for a week. Our room is next to the President's bedroom, but he's so busy all day, I hardly ever see him. Only at night, when Paderewski sits down with Sylwin for a brief game of cribbage before retiring, do I come in for a moment to say at once good morning and good night. You can see he's tired, but in a good mood, so the conference must be progressing satisfactorily. Once again he will demonstrate that nobody can represent Poland in the international field the way he does.

Aix-les-Bains is living up to its reputation as a fashionable spa. Very few of the people who come here intend to take the cure. In connection with the Conference of Foreign Ministers, crowds have flocked here from London and Paris just to be on the fringe of important events and to get a look at the statesmen who are trying to create a new order in war-weary Europe.

August 28, 1920. Mme. Paderewska goes to the baths every day. Left alone in the hotel, I have to look after Ping. He's a dog in a million, a born aristocrat. They say his ancestors resided in the Imperial Palace at Peking. Ping displays no interest whatsoever in the opposite sex, perhaps as a result of the skirmish in his youth which cost him an eye. He never barks and doesn't bite, but neither does he consider anyone except Mme. Paderewska important. Even the President is barely tolerated.

Because the reporters are always on the lookout for details about the private life of the Paderewskis, Ping has received a good deal of publicity. Whenever I go out for a walk, he's the pretext for my being asked all sorts of questions. I refrain from getting into a conversation with strangers because I know that such a seemingly innocent exchange of remarks might lead to the publication the next day of a lengthy interview with a "person close to Paderewski." To simplify matters I pretend not to understand French. It's not so easy when I speak French as fluently as Polish. I have to be careful not to answer in spite of myself.

I've met a lot of new people who've come down to Aix-les-Bains just because Paderewski is here. They keep getting in our way all day long and they all say they've been friends of the Paderewskis for years. But I don't believe anybody anymore and try my best not to get involved with them. It's quite a job to be aloof. Because I look so darn young, everyone thinks I must be naïve.

The other day I had the dubious pleasure of getting acquainted with one of these hangers-on, Mr. O. What a peculiar man! A complete stranger, he came up to me and handed me a gift. I was still more surprised when I unwrapped the present and saw a pair of embroidered red bedroom slippers that were so old-fashioned and hideous that even my great-grandmother wouldn't have been seen in them. My first reaction was to wonder what pockmarked Mr. O. was after. I found out soon enough. He started to commiserate me, bewailing the fact that I'm always alone and that although it's an honor to be part of Paderewski's entourage, there's no future in it. Private secretaries never get anywhere, he said. Now, he, Mr. O., has such connections in the Polish Foreign Office that he could easily get Sylwin a post at the Vatican or the Quirinal which would enable him to scale the heights of diplomatic success. I was thoroughly exasperated by this stupid talk and couldn't for the life of me understand why the Paderewskis didn't send the fellow packing. Mustering all my calm, I told him Sylwin and I are not interested in a future. I explained icily that we're truly grateful for the confidence the President bestows upon my husband, that we'll never disappoint him and that we feel the happiest and proudest people under the sun just because we can serve Paderewski. I'll wager Mr. O. would love to take Sylwin's place. Wouldn't that be lucky for the President!

Riond Bosson—September 14, 1920. The conference at Aix-les-Bains is now part of history. I was there all the time and I never even saw Lloyd George nor Clemenceau! I shall never admit it in Warsaw. My only consolation is that Sylwin got me a photograph with a personal dedication from both statesmen.

Yesterday Sylwin and the President left Aix-les-Bains

for Paris while Mme. Paderewska and I came to Switzerland to take care of some important matters at Riond Bosson before rejoining them in Paris. This is the first time the Paderewskis have been separated in all the years they've been married. Mme. Paderewska is so afraid of an attempt on the life of her husband that she accompanies him everywhere. When she cannot go with him, she waits for him in the car.

At parting, one of the delegates to the Conference presented Paderewski with a huge carton of cigarettes. As the President likes to smoke his own brand of cigarettes, he handed me the gift with instructions to leave it at Riond Bosson. That's when my troubles began.

I deliberately put the parcel in a noticeable place in the compartment reserved for Mme. Paderewska and myself, figuring that in case of customs inspection it wouldn't look as if we were trying to smuggle cigarettes over the Swiss border. Well, when they came in to check our passports at the frontier, they naturally noticed the great number of cigarettes. The next thing we knew, we had several customs officials in our compartment inquiring sharply as to the meaning of the contraband cigarettes. When I told them neither Mme. Paderewska nor I smoked, they tried to confiscate the cigarettes. I wouldn't let go of the carton and they made me leave the train and follow them. I was on the verge of tears. I *couldn't* give up the cigarettes and the train might start any minute. Mme. Paderewska would go on alone and we'd be accused of smuggling cigarettes into the bargain. What would the President have to say to all this?

At the customs office I lost my patience when another inspector commenced berating me. What, I demanded, was I supposed to do when these cigarettes had been given to Paderewski by a very important dignitary? Should I have thrown them away? The inspector smiled. "The next time your President receives a present of this kind, keep it out of sight. Don't provoke the customs officials."

I got back on the train just in time.

Paris—September 20, 1920. We've been back at the Ritz since September 16th. We're all of good cheer. The news from Poland keeps getting better and better. The Red Army's retreat from Warsaw has turned into a rout. Only a few months earlier it had seemed that the horde from the East would move across Poland and inundate Western Europe. Now it's fleeing in disorder, abandoning loot and weapons. Once again Poland has saved Christian civilization from Eastern barbarism.

There were no guests at lunch today, so I sat next to the President. I was filled with apprehension when oysters were served as an appetizer. I'd never tasted them in my life and never even had any desire to eat something that was still alive. Paderewski was quick to note my hesitation. "Don't you like oysters?" he asked. I admitted I'd never tried them before. "That's bad. Oysters are nutritious and good for the brain. But you must know how to prepare them. The important thing is not to spoil the cartilage because it's the tastiest part of the whole oyster." Suiting the action to his words, he delicately scooped the oyster out of its shell and generously sprinkled it with lemon juice. "Now, try this." I would have gladly declined, but I summoned a bright smile and bravely swallowed the slithery mollusk. The President was already preparing the next one. After I'd gotten a few down and my anxiety wore off, I discovered that oysters have quite a pleasant taste. From now on, oysters on the half shell will meet with my approval.

September 30, 1920. In the endless chain of receptions, visits, and conferences, we rarely spend an evening by ourselves. If the reception isn't too official, the President usually winds up the evening with a rubber of bridge. Aside from bridge, his favorite form of entertainment is the cinema. Often, after dinner, Paderewski invites all the dinner guests to the movies.

Today, at the dinner table, somebody mentioned that a good film was being shown in a cinema on the Champs

Elysées. Three taxis took the whole company to the theatre. When we entered, the house was so full that we all slipped into the last row. I don't know whether the picture had just begun or was about to end.

Before I had a chance to become oriented in the plot, the lights went on. I heard shouts and saw the audience rise to its feet. The orchestra struck up a tune which we recognized as an attempt at the Polish National Anthem. Everyone stood facing our row of chairs. When the orchestra finished playing, a veritable tempest sprang up: "Vive Paderewski!" "Vive la Pologne!" "Vive Paderewski!" The crowd surged toward us and a moment later I saw the President borne aloft in the direction of the door amid more cries of "Vive Paderewski!" Terrified, I tried to follow him and found myself also being swept streetward, although not on the shoulders of the French crowd. In the street Paderewski was surrounded by an enthusiastic mob and the Champs Elysées resounded with his name. I returned to the Ritz alone as did the rest of our theatre party.

The President has one regret—he didn't get to see the picture.

November 1920. The banquet Paderewski gave at the Ritz in honor of Marshal Foch was a great success for everyone but me. I was present only at the beginning. Important social and political function that it was, everybody who was anybody wanted to be invited. But the banquet hall could accommodate only two hundred. As a result, Sylwin and I suddenly became very popular. People left calling cards, telephoned us, invited us here and there, all in the hope that through us they'd get a coveted invitation to the banquet.

Luckily for us, the President took upon himself the difficult and thankless task of drawing up the seating plan for his two hundred guests. He did it better than an experienced chief of protocol could have done, too.

The night of the banquet I was feverish and dizzy, the

after-effects of poisoning from the lobster I had eaten. But I didn't tell a soul about the way I felt for fear I might not be permitted to attend the gala affair.

Slowly the guests assembled. I was standing near Mme. Paderewska when Marshal Foch entered. I was struck by his noble, charming, and prepossessing appearance. The Marshal was cordially greeted by his hosts and then Paderewski, seeing me standing shyly nearby, introduced me to the Marshal: "And this is my little daughter." The Frenchman was rather taken aback by the statement. He pressed my hand and with touching frankness and embarrassment murmured: "How could I have been ignorant of the existence of President Paderewski's daughter?"

"It's very simple, Monsieur le Maréchal," I replied, "I'm only the wife of the President's secretary. It's just that our President is such a good father to me." Marshal Foch was relieved he hadn't committed a faux pas and I was delighted to have had a few words with him.

Sylwin and I sat down at opposite ends of the tremendous lavishly set table. Already at the first course I felt so ill that I got up from the table, walked to the door by sheer will power, and quietly fainted away in the corridor before Sylwin had even been able to get to me. Fine thing! The guests naturally thought I'm expecting. Nobody suspected the unromantic lobster. I am just recovering from that serious illness.

As if He Were Playing Chopin

Riond Bosson — November 11, 1920. We've returned from Paris but not for long. The opening session of the League of Nations will be held at Geneva on November 15. Paderewski has accepted the appointment as first delegate and will head the Polish delegation. Sylwin is looking for suitable quarters in Geneva where we might all live while the League is in session.

Geneva — November 25, 1920. The Paderewskis, Sylwin and I, and two confidential secretaries, Leniutka Liibke and Miss Maria Kropiwnicka, are installed in an enormous apartment on the Quai du Mont Blanc.

I attend each session of the League of Nations. After the first few days of excitement the meetings have settled into a monotonous routine. Only the speeches of the more prominent delegates create fresh interest. They are delivered in one of the two official languages of the League — French and English. After each speech the translation is read, which is terribly boring. In the meantime, the delegates converse in low voices or slip out for a smoke. Paderewski alone hardly ever leaves his seat. He never engages in conversation during a speech; he listens attentively but makes no notes. I was surprised today to notice that during an exceptionally long and uninteresting speech he was sketching something on the program. At long last, the meeting drew to a close and the bored delegates filed out of the hall. I saw the President's program fall from the desk to the floor.

Curious to know what Paderewski had drawn on his program, I ran downstairs and tried to get into the assembly hall. The doorman stopped me, explaining that only delegates were admitted on the floor. In return, I explained to him that I belonged to Paderewski's household and that the President had forgotten his gloves on his seat. The program was lying on the floor and I hastily stuffed it into my pocketbook. Unable to restrain my curiosity any longer, I took it out as soon as I was in the corridor. I blinked when I saw an excellent drawing of the Peruvian delegate, who had been sitting near Paderewski.

At tea I asked the President: "Did you ever draw?" He looked at me with surprised interest. By way of reply, I triumphantly produced the program with the portrait.

"Oh, that," he laughed, "that Peruvian's face intrigued me, so I made a sketch of it."

I had my pen ready as I asked, "Won't you autograph it for me?"

I'm pleased as punch about this acquisition to my collection. I don't suppose anyone else in the world has a drawing by Paderewski — and an autographed one at that.

Geneva — December 4, 1920. This has been a red-letter day at the League because today Paderewski addressed the delegates. All week the League's secretariat had been besieged with requests for passes for this occasion.

Long before he was scheduled to speak, every seat on the floor was taken and the spectators' gallery was jammed with standees.

At last, Paderewski came up on the platform — a leonine figure radiating moral strength. Accustomed though I am to seeing him, my heart skipped a beat. The audience rose in a spontaneous gesture of welcome and burst into loud and long applause. Paderewski acknowledged the tribute with a dignified low bow and waited for the ovation to subside. From the first minute of his speech, the audience was so quiet you could have heard a pin drop. For more than an hour Paderewski addressed this assemblage of the world's greatest diplomats in French without notes and held them as spellbound as if he were playing Chopin for them. When he finished, he received another ovation lasting several minutes. Then, to everyone's undisguised astonishment, Paderewski launched into an English version of his own speech. He's the only delegate who has perfect command of both languages.

The meeting was adjourned following Paderewski's bilingual performance. To have any other speakers after him would only have been an anticlimax. Delegates and spectators gathered in knots in the corridors to exchange comments about the oration they'd just heard.

What the President's appreciative audience did not know

was how hard he had worked to make this—and, as a matter of fact, every speech of his—the masterpiece of clear thinking and brilliant verbal form that it was. Time ceases to exist for Paderewski when he is in the throes of composing a speech. If he works on it during the day, lunch or dinner are hours late. Nobody dares interrupt the President. So we all wait mournfully, stealing a snack as best we can, for none of us would dream of sitting down to a meal without him. Sometimes we wait so long that lunch practically runs into dinner. Woe to the guest who has been invited for such a day—he must wait with the rest of us.

When the President writes at night, he often works until the small hours of the morning. At such times we, too, go without sleep because nobody retires without bidding Paderewski good night. We all stay up, even Mme. Paderewska and her secretaries. Before the President finally goes to bed, he and Sylwin still have to play a game of cribbage. Sylwin yawns scandalously but plays; I'm generally so sleepy I'm groggy; only Paderewski shows no sign of fatigue and never yawns.

After he writes out his speech, the President commits it to memory word for word. For the meeting of the League of Nations today he accomplished the prodigious feat of memorizing two speeches, one in French and one in English.

December 11, 1920. Each delegation to the League of Nations is tendering a reception for the other delegations. It was Poland's turn yesterday. In reality, the Polish reception was given by Paderewski inasmuch as he footed the bill. Heretofore, all such affairs were for men only—pretty boring, too—while the poor diplomats' wives and daughters twiddled their thumbs at home. Paderewski was the first in Geneva to invite both the delegates *and* the fair sex, a step which met with the unqualified approval of the grateful ladies.

The supper and the ball that followed made all previous functions pale into insignificance, but they set Paderewski back ten thousand Swiss francs. Quite a sensation were the mountains of fine Havana cigars (ten thousand of them) which the President (who smokes only cigarettes) received from the Cuban delegate, Aguerro y Betancourt. I'm afraid the cigars were a greater hit than the ladies with the diplomats. But as the men were in the majority—mostly young unmarried secretaries or delegates who hadn't yet brought their families over—there was no dearth of dancing partners. I did not sit out a single dance. The delegate from Siam was the best dancer.

At one point one of the gentlemen headed in my direction to ask me for another dance, but noticing the activity around the cigars, he suddenly changed his mind and his course. Right he was, too, because I'd still be there while the cigars were dwindling fast. Sure enough, he bobbed up again some time later and we started to dance. He paid me a compliment about my dancing and without further ado asked me for a dancing date for tomorrow, all the while holding me tighter than was really necessary. I had an overwhelming desire to give him a piece of my mind, but as my rôle was more that of a hostess than of a guest, I had to be gracious and nice, confining my vengeance to a hearty wish that the cigars with which he'd stuffed his pockets might be crushed.

Judging by the number of requests for dates I received in the course of a single evening from these romantically inclined diplomats, I gather they must be frightfully bored in placid Geneva.

The President was constantly surrounded by delighted guests. Headed by the wife of the Chinese delegate, the charming Mrs. Wellington Koo, every lady present came up to thank him for his departure from the custom of stag parties.

Very few of the guests—only some elderly men and women— refrained from dancing. Of course the Paderewskis did not dance. They're too dignified and inspire too much respect to be asked to dance, I imagine.

And yet, the Paderewskis do dance—both of them! But only in the foyer at Riond Bosson when there is no company.

Sometimes after the evening rubber of bridge, when I'm so sleepy I can't wait to go upstairs, Mme. Paderewska suggests that we dance. Leniutka puts a record on the big phonograph that isn't used for years on end and we begin dancing around the billiard table. I was panic-stricken when the President first asked me to dance, and I'll never get used to such a dancing partner! He dances too well, too musically. He invents so many steps in each dance that it's difficult to follow in exact time with the music, to the tempo of which he sticks with minute precision.

Sylwin usually dances with Mme. Paderewska, Henryk Opienski with Mrs. Wilkonska, who tries to be sociable but complains even as she dances: *Boze, Boze!* Then we change partners. Our improvised dancing party lasts around ten minutes. None of us would qualify it as relaxation, but since it's all done for "reasons of health," to provide the President with a little exercise before bedtime, we all dance with a will.

December 20, 1920. Paderewski has resigned as a delegate to the League of Nations. His resignation has evoked a good deal of comment and regret in diplomatic circles. His withdrawal from the League will certainly weaken the prestige of the Polish delegation and the League as a whole will lose one of its staunchest supporters.

I don't know what prompted him to make this decision, but he did announce at the same time that he and his wife are planning to go to the United States to participate in the Polish-American Convention at Pittsburgh.

[When Paderewski returned to Switzerland from Poland in February, 1920, he faced the urgent necessity of attending to his disrupted finances. Very little had been done in that direction when he consented to represent Poland at the Council of the Ambassadors and, later, to accept the appointment as head of the Polish delegation to the League of Nations. It was inevitable that, opposing the new Polish government, Paderewski should find his views in conflict with those of the Warsaw Cabinet, and that the conflict should deter and discourage him in his task of representing his country abroad. When it finally became clear that the United States would not join the League, Paderewski lost his hope that the League would ever become the instrument of peace and justice Woodrow Wilson intended it to be. So, when his political difficulties became complicated by increasingly urgent financial problems, Paderewski decided to relinquish all his government duties and as a private citizen attend to his personal affairs. *S. S.*]

I'm overjoyed that Paderewski has asked Sylwin and me to accompany him. He fears, however, that Father won't agree to my going away so far for so long. I'm positive Father won't object.

At any rate, Sylwin and I are off for Warsaw to spend Christmas there.

Warsaw — December 22, 1920. My beloved capital has changed greatly since I was here last. You still see plenty of uniforms in the street, but the university students are back at their studies so as not to waste time until the peace treaty with the Soviets is signed. There seems to be feverish activity everywhere to repair the terrible ravages of the war. Not a single railroad station east of Warsaw has been spared and trains move across temporary bridges. Many families are in mourning for their men, but those who survived are full of optimism and energy. The one bitter note is the general regret that Paderewski, who did so much to liberate Poland, not only doesn't head the government but is away from his country.

Father isn't the least bit opposed to my going to America. He's glad that I'll get a chance to see that wonderful country.

Those Fantastic Towering Buildings

Riond Bosson — January 18, 1921. The Paderewskis were very glad to learn that we would both go with them. The house is literally upside down. Added to the never-ending pilgrimage of visitors are the hundred and one troubles that harass a prospective traveler: packing countless trunks and suitcases, writing a mass of letters, arranging the details of our journey to and stay in the United States.

It's all very hectic and we are exhausted. The only member of our expedition who is the picture of unconcern, who packs no bags and who doesn't have to worry about reservations is Ping. I wonder who thought up that expression about "a dog's life?"

Paris — February 1, 1921. After weeks of preparation, we finally left Riond Bosson. I'm sure we don't even know how many trunks, bags, bundles, and odds and ends have been taken along at the last minute with a view to packing them properly later on.

This time we've stopped at the Hotel du Palais d'Orsay, an enormous old-fashioned hotel in an outmoded section of Paris. Never in my life have I seen such a long corridor. I wondered why the President chose this ancient hostelry in preference to the Ritz. I soon had my answer. He stays at the Ritz when he's in Paris in an official capacity, but when he's here privately he stops at the Palais d'Orsay because he has a soft spot in his heart for it. He told us that many years ago when he became sufficiently affluent to afford a first-rate hotel, he stopped at the Palais d'Orsay. In those days the Hotel du Palais d'Orsay was one of the best in all of Paris. Now I understand why everybody in the place welcomes the President with such sincere friendliness and why he cordially shook hands with them all.

In spite of the faded splendor, the atmosphere is quite

homey. A special chef, a maître d'hôtel, and two old waiters who know Paderewski's likes and dislikes from the old days were assigned to the President.

The small sitting room of Paderewski's suite, graced by a magnificent Erard piano, was already filled with guests who had timed their arrival to coincide with our appearance. The maître d'hôtel came to take the order for dinner. Mme. Paderewska ordered, asking the President as she went along whether he approved each choice. Sylwin naturally couldn't resist the temptation and kept suggesting a different sauce or dressing for each dish.

Paderewski agreed to every suggestion. "And of course a chocolate soufflé with chocolate sauce for dessert, because Mr. Strakacz is fond of it," the President added. The maître d'hôtel solemnly wrote down "chocolate soufflé."

But when it came to ordering the wines, nobody volunteered an opinion. Paderewski made his own selection from the wine list, specifying the type and the vintage. We concluded the meal with champagne, because the President prefers champagne to any other wine—but it must be sweet.

On Board the SS La France—February 6, 1921. I still can't believe it's true. So we are really going to America! When the boat train pulled into Le Havre this afternoon my happiness was a little mixed with fear of seasickness, but the sight of the steamer reassured me. The *La France* is so huge, I do not think she will roll at all. Sylwin and I have a beautiful stateroom with private bath.

Coming aboard, we hurriedly unpacked and changed for dinner. Our party has unexpectedly been augmented by an American couple, Mr. and Mrs. Ernest Schelling. Schelling is a pianist and a composer and is one of the very few friends who call the President by his first name. He's very distinguished looking, gracious and gay. Mrs. Schelling is just as charming and dresses beautifully. Their home is in the States but they also have an estate in Switzerland.

We called for Leniutka [Helena Liibke] and the Schellings, and with them waited for the Paderewskis. The seven of us then went up to the tremendous dining room. All eyes turned to the President and followed him to his table. But it was a long time before he could sit down because every few seconds somebody kept coming up to shake his hand.

While we were standing around our table, I suddenly felt a little dizzy. The room seemed stifling. When we sat down, Paderewski turned to me and asked, "Well, how does our little girl feel, no seasickness yet?" In an instant I had pushed my chair back and virtually bounded out of the dining room in mortal terror that I might disgrace myself in full view of that brilliant public.

Sylwin followed me to our cabin and gleefully informed me that *La France* was still safely anchored in port and that she wouldn't sail until four o'clock in the morning!

New York — February 13, 1921. After a terribly stormy crossing (Sylwin and I were both mightily seasick in contrast with the Paderewskis, who are excellent sailors), we steamed into New York harbor.

At the pier a throng had gathered to greet the President. There were scores of photographers and camera men on hand, not counting the well-wishers and friends who had come just to catch a fleeting glimpse of Paderewski.

I was so fascinated by the skyscrapers twinkling with a million eyes — so colossal and strange in comparison with Europe — that I became separated from the President's party. Mr. and Mrs. Michal Kwapiszewski — she is a very nice American and he's a handsome young Pole with thick gray hair — came up to me, introduced themselves and offered to take me to the Gotham Hotel in their convertible car. They laughed when I practically lay down on the seat of the open car, the better to see those fantastic towering buildings lit up somewhere in the clouds.

The lobby of the Gotham was all astir with more reporters, and people for whom Paderewski must be quite a drawing card. A few minutes later the Paderewskis, Sylwin, and Leniutka drove up to the hotel and headed straight for the elevator. We, too, tried to push our way through to an elevator, but in the crowd I lost the Kwapiszewskis and had to get into an elevator filled with strangers.

We shot up so quickly and rode so long that my stomach sank and the pressure in my ears made me feel as if I were on the summit of Mont Blanc. Never before have I ridden in such a fast elevator. I got off at the last stop, but the absolute silence told me the Paderewskis were not around. After peeking here and there, I pushed the button and got back into the elevator. The ride down was even more upsetting. I got off at what I thought was the ground floor but it turned out to be another floor, and the Paderewskis were not there, either. Again I pushed the button, stepped into an elevator and, instead of landing on the ground floor, found myself back on the top floor. By now I was desperate. I couldn't say a thing in English and I couldn't even get to the ground floor to ask what the number of the Paderewski suite was. At last I hit upon a more considerate elevator which stopped at every floor. On the seventeenth floor the elevator door opened and there was the President standing directly in front of it, his eyes lighting up as he caught sight of me. "My dear child, I was worried about you and was going down to look for you! I was afraid you'd gotten lost."

How good the President is. He always senses and thinks about everything even if he doesn't say much. I suspect he realizes I lost my head when I saw this America.

February 14, 1921. After a perfect night's sleep, I awoke still feeling the ship's rolling. Sylwin rose early. No sooner did he go out of the room than someone tapped on the door and without waiting for an answer a man walked right into the middle of the room and addressed me from there. I didn't know what to do, especially as the fellow not only failed to react to my conversation of one word: "mistake," but looked as if he had every intention of remaining.

Slowly it dawned on me that he must be a reporter. Sylwin had warned me not to talk to anyone because these newshawks are ready to pounce on whatever I'd say and then write up Paderewski in the papers. I was afraid to utter a word, afraid to be rude, and afraid to appear ridiculous. Smiling my prettiest, I indicated by graceful gestures toward my bed and the door that I'd appreciate his leaving. My intruder obliged, though not too graciously. In a flash, I was out of bed and going toward the door to lock it, but before I could get to it, another reporter was coming in for a silent interview.

Because I was in my nightgown, I hastily ran into the bathroom and slammed the door behind me. Cautiously half-opening it a little later, I saw four new gentlemen calmly conversing in the middle of our bedroom, apparently waiting for Sylwin. When he finally returned, he politely asked the group to leave, explaining that he could not grant them an interview; he then prudently locked the door. When it comes to Paderewski, nothing seems to be sacred to American reporters!

February 18, 1921. I have gotten to know a great many Polish Americans, mostly clergy. They're kind, pleasant, and direct. And they love Paderewski. Whenever I meet a Polish American, I feel as if I've known him a long time. So many of the names are familiar to me because I've heard them mentioned in connection with the generous American aid sent to Poland after the World War. Paderewski himself often spoke of the priests and lay men and women who had extended a helping hand to assist him in rebuilding Poland. The gifts ran into millions of dollars, and all of them, large or small, were sent either to the White Cross that Mme. Paderewska founded, or in care of Paderewski himself.

The Poles over here love America and I have the feeling they would not stand for a word of criticism of their country. But their hearts belong to Poland and Paderewski is to them a symbol of their native land. They're so proud of him!

February 19, 1921. Everybody knows that the Paderewskis never go out alone. They like to attend private receptions with their entire "court" — Sylwin, Leniutka, and myself — while Sylwin invariably accompanies them to all official functions.

To give us the treat of an evening all to ourselves, the Schellings invited the Paderewskis to an intimate dinner at their home today.

As soon as Sylwin made sure that the President and Mme. Paderewska had left the hotel, he made a bee-line for the Steinway. In all the time that I've known the President he hasn't touched the piano, except for that one occasion in Riond Bosson when he acted as accompanist. Nevertheless, whenever Paderewski stops at a hotel in any part of the world, a Steinway concert piano is always waiting for him in the sitting room, put there with the compliments of the Steinway Company.

Coming out of our room into the corridor, I saw open doors all over the place. People came out of the elevators and listened raptly as Sylwin unconcernedly played a sentimental waltz. I hurried back into the suite to tell Sylwin that a crowd was gathering in the corridor under the misapprehension that the music issuing from the President's quarters was being played by Paderewski. At this, instead of quitting, Sylwin began a demonstration of concert keyboard technique and of a forceful use of the pedals. Peering through a crack in the neighboring door, I saw the corridor filled with people, all convinced they were listening to Paderewski. After a few resounding measures, Sylwin ended the practical joke. The audience lingered in the corridor for at least another five minutes and then melted away in disappointment.

Pittsburgh, Hotel William Penn — February 22, 1921. We're in Pittsburgh for a few days attending the Polish Convention. This was the chief reason for Paderewski's visit to the United States. It's a huge convention. I've met scores of Polish leaders from all sections of America. Some I know from Warsaw, Morges, or Paris. I was surprised to learn that almost all of the Poles here speak pretty good Polish, even though a good many of them were born in America and have never been to Poland. They all make a special effort to talk with Paderewski in Polish because they know nothing pleases him more. Whenever the President hears a child speak Polish, he simply beams. He believes every Pole should speak the tongue of his fathers, and he insists it is the sacred duty of every Polish mother to teach her children the Polish language. I remember that Paderewski once said at Riond Bosson that every child of a German mother always speaks German, because every German mother sees to it regardless of the nationality of her husband.

I attend the sessions of the Convention all day and find them very interesting. Sylwin and I have received tags bearing our names and the inscription "Honorary Deputy to the Convention," which give us free access everywhere. They wouldn't believe me in Warsaw if I were to tell them I was a deputy.

The President alternates between brilliant speeches in Polish and in English, as the occasion warrants. Without seeing the enthusiasm, admiration, and worship with which Paderewski is surrounded here, it is impossible to imagine the extent to which he has won the hearts of the delegates. He is being honored not only as a statesman and an artist, but as a great human being.

New York—February 29, 1921. The Paderewskis have decided to go to Paso Robles in California for an extended stay. I'm so happy. Now I shall get to see all of America.

But there always has to be a fly in the ointment. I still haven't gotten over the feeling of terror I experienced after the mess I made today by my ignorance of English.

Because the telephone in our room rings from morning till night, to avoid any confusion while Sylwin is away and an English call comes through, I learned how to say: "I am sorry, nobody is in." That was the reply I gave today to the hotel clerk when he announced the arrival of luncheon guests who had been invited by the Paderewskis without anyone telling me about it. The guests went away, and was there a row! Naturally I didn't admit I'd said what I did. The blame was put on the desk clerk who'd apparently rung the wrong room.

But Mme. Paderewska gave us no peace, she was so annoyed and upset. These turned-away guests were terribly important to her, they were some railroad "big shots" who had it in their power to permit Ping to ride with us instead of in the baggage car. Mme. Paderewska would never consent to be separated from Ping. That dog even goes to the movies, being carried in under the steamer rug in defiance of regulations. How could he be expected to travel alone all the way to California? After today's unfortunate incident, the Paderewskis have decided not to ask railroad officials for the special permission.

This has taught me a lesson about being more careful in answering the phone. But I wish I knew what to say instead of that neat sentence that proved so treacherous.

There are always so many guests, so many people who are forever asking me about something, that I run out on Fifth Avenue whenever I get the chance. I like everything here: the American women with their beautiful legs and shapely ankles, dressed in fine furs the like of which you don't see even in Paris; the superb window displays; and above all I like the feeling of freedom. I like to be alone at times, but Mme. Paderewska frowns upon such heresy. She'd prefer seeing me around all day. She must have said something about it to the President because for the first time he rebuked me, but so delicately and tenderly, that I felt quite unhappy. He asked me why I'm always hiding and avoiding the company of Mme. Paderewska instead of being with her. I told him frankly that since I don't feel I'm needed, and inasmuch as there already are so many people around her, I tactfully make myself scarce. To this the President replied with a touch of irritation, "There is no need to be *too* tactful." And Mme. Paderewska amplified this by remarking: "A person could live with you for a hundred years and still not get close to you." I didn't answer because I'd rather take walks along Fifth Avenue.

They did find something for me to do, though, to keep me busy inside the suite. I'm supposed to change the water of the flowers with which the sitting room is filled, check to see whom they're from, and keep the bouquets fresh looking. I've done it so many times I've lost count. Sometimes there are baskets of beautiful flowers for me, too, but they all have to go to the general sitting room. How I'd love to have them in my own room. I'd really enjoy caring for them then.

So, whenever I can, I skip out on Fifth Avenue. There are plenty of people milling around the Paderewskis as it is. And I feel perfectly fine taking in the sights of New York.

On the Train for Chicago—March 20, 1921. Our departure for California today was another adventure. We left the hotel in two taxicabs. The Paderewskis, Sylwin, and I rode in the first; and Leniutka and Augusta (the colored maid who joins the Paderewskis whenever they come to America) followed with the usual mountain of assorted suitcases and traveling bags. That luggage plagues our existence. There are so many pieces, at least one hundred, that we can't keep track of them all and something is forever getting lost.

I thought we'd never get to the station on time. The President doesn't believe in hurrying and always leaves at the very last minute. It's bad enough when we're going on a short trip but worse when we were supposed to travel five days and six nights. The railroad fare for the six of us had cost a small fortune. It wouldn't have been very funny if we'd missed that train.

To make matters worse, a crowd gathered around Paderewski in the hotel lobby. The President moved along exasperatingly slowly, pausing every few seconds to shake someone's hand or to give a generous tip.

I breathed more easily when we were finally sitting in

the taxi. Sylwin held the President's medium-size pigskin bag, which we all know is the most important, even though we haven't the slightest idea what's in it. It's the only bag Paderewski packs himself and the only one he keeps an eye on to make sure it doesn't disappear.

We were at the station in plenty of time, but two minutes before train time Leniutka, Augusta, and most of our luggage still hadn't shown up. Unable to account for their absence, we got on the train which was about to start. Just then Augusta appeared, squealing hysterically, and flung herself into Mme. Paderewska's arms with such force that she almost knocked her down. Behind her, Leniutka came running, her hair streaming. Everybody on the platform began pitching suitcases into the train. The last bag was thrown in just as the train started moving. Augusta kept shrieking her happiness at having caught the train and it was impossible to quiet her. Even the President had been worried by the episode. Only Ping, concealed in his specially constructed suitcase, failed to react, knowing he was traveling incognito.

Our feeling of relaxation soon suffered a shock. When the conductor came for the tickets, it developed that Sylwin had left all of them from New York to San Francisco and Paso Robles in the hotel! Mme. Paderewska scolded him roundly for such absent-mindedness. But it's Paderewski, so the conductor made no issue of it. Receiving a promise that the tickets would be delivered to him, he merely made a note of the incident.

Chicago, Hotel Congress — March 22, 1921. Chicago is such a huge city its unnumbered streets are an invitation to get lost. I took a taxi to visit my American aunt who happens to be staying here with Josette and Evelina, my cousins, and the fare was $8.40! I lost all desire for further exploring at that price. Besides, I was scared stiff the taxi driver was abducting me, because I had no idea a city could be that immense. I, for one, am glad we're resuming our journey tomorrow.

San Francisco—March 25, 1921. The trip to California was like living in a fairy tale. I felt spellbound by the abundance of breathtakingly beautiful views. The Paderewskis have made this trip so many times it no longer leaves any impression on them, but I kept my eyes glued to the window and shall never forget this train ride. Everyone else was relieved when the journey was finally over, but I could travel like this for weeks and months without wearying of it. Probably no one was happier than Ping to arrive in California. When the poor dog was lifted out of the bag, he couldn't stand on his legs. Throughout the entire trip Ping wouldn't budge from his little trunk, refusing food and other ministrations. All the railroad help were aware of Ping's presence and even hinted at an airing with their blessing, but this descendant of Chinese canine aristocracy must have realized his anomalous position in a passenger car and prudently stuck to his valise.

San Francisco is enchanting. The Paderewskis have stopped here for a day just to show us the town. They drove us around everywhere and were delighted with our pleasure and wonder.

We spent much time visiting Chinatown. The President is fond of this part of the city. No wonder, when he has such a fine collection of Chinese art in Riond Bosson.

Paso Robles, California—March 26, 1921. Last evening we left San Francisco for the President's ranch at Paso Robles.

At midnight our train slowed down and the conductor called out our station. Looking through the window we saw the sky luridly aglow. Even the air particles seemed to be caught in a fiery dance. My first thought was that the station was burning down.

The train stopped in front of a tiny building, the Paso

Robles Station. The concourse out to greet the Paderewskis
was so great it was almost impossible to alight from the
train. Before I could collect my wits, I saw the members of
this self-designated reception committee grabbing a suitcase apiece. I ran after a fellow making off with Paderewski's
precious pigskin bag, but I soon realized there was nothing
to fear. These were all friends. Looking around in search
of the President, I saw him and Mme. Paderewska seated in a
big open car.

I felt like rubbing my eyes to make sure the whole thing
wasn't a dream. In spite of the press, there was no hubbub;
it was all so dignified, solemn, and majestic. The car with the
Paderewskis in it inched along between a guard of honor
consisting of two rows of automobiles, in military formation,
filled with people holding the flaming torches that turned
night into day. Small children walked backward in front of
the slowly moving car and strewed the ground with flowers.
Behind the Paderewskis came the public, each marcher armed
with part of our baggage—our multitude of bags for once
serving a useful purpose. There were no shouts, no cheers,
but all the cars in the honor guard tooted a march on their
horns until we got to the Paso Robles Hotel some fifteen
minutes later.

Paso Robles Hotel—April 6, 1921. I don't think there can be
any country in the world more beautiful than California.
Each day is lovelier than the one before. For the first time
since I have been with the Paderewskis, we have relative
freedom. Paso Robles is a miniature town with only two
streets, and the countryside is uninhabited. Hence, the
Paderewskis have few visitors, while the people in our hotel
have by this time become accustomed to seeing the President
daily and no longer importune him.

Every day we go on long walks and spend hours wandering around the President's property. There is no house on
the land. That's why we're staying at the hotel. Both the
Paderewskis take a deep interest in their Rancho.

The President also owns an oil field near Santa Maria. We motored down to have a look at it the other day. Paderewski peered inside the oil-well derrick and put questions to the engineers in charge of drilling operations. Their explanations sounded optimistic. However the field he bought is the only one in the entire area that has not yet produced oil. It seems to me the President has never yet made a shrewd business deal.

Evening means movie-time for us, for although Paso Robles is only a two-street town, it boasts no less than two moving picture houses, with a program change daily and with two changes on Sunday, which means that Sundays we go both afternoon and evening. "We" means all of us, including Ping hidden underneath the blanket.

Paderewski is very fond of the movies and always enjoys himself capitally. Neither the musical accompaniment nor uncomfortable chairs can ever spoil his enjoyment of a film.

I don't care too much for the cinema, but by dint of going every day, I've become used to it. We've luckily hit upon a couple of good pictures lately with Mary Pickford and Douglas Fairbanks. Anyway, it's a pleasure to go just to see the President having such a grand time.

April 12, 1921. I'm sorry to say we're leaving Paso Robles today. I wouldn't mind staying here all my life. It's been so wonderful, every minute of it, that I'm ashamed to confess I missed no one and nothing. My only consolation is that I'll see Hollywood on our way back.

Chicago—April 16, 1921. We spent all day in Hollywood. The Paderewskis took us around everywhere. I wish I knew what part of California I like best. Whatever I see appeals to me. I'd gladly live anywhere in California. I'm ashamed of myself but I cried when leaving California. I know I'll never be so happy as I've been here and I shall always dream of returning.

We're stopping here for a day between trains. Sylwin

and I are traveling alone, saddened because we've left the Paderewskis in Los Angeles with Leniutka. They've gone back to Paso Robles.

The President instructed Sylwin to accompany Bishop Rhode, Father General Zapala, head of the Resurrectionist Fathers, and Rev. Celichowski on their first trip to Poland. We're hurrying to New York to meet them there.

New York, Hotel Gotham — April 18, 1921. In two days we sail for Europe with the highest Polish dignitaries of the Catholic clergy in America. It's quite an honor for us and a mark of trust, but I'd much rather stay in the United States. The atmosphere here is so different from our postwar Europe that I feel as if I were on another planet. If Europe were more like America, maybe we wouldn't have those terrible wars. . . .

On our way back from California to New York, an American who had become friendly with us on the train said to Sylwin: "You're making a mistake by leaving this country. You seem to be a capable and energetic fellow. We need young people like you here, we appreciate them and we give them a chance to get ahead."

I simply have to visit America once more before I die.

It's a Girl!

Warsaw — March 1922. March 17th at two-thirty in the afternoon, I gave birth to a daughter.

Care must be taken to safeguard her good looks, so Grandmother Strakacz christened her with water, while I asked for the scissors and with the greatest self-confidence in the world, clipped the infant's eyelashes. I once read somewhere that in Sweden they always trim a new-born baby's eyelashes, which accounts for the fact that Swedes have such lovely long lashes.

At my request, our butler telephoned the coiffeur to come at once and bring a razor. He appeared a half hour later and learned to his horror that he was expected to shave the head of a three-hour-old young lady. Mr. Bronislaw tactfully suggested it might be advisable to wait at least a few days, but I would not hear of any delay. If I could cut off her lashes, he should be able to give her a haircut, especially since she was born with a respectable crop of hair. Realizing he could not hope to change my mind, he grimly prepared to shave the tiny head, his entire demeanor indicating he was about to perform some perfectly terrible operation. I watched with satisfaction, happy in the thought that my little girl would at least have alluring eyelashes and beautiful tresses!

May 31, 1922. Anetka yells day and night so that no one gets any sleep. Maybe she'll be a singer. At any rate she's certainly training her voice.

I've been so sick, I almost died. The doctors couldn't figure out why I contracted peritonitis. I look a fright, I'm ashamed to go into the street. My weight is down to ninety-seven pounds.

Sylwin and I have decided a trip to Paris would be the best medicine for me. From there we shall go to Riond Bosson to visit the Paderewskis.

Julin, Poland—June 16, 1922. The Paderewskis have bought Julin, an estate near Lochów, which they intend to turn into a school of agriculture for girls, with special emphasis on scientific chicken farming. Engineer Mielczarek will put up chicken coops similar to those at Riond Bosson. Because the main building at Julin is as yet unoccupied and Sylwin has been commissioned to supervise the alterations, we've come down for a few weeks with Anetka, her nurse, and her grandmother.

Paris—July 8, 1922. Paris! I'm so glad to taste a little freedom again. The apple of my eye doesn't yell any more, which assures us of a good night's rest. When I walk down the boulevards of Paris I almost feel well.

Riond Bosson—July 16, 1922. The Paderewskis were very happy to see us. They wanted to hear all about Anetka. The President would like us to bring Anetka down to Riond Bosson. Mme. Wilkonska turned ashen at the very thought that we might accept the invitation. I can't blame the poor woman who has her hands full running this complex household with its unending procession of exacting guests. The Paderewskis like to be surrounded by people, but Mrs. Wilkonska has to figure out how they're all to be fed and housed.

We're going back soon. Sylwin is trying to reserve a freight car while I'm selecting chicks which we'll take to Julin. I had experience in raising chickens before I married and I enjoy it, so I'll have something to keep me busy at Julin.

Julin—August 20, 1922. All the chickens from Mme. Paderewska's poultry farm arrived alive and well. The chicken coops are a duplicate of Riond Bosson's. Thanks to Mme. Paderewska, Julin will have the first school of scientific poultry husbandry in Poland.

Weisser Hirsch, near Dresden, Saxony—Dr. Lahmann's Sanatorium—November 15, 1922. I'm at Dr. Lahmann's famous sanatorium without in the least expecting to be here. I've been ailing, nervous, and underweight for so long that Sylwin literally forced me to come. We parted in Berlin, Sylwin going on to the Paderewskis in Switzerland.

I arrived this morning shedding copious tears of self-pity because I was all alone in a strange place. But so many funny things happened during the day that now I feel lighthearted.

You can certainly tell this is a German place by its order, organization, and strict discipline.

The first thing I did was report to the director. I walked into the waiting room simultaneously with a strikingly handsome gentleman. He was so distinguished looking I wondered idly who he was. A few minutes later, however, I was so furious with him, I wouldn't have cared if he'd turned out to be the King of England. When the medical assistant opened the door and looked around the room to determine who was to see the director next, I got up and headed for the doctor's office. At that, my Adonis jumped up from his chair, dashed in the same direction, collided with me in the doorway, and before I knew what had hit me, slipped into the director's office ahead of me. After half an hour this strange man emerged and profusely apologized to me in German for having shoved me aside, explaining that he always has to be first because his nerves do not permit him to wait for the doctor. In my haughtiest German I retorted that my nerves dislike waiting for doctors too. The director gave me a cursory examination and opined: "Your tissues are eaten away, you'll never be well." Then he assigned me to the specialist under whose care I'm supposed to be during my stay here.

Quite an original diagnosis, I must say. I don't know what it's all about, but it's a fine prospect to be an invalid all my life! I don't trust these Germans. Why did I ever come here to begin with?

At noon I went down to the huge dining hall, where each guest's place is indicated by a special placecard on the table at which his diet entitles him to sit. My table is reserved for those who have to gain a lot. Every course was served cut up into tiny pieces, as if I were a dog. I asked for a glass of water. Do you have a water card, they demanded. No, but I'm thirsty. Result: I got no water. Each of us at the table was eating something different, no two prescriptions seemed to be alike. The further the meal progressed, the less I could force anything down.

A scarecrow like myself shared my table. It didn't take me long to see she was Polish too, an actress, whose nerves were in a worse state than mine and a little wacky to boot. I complained to her that they wouldn't even give me a drink of water. To add insult to injury, I had to watch my neighbor sip a tall glass of my favorite bilberry drink. You can have it after lunch, she laughed.

The mid-day repast over, my compatriot urged me to accompany her a little way so that she could show me something interesting. A three-minute walk and we were inside another building. I simply couldn't believe the evidence of my eyes. Men and women who had just finished a carefully planned meal in Dr. Lahmann's renowned sanatorium were already seated or in the process of pulling up chairs around small cozy tables, and were unconcernedly munching Swiss cheese, frankfurters, and sandwiches, washing it all down with beer, tea, or coffee. In other words, they were eating everything that had been ruled out for them by their physicians!

Hurrying back to my room in the Villa Mathilde to unpack my things, I was surprised to find a letter addressed to me in an unknown handwriting. Tearing the envelope I extracted two tickets to the Dresden Opera together with an invitation and a request to escort me to tomorrow's performance from the gentleman who so rudely bumped into me in the doorway to the director's office.

I know that it's next to impossible to get tickets to the Dresden Opera, they're sold out months in advance; but after all, I can't go with a complete stranger. I waited until dinnertime to return the embarrassing present.

Coming into the dining room in the main building I noticed my opera fancier was seated at another table — his diet must be radically different from mine. When he saw where I was sitting, he insisted on being transferred to my table. For his pains he received a tongue-lashing from the waitress, who indignantly informed him that the seating arrangement was prescribed by the doctor and could not be changed at the whim of a guest. After dinner, Mr. von K. was formally introduced to me. Fortunately, he's not a German, but an honest-to-goodness Hungarian from Budapest. I liked him right off—he's very nice and full of fun—and handsome as the dickens. But I got it through his head that I have absolutely no intention of going to the opera with him. I feel sorry for him because he was so genuinely disappointed. He told me he thought he'd be giving me pleasure because when he first set eyes on me and heard my voice, he was sure I must be a singer.

December 12, 1922. My sojourn in Dr. Lahmann's sanatorium is getting a bit too complicated for me, so complicated, in fact, that I've been thinking of complaining to the director. Mr. von K. has been making a perfect nuisance of himself, following me around everywhere and displaying fits of jealousy whenever I talk to anybody else. It was with real satisfaction that I learned the director wanted to see me in his office. Only I still wasn't quite sure how to go about asking him to cool the ardor of the Hungarian gentleman, who aside from his possessiveness is very pleasant.

I didn't have to worry about the way to phrase my complaint, because the minute I walked into his office the doctor took my hands and said: "What's this I hear about you turning my sanatorium topsy-turvy? Certain patients can't eat or sleep on account of you. Instead of getting better, they get attacks of nerves."

This was too much. Up to now I hadn't told these Germans who I am, but the director's smug accusation made me blurt out: "I would appreciate it, Doctor, if you treated me with greater respect. I'm a Pole and a member of President Paderewski's household, so that my behavior must always be above reproach. I didn't come here to seek adventure and you may be sure that now that I know this is a lunatic asylum I won't come again!"

He caught hold of my hands again and responded soothingly that he wasn't a lunatic, but a doctor, and that he, too, liked me very much: "Aber Sie sind wie die kleine Mimosa Blume aus einen Wintergarten, die man darf nicht berühren." I thanked him for the compliment and made a hasty exit.

December 15, 1922. Three days of peace and quiet. No sign of my Hungarian. I didn't even inquire whether he left. At any rate, his place at the dining table has been empty.

Upon returning to my room in the Villa Mathilde this afternoon I found a big flat cardboard box on the table. When I opened it and saw the lovely black evening gown it contained, my first reaction was that there must be some mistake. It was no mistake! The card enclosed with the dress was from Mr. von K. Having learned my identity, he was inviting me to a dinner in my honor in Dresden's most exclusive club. "You will meet Paderewski's friends and admirers, whom I have invited especially for you."

Running into Mr. von K. at dinner, I asked him the meaning of the dress and the invitation. Did he actually believe I would accept a gown from him? Whereupon, this odd individual explained that the dress was bought for his wife, who is about my size, but inasmuch as I've always refused to go out with him, pleading the lack of a long dress, he had sent it to me to make sure I wouldn't turn down his invitation this time.

I didn't go to the Dresden Club with him but I did wire Sylwin that my cure was over and that he was to fetch me at once.

December 16, 1922. I showed Mr. von K. Sylwin's reply announcing his arrival for the eighteenth.

This evening there was a magnificent box of chocolates in my room. The card read: "To the beautiful, proud Polish woman whom I shall never forget." He's gone at last.

Warsaw—June 2, 1923. How sweet of the Paderewskis to have invited us to Riond Bosson for the summer—and with Anetka no less. But I am definitely against accepting.

Anetka is still too little. She would be too much trouble for me and for a household where there are only adults.

I'm renting a summer house at Wolomin, near Warsaw. The cook, maid, Anetka's nurse, and of course my mother-in-law, who dotes on Anetka, are going to that sandy resort. Meanwhile Sylwin and I shall go to Switzerland for a few days to thank the Paderewskis for their invitation.

Riond Bosson — June 15, 1923. Both the President and Mme. Paderewska are very glad to have us around, even though there is little opportunity for getting really close to them. The house is perpetually overflowing with guests, and Mrs. Wilkonska's recurring refrain is that they'll be the death of her one of these days. Only Sylwin has the chance of conversing with the President alone. For the rest of us, arrival at Riond Bosson means — after exchanging a few sentences of greeting — fading into the background of Paderewski's entourage, which expands, shrinks, or changes, but which is merely an entourage. I never open my mouth anyway, (nobody in Warsaw would believe that). I rather confine myself to the rôle of a listener. And you can certainly learn plenty when the President talks.

June 18, 1923. For the first time since heaven knows when there were no guests at afternoon tea today. We gathered around the table in an informal group, with Mrs. Wilkonska at the head of the table pouring the tea. Woe to anyone who would try to supplant her in this rôle!

While he has his tea, the President usually reads all the papers brought by the afternoon post. All other mail is brought upstairs and placed on the desk in his study. There are probably more letters delivered twice each day to the President than come in a month to any other private family.

Today Paderewski sat down next to me, glanced at the papers, and suddenly said to me in an injured tone: "I must reproach you about something." I looked at him surprised and horrified. "You didn't ask me to be Anetka's godfather."

I grew radiant with happiness and hastened to explain: "But, Mr. President, Anetka hasn't been christened yet. She'll wait for you and Mme. Paderewska to be her godparents even if it means years of waiting. Only I didn't dare to ask you. Besides, Anetka is waiting until you come to Poland for her christening." A fleeting glimmer of sadness in his eyes, and the President responded: "Oh, well, that's different. That makes me happy because I'd like to be Anetka's godfather."

I'm delighted and proud that the President suggested being my child's godfather of his own accord.

The King and Queen Applauded

Warsaw — May 14, 1924. Again we've been invited by the Paderewskis to bring Anetka to Riond Bosson. And again I've decided not to go. Anetka is still little. Taking the nurse along would be too expensive and I couldn't manage by myself.

I shall take Anetka to Gdynia, to spend my first vacation at the Polish seashore, but I'm nursing the quiet hope that the Paderewskis will come to Poland in the fall so that we can have our belated christening. Another reason why I'm reluctant to take Anetka to Switzerland is that I'd like her to be baptised in Poland.

The President has been invited by the University of Poznan to receive an honorary doctorate. Sylwin is going to Switzerland in connection with this matter. We hope the President will not decline the invitation.

Brussels, Belgium — May 26, 1924. For the first time in my life I went to a recital by Paderewski. I doubt whether I can do justice to the occasion. But let me begin at the beginning. Queen Elizabeth of Belgium asked the President to give a concert in Brussels, the proceeds to be donated to Belgian charities. The President agreed and he and Mme. Paderewska were forthwith invited to stay at King Albert's Laeken Palace. Leniutka is there with them. Sylwin and I came from Warsaw for the concert and are staying at the same hotel with the Gorskis (Mme. Paderewska's son and daughter-in-law).

The concert hall was filled to the rafters when we came into the box that we shared with the Gorskis. In whatever direction I looked I was dazzled by the sumptuous gowns and sparkling gems worn by the ladies of that distinguished audience. Only the royal box was as yet unoccupied, a tiny void in the sea of faces.

Mme. Paderewska was not with us. Whenever her husband plays, she remains backstage with him from his first number to the last.

The King and Queen finally entered their box. As one the audience rose, bowing in their direction. They fell to my liking at once—kind, noble faces and truly regal in bearing. But I didn't have too much time to study the royal couple, because just as we'd resumed our seats, Paderewski walked on the stage. Strangely enough, though I've seen him and spoken with him so many times, the President's appearance made more of an impression on me than I had anticipated.

A moment later we were witnessing an unprecedented act of tribute: the King and Queen had risen to their feet and were applauding Paderewski together with the audience, which responded with redoubled clapping to Their Majesties' disarming violation of protocol.

Soon after the President began to play, the King's aide disappeared from the royal box. He'd been sent to extend an invitation to Mme. Paderewska to join Their Majesties in their box. Mme. Paderewska was tempted to accept, but she ended by expressing her thanks for the honor; she declined on the ground that since she never leaves her husband alone backstage during a concert, a departure from her customary habit might distract the President while he was playing. It was not until the concert was almost over that Mme. Paderewska came up and sat at the King's right.

What can I write about the President's performance? I'm no critic. Anything I'd try to say would sound presumptuous. I was stirred to the core. As I listened I imagined that Paderewski was not playing on the piano, that there were no pedals nor keyboard, but that limpid heavenly music was somehow floating down to us through his magic touch.

May 27, 1924. The Gorskis, Sylwin, and I were already on the Paris Express waiting for the Paderewskis and Leniutka. An impressive limousine drove up on the platform and pulled up at the coach reserved for the President. Leopold, the youthful Belgian Crown Prince, had accompanied the Paderewskis to the station in a court car, and they literally stepped from the automobile into the train. Brussels has accorded a truly royal welcome to Paderewski.

Riond Bosson — May 29, 1924. The first thing Leniutka did after we got to Riond Bosson was to take out of the trunk two silver-framed photographs surmounted by the royal coat of arms. The picture of the King bore the dedication: *"Au libérateur de la Pologne et à l'incomparable artiste I. J. Paderewski — Albert. Bruxelles — Laeken 27 mai 1924 an."* The Queen had autographed her photograph: *"Souvenir d'admiration et de reconnaissance au Grand Maître Paderewski — Elisabeth — 27 mai 1924 an. — Bruxelles, Laeken."*

We placed the pictures on one of the Steinways in the drawing room on either side of the huge photograph of Queen Victoria.

The Paderewskis' Godchild

Poznan, Poland — November 18, 1924. The Paderewskis have come to Poznan, where the University will confer an honorary doctorate upon the President. The Hotel Bazar at which we're staying with the Paderewskis doesn't have a single vacant room. It looks as if all the prominent families of Poznania have sent their representatives to welcome the President. I meet new people every day, some of them distant relations whom I've never seen before. I feel perfectly at home among these cultured, sincere, and cordial men and women. I think that Paderewski is happy to be with them, too, because they're people who appreciate his worth and believe his self-imposed exile was a stroke of ill fortune for Poland. They are constantly furnishing the President with proof of their admiration, love, and respect. But if the President is happy, his innate modesty, and to a certain extent, I suppose, his feeling of reserve, prevent him from showing it outwardly. It is my impression that, despite his love for Poland and even though he has never complained to a soul, Paderewski cannot forgive the Polish politicians for the injury they have done in rejecting his good offices. Whenever the conversation switched to Poland at Riond Bosson or on some trip, a shadow of sadness would flit over the President's face, though no word of bitterness passed his lips.

Anetka and her nurse, who has now advanced to the position of governess, are at Skoraszewice, the estate of Mr. and Mrs. Sypniewski, which is only a few miles from Poznan. Mrs. Maria Sypniewska with whom I became acquainted at the seashore, suggested that we hold Anetka's christening at her home. The Paderewskis agreed, and Sylwin and I have decided it would be better to have the ceremony in the Province of Poznan among people we don't know too well but who are loyal friends of the President than to risk it in Warsaw where we have too many friends, some of whom not so long ago gave the President a bit of rough treatment and contributed their share to the fall of his cabinet.

My only regret is that Father, who worships his grandchild, will not be present.

Skoraszewice, Poland — November 22, 1924. This was Anetka's day. What a shame that she's so little she won't remember any of it. Even the weather was perfect, sunny with a nip of frost in the air. The christening was set for the afternoon, but our guests from near and far started arriving early in the morning so that by lunchtime the house was filled with them.

Anetka was resplendent in a white lace dress and gray squirrel wrap. When we combed her hair into a million ringlets, she looked exactly like a little poodle. The effect was so comical that when the Paderewskis arrived with Sylwin at four o'clock, my husband wanted to know what on earth I had done to the little one's head, and the President lifted Anetka high up into the air, laughing heartily the while. The imp solemnly stared straight into his face and out of the clear sky asked whether the man had his own teeth! That's Anetka all over, you never know what she'll say next. The President indulgently reassured her, "They are my own, see?" tapping his finger against them.

After the introductions had been made, we went to church. A landau drawn by four spirited Arabian stallions — the pick of Count R.'s famous stud — drew up in front of the manor to transport the Paderewskis and their prospective godchild the short distance to church. Most of the guests covered the ground on foot. They didn't have far to go because the tiny wooden church with its slender spire and belfry, buttressed on three sides to keep it from listing, stands in the center of the Skoraszewice Park — one of the oldest and loveliest relics in this part of Poland. The Pastor came out of his little church to greet the Paderewskis. A throng of peasants waiting on the spot bowed their bare heads as if the President were the bishop himself.

It was an unforgettable picture — that ancient careening temple serving as a background for the leonine silvery mane of Paderewski, who solicitously bent over Anetka, and each time the priest dashed holy water on her, stubbornly wiped her head to make sure she didn't catch a cold. For once Anetka sensed the solemnity of the occasion or responded to the President's personality, because to my amazement she

stood there quietly and humbly in front of the Paderewskis.
Overwhelmed by the presence of Paderewski, the priest
forgot with what name Anetka was to be christened. It
had to be Aniela, of course, because it's traditional in our
family. The priest turned to me and asked what name I
wished to give. I was so moved by the sight of the President
that I suddenly experienced the desire to please him and
unhesitatingly announced: Helena-Aniela, in honor of Mme.
Paderewska. I became aware of Sylwin's despairing expression and of his even more desperate attempt to convey to
me by inconspicuous gestures that this was not on the program. Too late. It was done—Father K. was already christening Helena-Aniela.

Supper and speeches followed upon our return from
church. I have no recollection of what was said, I don't
even remember a word of Paderewski's toast because I was
so terrified at the thought that Sylwin would have to make
the concluding speech. I'd never heard him address a group,
and here he was about to make his debut in front of the master orator Paderewski. I couldn't for the life of me imagine
what he'd say.

I remember Sylwin's every word. He spoke beautifully,
but he said to me later, "You were looking at me with such
horror-stricken eyes I thought I'd become tongue-tied."

Riond Bosson—May 1925. We are paying our usual pre-
vacation visit to the Paderewskis. For the summer I have
rented a cottage near Jablonna to enable Sylwin to spend
his week ends with us. Sylwin has little time for anything
outside of managing the *Rzeczpospolita*, Paderewski's own
newspaper in Warsaw. That's one of the reasons why we
have been in Poland these last few years. The President is
leading a purely private life now and without the newspaper
Sylwin would have little to do. Leniutka is quite capable of
being secretary to both of the Paderewskis. She is so familiar
with their habits and is such a practical and sensible person
that she could take any man's place.

Today, the President gave me, or rather Anetka, a truly magnificent and heartwarming gift. After tea he went up to his study for a moment. When he came down again, he called me into the foyer and said: "Aniela, I have something here. It's for Anetka. For her hope chest." And he handed me a very heavy pouch of coarse white linen held together with a black drawstring that bore a suspicious resemblance to a man's shoelace. I untied the bag and gaped at the glittering collection of gold coins—Russian rubles, French and Swiss gold francs, some ducats, and gold dollars. The President smiled and said: "I sewed this pouch myself. When I began saving money, I put it into this homemade bag. I want Anetka to have it now." This was the first time I heard the President refer to his own person with pride. I was moved to tears, even more by the present of the pouch itself, stitched so carefully and evenly by Paderewski's hands, than by the gold it contained.

Coup d'Etat in Warsaw

Warsaw—May 15, 1926. The revolution is over, thank God. What a ghastly experience. I shall never forget these past three days as long as I live. I did not write in my diary during all the shooting, but I certainly want to keep a record of these momentous events and I'm going to put it all down as it happened day by day:

May 12, 1926. The city was strangely restless. Even our home seemed different than usual. The doorbell had been ringing almost continuously since two o'clock in the afternoon. Zygmunt H. and his wife, Captain O., Captain S. S., Major U., lawyer M., Monsignor K., and a score of other officers had been dropping in, gathering in knots all over the house and holding mysterious discussions in low voices.

Everybody was brimming over with suppressed excitement, and every so often one of the military men ran into the room facing Mokotowska Street, or into the drawing room, which gives on the Square of the Three Crosses, or into our bedroom, whose windows open onto the Aleje Ujazdowskie.

All this strange behavior became clear to me when Sylwin whispered that Pilsudski was preparing a coup d'état, that the revolution might break out any minute, and that our house was swarming with officers because it offered the best vantage point for observing the course of events.

[From the time Paderewski resigned as prime minister (December, 1919) until May, 1923, Pilsudski's strong personality shaped the destinies of the Polish State practically unchallenged. Pilsudski seldom acted directly, thus avoiding personal political responsibility. He refused to accept the Presidency of Poland, but suggested the election to that high office of a man quite worthy, but almost totally unknown in Poland. Such a state of affairs finally produced a reaction: a normalization of the political conditions was urged from many quarters. A strong government of national unity formed under the leadership of the peasant leader, Wincenty Witos, declared that it would assume both real power and responsibility. Pilsudski considered this action a personal insult, and after issuing strong statements to the press, he resigned as Chief of Staff (the office of his choice), and in the middle of May, 1923, he retired to private life. Pilsudski remained in semi-retirement until the successful military coup of May 12 to 15, 1926, prepared and executed by Pilsudski's followers, restored him to power. *S. S.*]

I had Andrzej make a lot of our famous black coffee, which our guests gratefully consumed in vast quantities. Suddenly at around four in the afternoon, we heard shouting and tumult in the street. We all rushed out to the balcony on the Aleje Ujazdowskie, onto which our bedroom opens, in time to see a cordon of soldiers closing the Aleje to traffic at the point where that street runs into the Square of the Three Crosses. At that very moment a bullet whiningly whizzed between our heads and neatly cut down my beloved araucaria plant. It was a miracle that not one of the more than twenty people on the balcony was hurt. We hastily retreated into the room. I dashed for the nursery, which was a vulnerable corner room. I carried Anetka out and installed her in the hallway, instructing the nurse to remain there with her. Our uniformed friends skipped out one by one without taking leave of us. I knew perfectly well on which side each of them had gone to fight.

The remaining guests also left, trying to figure out the quickest means of getting to their homes. My brother Tadeusz went upstairs, where the offices of the Ostrowiecki Works, of which he is Managing Director, are located, to await further developments. Sylwin and Monsignor Kaczynski hurried to the office of the *Rzeczpospolita* on Szpitalna Street. Since it is an opposition paper to the Pilsudski coup it runs the risk of being raided.

[Before leaving Poland in 1920, Paderewski founded in Warsaw a daily paper under the name of *Rzeczpospolita* (The Republic). The *Rzeczpospolita* was to continue the policies of Paderewski, and to become a standard-bearer of a middle-of-the-road democratic opposition. The paper, widely publicized as a Paderewski organ, became both popular and influential; it was never, however, financially a success. Paderewski sold it in the middle twenties to Wojciech Korfanty, the head of the Polish Christian-Democratic Party. The *Rzeczpospolita* appearing now in Warsaw is under complete Communist control, like the rest of the press in Communist-dominated Poland. *S. S.*]

I was left all alone with Father, Anetka, and the servants. A new complication: Every day after he's finished his work in the factory and has had his dinner, Father goes to the Lourse Cafe for a demi-tasse. He permits nothing to interfere with his daily custom. I begged him not to go today, but my pleas and arguments fell on deaf ears. Even if it means walking between bullets, Father must have his demi-tasse and read his papers at Lourse's.

I was not alone for long. Some of the guests had been unable to get through to their homes and returned here.

Father was back soon, too, thoroughly disappointed. He'd gotten to the Cafe only to find it closed. What has a revolution got to do with a coffee-house? he mournfully inquired. After all, they won't be fighting long. And with all the unconcern in the world he settled down to read his newspapers in the dining room. Father is an incurable optimist.

I didn't feel calm at all, though. Worried about Sylwin, I called the newspaper office, but the telephone was dead.

The doorbell rang again. Andrzej admitted five French-speaking Belgians who had arrived for a stockholders' meeting of the Ostrowiecki Works. They'd called on Tadeusz in his office and then tried to make their way back to the Hotel Bristol where they'd put up. Not only did they fail to get to the Hotel, but Monsieur N. was whacked over the shoulder with the butt end of a gun when he insisted on his rights. He was quite incensed about it, and still didn't realize he'd been caught in a revolution.

The house had filled up again with people. They were shooting in earnest now. We removed Anetka's mattress from the crib and put her to sleep on it under a table in the corridor. There were no windows around so she was perfectly safe. The cook prepared supper, but working in the kitchen is no lark when its windows face Mokotowska Street. As it was too dark to tell where the bullets were flying thickest, we congregated in the dining room, the windows of which give on the courtyard, affording relative peace and quiet.

It was time to think of bed—quite a problem with so many guests. We had enough bedding and rooms for everybody, but the rub was that all the bedrooms in our triple-exposure building face the street and hardly offered assurance of a safe and restful night. We coped with the situation by going from room to room, stooping as low as we could, removing the mattresses and pillows from the beds and carrying them into the corridor, where we placed them on the floor, one next to the other. Everybody retired without undressing, because even our bathroom presented a target for

stray bullets. We've always been proud of the air and sun-
light our many windows bring into our house but they certainly are a nuisance when a revolution chooses our Square
for its headquarters.

As was to be expected, Father refused to permit his bed
to be touched, insisting he was going to sleep in his room.
"They won't be shooting at each other during the night.
You'll see, they'll catch some sleep themselves." Father's
pooh-poohing didn't reassure me, because his room is the
most exposed of them all, with windows on both the Square
and the Aleje Ujazdowskie.

May 13, 1926. By morning the shooting seemed to have died
down. Taking advantage of the lull, our guests queued up
for ablutions in the bathroom. Father emerged from the
bathroom looking very sheepish. He led me to his room and
shamefacedly pointed to the window, saying, "I should never
have expected it, but those rascals must have done some
shooting during the night." When I looked I froze with
horror. The large windowpane facing the balcony on the
Square was cracked and had a tiny hole in it. There was a
similar hole in the bed's mahogany headboard and a third
blackened hole in the pillow. The rifle bullet was embedded
in the pillow's downy contents. It probably missed Father's
head by inches.

What a horrible day! One frightening thing after another
happened. First thing in the morning all the servants dispersed in search of food, as there wasn't a scrap of nourishment in the house. Our maid triumphantly brought back a
quart of milk, Andrzej procured a whole ham and a large bag
of coffee, the cook dragged in a sack of lima beans.

The nurse had been holding Anetka in her arms all morning to keep her from running into a room. All of a sudden I
noticed the child had become white as a sheet and was staring
at me with stark terror in her eyes. It turned out the cook
had given her a large lima bean to play with, which Anetka
had stuck so far up her nose that something was happening

to her. To add to the confusion, at that precise instant a deafening salvo rattled our windowpanes and shook our walls to their foundations. Oblivious to everything, I dashed into the bathroom and got the pincers from the medicine chest. A second later, with a sure hand that would be an utter impossibility under normal conditions, I inserted the pincers up the frightened child's nose and pulled out the deeply wedged lima bean. I sighed with relief, the nurse groaned "Mother of God," and Anetka solemnly remarked: "Granddaddy, that wasn't funny at all!"

Our windowpanes were in the throes of a relentless St. Vitus dance. The unharnessed horses of the First Regiment of Light Artillery were standing in our courtyard, while the cannon on Mokotowska Street were blasting away directly under our windows. We crawled into our rooms and opened all the windows to prevent the panes from shattering.

All day, young boys armed with rifles, wearing military caps and sporting military buttons on their jackets, had been turning up at our kitchen door. The first one appeared around noon. "Please, lady, I don't want to fight, please hide me," while he stared hungrily at the steaming pots and pans on the stove. "I haven't eaten since yesterday." Andrzej, delighted that he would have company in eating, gave the lad a heaping plate of lima beans. Meanwhile, we ripped off the buttons with the eagles on them and consigned them as well as the military cap to the fire. The maid and the cook sewed on black horn buttons in their stead. Sylwin's hats were all too big, but Tadeusz's was all right, and the happy boy, transformed into a civilian, made his departure by the front door.

The grapevine service must have been efficient because the same scene was repeated several times. But the kitchen fire never goes out, there were plenty of lima beans and there was no dearth of caps and hats—those of father, Sylwin, Jan, and Tadeusz were all requisitioned. Nor was there a lack of buttons. Father is a button collector, he even picks them up from the street. They came in very handy, these boxes of assorted buttons which we sewed on for the boys who did not want to take sides in the revolution.

It was time for supper. Tadeusz was dreadfully upset because the Eleventh Lancers Regiment ousted everyone from the office and set up a position there. They placed machine guns in the windows and were going to attempt to silence the machine gun which was on the roof of the Strzalecki house in the Aleje Ujazdowskie. This meant that we would *really* be caught in the cross-fire. It was too much to hope that the other side wouldn't shoot at our machine guns. I didn't know how our friends were faring. We were still an unconquered position of the Pilsudski camp. In view of these developments I wondered whether it wouldn't be wiser to take Anetka down to the cellar for the night, but nobody felt like taking shelter below ground. I had absolutely no idea what was going on in the office of the *Rzeczpospolita* and no news from Sylwin. Tadeusz was in despair for fear they would demolish the offices of the Ostrowiecki Works.

It was close to midnight. We were all seated around the table in the dining room. Nobody was in a hurry to go to sleep on the floor in the corridor. Even though we were in the very middle of the shooting, we didn't know which side was winning or how long the fracas was to continue.

The doorbell again! I kicked a mattress away from the front door and let in an officer wearing a cap with a white stripe from the Eleventh Lancers Regiment. The newcomer saluted me and walked on top of the mattresses into the dining room where he settled himself in the chair vacated by me. It was pretty obvious that he was drunk. Keeping his cap on, the captain announced: "I'm hungry and would like something to eat. If you don't give it to me, see what I have," and he took a hand grenade from his pocket, playfully tossing it up into the air.

"Why shouldn't I give you something to eat?" I told him. At the same time I was painfully aware of the fact that the house was completely bare of food, that I didn't even have milk or a roll for Anetka's breakfast the next day. The officer was still toying with the grenade, so I tried a new tack: "You will get something to eat, captain, I don't know what it'll be, whatever I can scrape up. But please put that grenade away. Whom do you propose to scare with it—me or my four-year-old daughter who's sleeping under the table? You've a daughter her age yourself, I know who you are, I'm Zosia K.'s friend." (Lawyer M. had told me in a whisper that this was Captain P., the husband of my former classmate, who had left him because he's such a drunkard and a bounder.)

Having thus spoken my mind, I dashed over to our care-taker's apartment. I swiped his last three eggs and roused Jadzia, the maid, who sleepily but obediently scrambled them. The jittery officer ravenously devoured this not very sub-stantial meal and went upstairs to Tadeusz's office, where he was quartered with his squadron, promising that he would soon put out of commission the machine gun on the Strzalecki house.

May 14, 1926. The next day not only was there less shoot-ing outside but our contact with the outer world was being reestablished, though our building was still in the hands of the rebels. At eleven o'clock came the blessed sound of a ringing telephone. Joyfully I ran to answer it. Maybe the revolution was over. That must be Sylwin calling! Lifting the receiver, I heard my name pronounced by an unknown hoarse voice. It was Captain S. but his voice was so changed it was unrecognizable.

"Where are you calling from?"

"From the trenches in the Aleje Jerozolimskie. I've just learned of the arrest of Marjan Borzecki and Konstanty Lenc. What about your husband?"

"My husband is in the office of the *Rzeczpospolita*. You can go there and arrest him."

"How can you talk like that? After all, I'm calling to in-quire about you both."

But I didn't relent. "If they told you to arrest Sylwin,

you'd have to do it. At any rate, thank you for thinking of us," and I put down the phone.

We kept hearing of the arrest of various political leaders. Another phone call and the previous scene was repeated. I really should have been getting concerned about Sylwin, but if he had been arrested, I'd have heard about it by then. It was funny, our political adversaries were more worried about Sylwin's safety than I was. Maybe I was naïve to think so, but I had the feeling that nothing would happen to my husband. Father was a figure to be reckoned with, Tadeusz was an internationally known industrialist, and Paderewski would surely move heaven and earth if Sylwin should come to grief! I could afford to be impudent, daring them to arrest Sylwin. To be perfectly honest, I was an ingrate. They were sincerely anxious to help me, these Pilsudski followers with whom we've had so many heated political discussions in the past.

Captain S. called again. Politely but firmly I told him I hadn't heard from Sylwin for three days, but that I would appreciate it if he would desist from telephoning me, inasmuch as the gulf between us after what had happened was too great. I knew I'd hurt him but there was no other way out of this messy situation.

I was worried about my friend Michasia though. I had heard how her husband, Marjan, resisted his arrest. All alone in the house with her infant son, Michasia must be heartbroken. It was almost six o'clock. The shooting seemed to be at an end. Father was all set to go to his Lourse Cafe. I raised no objection, because I wanted to get to Michasia on Danilowiczowska Street myself. Dressing to look like a servant, I grabbed a quart container and slipped out of the house. Before I got very far, a patrol stopped me. I explained I was looking for milk for my child. Where? On Szpitalna Street, because there was none to be had around here. I broke into a run along the deserted streets. The stores were closed, their windows boarded up. Occasionally someone stole into a building entrance hoping to find the store's rear door open.

Carried on wings of fear, I reached the Theatre Square. The City Hall and the Opera were surrounded by troops. I could see my milk story wouldn't do me any good here, where there wasn't a grocery within blocks. Concealing my container in a doorway, I thought up a different strategy. A few minutes later, I was challenged with the usual questions. This time I related how I had just been to the drugstore to get some medicine for my sick child. "I don't know what to do, the drugstore is closed." I was admonished to return home immediately. I thanked them and went on to Michasia's home on Danilowiczowska Street.

I was amazed to find Michasia grief-stricken but calm and collected. I could only marvel at her self-control. She had a visitor, General — —, an important Pilsudski man who is in love with her and offered to appeal to Pilsudski for her husband's release on the grounds of frail health. Michasia replied that her husband had not let himself be arrested voluntarily, but had been taken away by force, and that he would probably be very angry if she pleaded in his behalf with Pilsudski or any other foe. I invited Michasia and her son to our house (the general could help us pass through the patrols) but Michasia would not leave. Suppose a message came from her husband? There was nothing more I could do except kiss her and tell her to keep her chin up.

To avoid meeting the same patrols, I took a round-about route home — by way of Krakowskie Przedmiescie. I made a slight detour to pick up my milk pail and then scour the city for milk until at last I was finally safe in my own house.

Before I even had a chance to take off my hat, in walked Sylwin. He had been at the newspaper office keeping an eye on the printing press and the editorial room throughout the entire time.

May 18, 1926. A six-week social boycott of the Pilsudski adherents has been put into effect. No one of our circle receives one of them in his home. What a terrible atmosphere in Warsaw. It's unpleasant to go out into the street. People cold-shoulder each other.

Hearing that there are many wounded in the hospitals, which are not prepared to care for all these extra patients, I volunteered my services to the Ujazdowski Hospital without being sure that they would be accepted. The physician on duty asked me what I could do and what my name was. To forestall being dismissed later, I took a deep breath and recited my litany. "My name is Aniela Strakacz, *nee* Karszo-Siedlewska, and I've had four years hospital experience during the War as a volunteer nurse in surgery, including a year in Pavilion IX of the Ujazdowski Hospital." A little flustered by my determined eloquence, the doctor left the room. Presently he returned with a pass and directed me to the main Pavilion. Nothing has changed in the years I've been away. I recognized every ward and my thoughts went back to my girlhood.

Well, I was doomed to disappointment. Instead of being assigned to nursing duty, the head doctor delegated me to the pantry. There is a shortage of food which is being alleviated by gifts from the community. My responsibility is to divide the provisions so that each ward might get an equal share. Considering that I've never done anything like this before, it was a bit disconcerting suddenly to find myself quartermaster of the Ujazdowski Hospital. But I had to make the best of my appointment. I set about cultivating the good will of the chef, made an inspection tour of my new kingdom, and put to work the four orderlies assigned to help me in the storeroom.

May 24, 1926. Captain S. came to see me today at the hospital. I was amazed at the change that had come over him. His face was haggard and even his eyes seemed a different color.

"I expected you to come in civilian clothes," I started out reproachfully. I hate the sight of uniforms and besides I don't want to be seen receiving military men at the hospital. He flared up at once: "I'm a Pilsudski man and I will not take off my uniform." Then his voice broke! "You wouldn't receive me at your home now. This social boycott is driving me mad. Everyone shuns me, nobody wants to shake hands with me. People I know cross to the other side of the street to avoid saying hello to me. You'll see Pilsudski will be a great leader, but what kind of a life is there for me? I'm finished. I know I'll go insane if this keeps up."

"Don't take it so tragically," I consoled him, "What's happened, has happened. Let Pilsudski worry about losing his mind, you just get hold of yourself. Things simply have to get back to normal. Come to my box at the Horse Show on May 31—it's Box 32, for the press."

The Captain stared at me disbelievingly. "Isn't that your name day?"

"Yes, but I'm not having a party this year. I shall be at the Horse Show."

"But none of your friends will want to shake hands with me."

"Good manners and good breeding are a must in my box. In it everybody will shake hands with you," I retorted.

May 31, 1926. We had perfect weather for the Horse Show today. The usual crowds were there, but it wasn't the same as in previous years when people used to stop and talk to each other and visit in the various boxes. The tension today was unbearable what with the wholesale snubbing.

My box was packed with officers of the opposition, all of them in uniform. When Captain S. entered the box, there was genuine consternation among its occupants. An ominous rumble greeted the audacity of this well-known Pilsudski supporter and top-flight horseman who thought he could crash our box! So without losing a minute's time, I announced in a loud and emphatic voice: "I've invited Captain S. to my box. Let's end this civil war, at least in my house. Now please shake hands." There was more grumbling, but everybody held out his hand to the Captain. "And now, gentlemen, you may quarrel to your hearts' content, but please don't leave my box. This is my name day!" The wave of humanity strolling past our box turned surprised eyes at the assortment of my guests. (A few more Pilsudski followers had reinforced Captain S.) I don't care what others think. I was the first to break this senseless social boycott of the Pilsudski camp. We are all Poles and we can't treat each other like enemies in our own land. I don't care for Pilsudski or for his adherents, but we should finally learn not to mix politics with social life and friendship. Divergent political views should certainly not affect personal relations.

That is how Paderewski always reacted, even though he has been so slighted by a clique of Polish politicians that he prefers to live abroad. You never hear him taking digs at his compatriots.

Now that Pilsudski is in power, there is no room for Paderewski in Poland.

A Twenty-four Hour Cure

Warsaw—September 2, 1927. This is a real madhouse. Yesterday I returned with Anetka from Gdynia where we spent our summer vacation at the seashore, and tomorrow Sylwin and I are leaving for Paris. For months now my health has been very poor. The vacation at Gdynia failed to bring about any improvement. Sylwin arranged his vacation at the *Rzeczpospolita* so he could be free to go with me to France after my return from Gdynia. We have to hurry as Sylwin must be back in his office in October.

Paris—September 10, 1927. We are at a loss where to go from here. The Paderewskis are touring in Australia, so the usual trip to Riond Bosson is out. While they are away, the house is practically closed and Mrs. Wilkonska is hoarding her monthly allowances for the time of their return. At such periods no visitors are welcome.

Juan-les-Pins on the French Riviera—September 30, 1927. We have had a wonderful time here but soon shall have to return home. I had hoped so much that the warm sun of the Riviera would restore my strength, but it has not. I still feel miserable.

Warsaw—December 1927. We are worried at the lack of news from the President. We only know from the papers that his Australian tour is quite a success. How could it be otherwise? He has given several concerts for the benefit of the Australian Legion. I remember once hearing the President say that the sacrifices of the Allied Armies were a decisive factor in the regaining of Poland's independence. It somehow happened that nobody has expressed the gratitude of the Polish people for that contribution. Paderewski has taken it upon himself to do so, and in his own inimitable style. He has decided to offer the entire proceeds of several recitals to the respective war veterans organizations in each allied country.

May 10, 1928. For six months I have made no entry in my diary, but, after all, what is the use? The whole winter has been so awful! Five doctors in Warsaw have had a look at me, but not one of them has helped me. Today I saw Dr. S., a well-known internist, who examined me and pronounced me a victim of intestinal tuberculosis. He prescribed a diet of rice and fifteen to twenty-five drops of opium daily. To raise my spirits he promised the possibility of recovery after four years if I lie perfectly still at a health resort. He recommended Anin, a locality near Warsaw frequented by consumptives who are less serious cases than those sent to Otwock, but who face the prospect of tuberculosis just the same. True, I am down to ninety-two pounds, I lose a few more every time I have a little walk, and I have cramps after everything I eat, but it's hard to believe I am consumptive!

Anin, Poland—July 25, 1928. I have been here already three months. Anetka and her nursemaid are with me. It's like being in a desert. I spend days lying in the woods in front of the bungalow we occupy and feast on boiled rice and opium. I am no worse, but I can't say I am any better either. Weak and exhausted, I am indifferent to everything and everybody.

However, it looks as if my friends are not yet indifferent to me. I have plenty of visitors day in and day out. I am not too pleased about it because I can imagine how attractive I must look with my sunken cheeks.

So many men have been coming to see me, and so often, that the intrigued owner of my pension finally asked Anetka's nurse which of them is really my husband. Naturally my landlady did not get a very satisfactory reply because Sylwin is in Switzerland. He certainly will not leave Riond Bosson until after the President's name day, July 31st.

August 3, 1928. Finally my landlady made Sylwin's acquaintance. He came to see me directly from the train that brought him from Switzerland. And he came with astounding news: in two days we will go to Switzerland, Anetka included. When Sylwin mentioned my condition to the President, giving it as the reason for his early departure, the very suggestion that they had made a consumptive out of me aroused Paderewski's indignation. He immediately wrote a long telegram urging me to come with Anetka to Riond Bosson. Then on second thought, the President decided that it would be too difficult for me to travel alone with the child, so he dispatched Sylwin right away to bring me safely to Riond Bosson.

Riond Bosson — August 6, 1928. We arrived this morning, tired but happy. It is Anetka's first trip abroad, and she is as excited as I am to see the President.

Paderewski welcomed us in his usual tender and cordial way: "My dear children, how good that you and Anetka have come." But as for Mrs. Wilkonska. . . ! It is a good thing the President did not see how she received us. Breathing heavily out of sheer despair, she said nothing, but I could

read her thoughts plainly enough: that's all we needed here—
to have her come; she is sick herself, so she brings the child
too; now they will stay here forever! If I did not know Mrs.
Wilkonska so well, I would be insulted and take Anetka
away, but Mrs. Wilkonska will be as gentle as a lamb when
she finds out I have only come down for treatment and will
leave for Warsaw with Anetka after that.

Just about one hour after I got here, Sylwin drove me to
Lausanne, to the clinic operated by the famous Dr. X. We
had to hurry because an appointment had been made for me
in advance. This clinic is always full. They say the hotels of
Lausanne are crammed with visitors from all over the world
who wait for weeks not only to get a room at the clinic but
merely to be interviewed by Dr. X. The explanation for my
being accepted out of turn is simple—Paderewski requested
it.

The Clinic, Lausanne—August 7, 1928. The whole thing's incredible. In Warsaw they kept me on a rice and opium diet
for six months and made a tubercular case out of me. Here
I've been cured in twenty-four hours! I'm dead tired and exhausted now, but at least I'm rid of my tapeworm. It was the
tapeworm, which I must have swallowed in an undercooked
fish, that was undermining my health all this time.

Sylwin thinks maybe he has a tapeworm, too, because he
has been having stomach trouble lately. He's going to see
Dr. M. at Morges about it.

Lausanne—August 15, 1928. Sylwin telephoned to let me
know that after going through the same pleasant routine that
I went through, he was found to have no less than two tapeworms. "You've no idea how relieved and happy I am," he
exulted. "I've telegraphed Tadeusz we both had tapeworms.
Maybe he has one too, because he's always complaining about
his stomach."

August 22, 1928. The wire we got from my brother today is
the funniest thing I've seen in a long time: "Related contents

of your telegram at directors meeting of Ostrowiecki Works. We all submitted to examination. It developed I had tapeworm. So did Felo F. So did Director R., Director Z., and Director M."

We now recall that a year ago last May all of us dined together at a restaurant in Warsaw. That's probably when we ate that undercooked fish!

Riond Bosson — September 23, 1928. It has been two weeks since I left the clinic and came to Riond Bosson. Pretty soon we shall be leaving for Warsaw. I am gaining in strength almost daily, thanks to all the food which Mrs. Wilkonska stuffs me with. However this visit hasn't all been enjoyable, at least as far as I am concerned. Though two years have already passed since the Pilsudski coup in Poland, the "betrayal" of Paderewski by the Poles, as Mrs. Wilkonska puts it, remains a constant source of wrath and indignation to her. She never misses an opportunity to raise this subject, though never in the presence of the President. I promised myself never to argue with her, but she is sometimes really exasperating. Once, in the midst of a particularly angry tirade, when she was indiscriminate by indicting all the Poles, the President walked into the dining room and silently stood behind her chair. I saw the President and froze to death. Something in my expression must have betrayed the situation, because Mrs. Wilkonska turned her head and, realizing that the President was angry, tried to avoid discussion by suggesting tea for us all. I feared an explosion, but Paderewski agreed as if nothing had happened, and we all sat down at the table. I breathed with relief and considered the incident closed. But it was not.

As soon as tea was served, the President in a seemingly dispassionate voice started a stern lecture that made Mrs. Wilkonska puff with restrained anger. "You see, Antosieczka," he said, "it is too bad that you seem to have forgotten, that Aniela is recovering from an illness, and that all unnecessary emotions should be spared her." Again I froze in my seat, hating the very idea of becoming involved in this incident and, through no fault of mine, antagonizing Mrs. Wilkonska.

The President continued: "When one discusses serious subjects, proper terms should be used. You said that the Polish nation betrayed me. First of all, it is unjust and untrue to accuse the nation as a whole for what happened in Poland two years ago. It was a military coup, planned and perpetrated by a few unscrupulous politicians, supported by a bunch of hot-headed officers, in which the nation took practically no part. Secondly, it is ridiculous to say that I was betrayed by that act of revolt because no allegiance was due me from the Poles."

A little pause followed, and I thought with relief that it was all over. I did not dare to look at Mrs. Wilkonska, and I felt very miserable.

However, after a while the President went on: "In my opinion, it was a crime against the nation. A revolution in a democracy is always a crime. Democracy implies the rule of the majority and evolution instead of revolution. The very foundation of a democracy is freedom not coercion, rule by law not by force. These basic principles were wantonly violated in Poland. Because they knew only too well that they lacked the support of the majority, they decided to impose themselves by force. Some revolutions in the past, as a paramount reaction of the people against tyranny and oppression, have contributed to a much desired house-cleaning, have introduced long over-due reforms, and have given a nation a new unhampered start. But to be of this beneficial type, a revolution must express the will of the majority, it must restore to the people the sovereign power in the State. This was not the case in Poland. There the military coup was perpetrated neither by the people nor for the people. A group of ambitious men, considering themselves above the nation—a kind of an elite—and predestined to rule over the rest, by force if necessary, took over the power. Haughtily they made it known that they knew best what was good for the future of Poland, and that the common man had to obey or else. From such a self-appointed mission to dictatorship there is only one step, and usually this step is or has to be taken. I know my nation too well to believe that it would agree to be permanently enslaved. I fear for Poland the acts of an uncontrolled government, but I fear even more internal strifes at a time when national unity is essential. In addressing the Polish Parliament in 1919, I pointed out that our country can reasonably look forward to ten years of peace, ten years of opportunity for constructive work in repairing the devastation of war and in strengthening and developing our economy. Maybe I was a pessimist in my guess. Maybe another ten years of peace did lie ahead. But now, with our unity destroyed, how can we take advantage of these years to come? Placed between Russia and Germany, Poland is doomed to face another aggression. When this ominous hour strikes, will Poland be ready to defend herself? Will she have regained her unity — her only hope for survival?"

It was quite unusual for the President to speak to our family group so openly and on a subject of such importance. He must have realized our surprise, because, for the first time looking straight at Mrs. Wilkonska, and obviously desirous of lessening the tension, he added with a warm smile: "That is why I cannot blame you too much because I share your anxiety about the future of Poland."

For the first time I have had to ask Sylwin to help me out with writing down the President's remarks. I didn't tell him that I needed them for my diary. I simply said that I wanted them for the purpose of repeating them to our friends in Warsaw in their authentic form, which is partially true because each time we return from Riond Bosson I have to answer many eager questions about what Paderewski said about this or that.

"Appendectomy Late but Successful"

Warsaw — September 26, 1929. We received a telegram from Leniutka informing us that the President is gravely ill in a Lausanne Clinic, though his life is in no imminent danger, and Sylwin has left in a hurry for Switzerland. Before he left, I begged him to write me all the details upon his arrival in Riond Bosson. I am terribly worried.

October 3, 1929. I received only a short wire from Sylwin. It reads "President on way to recovery — appendectomy late but successful."

Today, however, I received a long letter from dear Leniutka. I quote it in part: "On the morning of September 22, the President suffered an attack of acute pain in his abdomen. Nevertheless he joined us at luncheon, though he did not eat much and retired immediately afterward. Dr. Raoul Masson, the family doctor, made a diagnosis of probable appendicitis. He returned twice the same day, and after his third visit, was positive of his diagnosis. He immediately telephoned to the famous surgeon, Dr. Jacques Roux, in Lausanne, who came hastily and about ten o'clock in the evening confirmed his colleague's opinion. Both doctors were sure that an appendectomy should be performed without delay. However, Dr. J. R. did not want to assume the responsibility himself, or else he did not have enough courage to decide, when Paderewski's life hung in the balance, so he telephoned his uncle, old Dr. Cesar Roux, a top-flight surgeon who has given up operating because of a weak heart, but who has bequeathed his fame and his knowledge to young Dr. J. R. When he heard his nephew's report, old Dr. R. advised him not to delay operating for another minute. The President, when informed about the situation, agreed to be moved by ambulance to the clinic. However, he insisted on first seeing his attorney Maître Gonvers, with whom he remained for two hours behind the closed doors of his studio. Only around midnight did the ambulance carrying the President and the two doctors leave Riond Bosson, and at one o'clock in the morning Mr. Paderewski was already on the operating table.

"As it appeared later, the operation was performed under extremely dangerous conditions: the appendix had ruptured and pus had already spread all over the abdomen. A general infection was setting in.

"Nevertheless, the day after the operation the President was feeling so well that we all looked with hopeful confidence towards his complete recovery. During the past week the President has been making such progress that at any moment now he should be permitted to leave his bed and sit up in an armchair."

October 20, 1929. Ten days ago Sylwin returned from Switzerland. The President was doing fine, he told me. But yesterday we received a new letter from Leniutka containing the sad message that the infection had developed into phlebitis in both legs. For a few days it looked as if the doctors would be unable to save the President's life. Though the immediate danger has subsided, the President will remain bedridden for several weeks at the clinic.

December 23, 1929. Good news reached us from Riond Bosson: the President has returned home! Though still extremely weak and worn out, he feels much better. The poor President is facing a long period of convalescence because it is time and nature, rather than medicine, that can restore his health. He will have to spend long weary days in a club chair, his legs reposing on an adjoining chair. How sad, that science can do so little for him. We are praying for him; that seems to be the only thing we can do.

February 20, 1930. At the suggestion of the doctors, Mme. Paderewska left with Leniutka and Soeur Paule, Mme. Paderewska's devoted nurse, for the French Riviera. They left

early in January and live in a rented cottage in Nice. Leniutka's mother is with them. Because of her illness, the doctors
considered the presence of Mme. Paderewska in Riond Bosson an unfavorable factor in the President's cure, for which
absolute rest and the elimination of all possible worries are
essential. However, the President apparently did not enjoy
the solitude of Riond Bosson too much. Two weeks later, he
followed his wife to the Riviera.

Providence must have guided his steps, when, after a
short stay in Monte Carlo and Nice, the President went to
Paris. And there the miracle happened. His old friend Mr.
Blondel, the head of the House of Erard, famous French
pianomakers, a man of great distinction and high culture, a
friend of many prominent artists, told Paderewski that he
knew a French doctor, Raoul Choussaud, who specializes in
treating phlebitis. Mr. Blondel urged the President to see
Dr. Ch. immediately and to submit to his treatment. The cure
consists of the external application of a special liquid in-
vented by Dr. Ch. Both legs are bandaged for three days, and
after a day's rest, a new application is made. The President
has greatly improved after only a few applications".

Riond Bosson—April 1930. The President does not look as
bad as I expected him to after his illness, though I can't share
Sylwin's optimism in finding him completely recovered. Of
course, I did not see the President during his illness and that
makes a lot of difference. On one thing, however, we are in
full accord: the recent ordeal has not in the least affected the
President's personal charm and his good humor. He has remained what he was—a lovable soul with a good, warm, and
ready smile, never mindful of his own troubles, but always
thinking about others.

Dr. Raoul Ch. came down from Paris after we arrived.
He is treated around here like a savior. No wonder, for he
saved the President's life. The President will remain under
Dr. Ch's. care for many months to come and will have to
undergo his treatments at regular intervals.

Taller than the average Frenchman, slim, this doctor with the youthful gestures and the smooth unwrinkled skin of a young girl does not look anywhere near the fifty years he's supposed to be. The big eyes beneath his bald head are so wise and disarming that I have been under the spell of his winning personality from the start.

We quickly became good friends, Dr. Ch. and I. Although everybody likes the doctor, they all flee from him after an hour's conversation, for he talks only about medicine, philosophizing about it into the bargain. But I could listen to him for hours without getting bored, because I have always been interested in subjects pertaining to natural history or medical science.

So I am subjected to what amounts to several-hours-long scientific lectures, for I can't interrupt by asking a question when I don't understand something, because the doctor does not like his trend of thought to be broken. His sole reply is "*Chut, petite sotte*," and he goes on outlining his medical knowledge and theory before me.

A typical Frenchman from the provinces, though living in Paris, Dr. Ch. regards us as people from another planet. He's never lived with foreigners before, and particularly in such an unusual Polish home as Paderewski's. "*Ah, les fous, les fous*," he keeps repeating, even in front of the President. Very accurate, systematic, health-minded, and pedantic, he cannot adjust to our way of life, although he is a little impressed by the fact that we make time and the world conform to us rather than the other way around.

"*Ah, les fous*," he exclaims, but smiles expansively when he sees all the rich courses served twice a day—soup, eggs, meat, two kinds of wine, puddings.

"*Ah, les fous*," and declining each dish with emotional protestations, he ends up eating everything with relish, washing it down with the best French white and red wine. But he has his meals served separately because he draws the line at waiting beyond the regular lunch or dinner period the way we do. He does join the rest of us at our delayed meals, but only for a *"fruit mûr cru"* — a ripe raw fruit, which he recommends as a fitting conclusion for every single meal.

Even though he shares our adoration of the President, Dr. Ch. is the first person who has ever had the courage to tell the President in no uncertain terms that the life he leads is thoroughly unhealthful. The good doctor backs up his dire predictions by scholarly dissertations on the value of a wholesome diet and the ill effects of certain foods. The President listens patiently and indulgently, but he never keeps up the conversation on this subject. He is too fond of good eating to change his habits now, particularly since he has never suffered any digestive disturbances because of it. Dr. Ch. really feels at home here. He is returning to Paris regretfully, and so we go to Warsaw.

Orlowo on the Baltic, Poland—July 10, 1930. This summer Sylwin left for Riond Bosson alone, I declined an invitation to go there, not thinking it proper to intrude on the President who was still under treatment. Early in the season both Anetka and I went to the Ciechocinek Spa. After a four weeks' cure, we have come to this seashore resort for the rest of the summer.

August 4, 1930. Sylwin came down by plane, but is returning to Warsaw tomorrow. I am deeply afflicted by the news about Mme. Paderewska's illness. It is a hopeless case of sclerosis of the brain. She is paying a heavy price for her restless activity during the past years. As a matter of fact, Mme. Paderewska has already been ill for two years, but by tacit agreement nobody ever mentioned it. The first symptoms of the progressing illness irritated rather than worried the President. She had difficulty in following conversations, in recognizing people, and sometimes even in answering simple questions. But in the beginning a short rest would restore her to normalcy. However, gradually the clearness of her thoughts became more and more beclouded. Now the lucid moments appear at irregular intervals, and for a short time only. The President, somehow, cannot reconcile himself to the situation, neither can he bring himself to treat Mme. Paderewska as an invalid. It is a tragedy for the President to see his beloved wife in such a condition, but it is a greater tragedy for Mme. Paderewska herself. Unfortunately, in her lucid moments, she is fully aware of her affliction. It is really touching, that her main concern is not for herself but for the President. The question of who is going to take care of him when she becomes fully incapacitated worries her day and night. On one occasion this summer, she took Sylwin aside and, looking into his eyes, she said: "Sylwin dear, you must promise me never to leave Ignace. No matter what happens, you will stay with Ignace and take care of him! Now, is it a promise?" Sylwin was deeply touched. He tried to comfort Mme. Paderewska by asserting his devotion to both the President and herself, but she meant to obtain a formal assurance from him which, of course, he gave. Obviously relieved, Mme. Paderewska kissed him affectionately and added: "I trust you. You do not realize how much your promise means to me. It restores my peace of mind." I was moved to tears when Sylwin related this incident to me. Of course, promise or no promise, Sylwin would never leave the President and would always be on hand whenever needed.

Every Concert a Triumph

August 15, 1930. Yesterday, late in the evening, Sylwin telephoned from Warsaw to tell me that the President had wired him to come immediately to Riond Bosson to discuss an important and urgent subject. He is taking the next train, and I am wondering what this is all about.

Warsaw—September 2, 1930. The weather was so beautiful I hated to return to the city, but I received a telegram from

Sylwin which alarmed and unnerved me: "Come to Paris immediately. Am accompanying the President on American concert tour. Sailing the tenth."

This is an unexpected blow, but what can I do? Tomorrow night I am taking the Paris train.

Paris — September 4, 1930. Having arrived in Paris this evening, I learned that the President has signed a contract for eighty-seven concerts in the United States. The tour will last eight months. It was out of the question for Mme. Paderewska to accompany the President. She lives in complete seclusion at Riond Bosson under Leniutka's care. Now the President will be alone, without his wife, from whom he has never been separated even for a day unless it was absolutely necessary. That is why the President needs Sylwin. But I cannot become reconciled to the idea that I am going to be alone for eight long months.

September 10, 1930. The President and Sylwin sail for America tomorrow morning. I am inconsolable.

September 11, 1930. Our last night together was a nightmare. I promised myself I would be brave and understanding, but it was beyond me. I wept gallons of tears and poor Sylwin was worried sick. He could not refuse the President and he felt miserable about leaving me for such a long time in my distraught state. Morning came and we had not succeeded in comforting each other.

It was time to pack the last-minute bags and leave for the boat train. We got into the huge automobile that was already laden with luggage. Pale, with bowed head, the President looked very sad. I clenched my teeth. I would not cry in front of Paderewski. I would not add to his worries. I know he's a frightfully lonely man without his invalid wife. I know Sylwin now means everything to him. To keep from bursting into tears, I didn't say a word. Neither did Sylwin. We understood each other perfectly. I kissed the President and Sylwin and made the sign of the cross over them. The train left and I was in Paris alone.

September 12, 1930. I packed my things and moved to a cheaper and more modest hotel. In spite of all my common sense, I feel deeply hurt that Paderewski and Sylwin had not even asked me whether I agreed to Sylwin's departure for so many months. Moreover I'm almost broke, I do not even have enough money to get back to Warsaw. I did mention to Sylwin that I'd spent too much in Paris and had run out of funds, but he replied he'd send me some money from America. He had none now and wouldn't ask the President to lend him a few thousand francs for anything in the world. Sylwin is just about the only person who doesn't touch the President for money. On the contrary, we both try to cut down on Paderewski's expenses wherever we can. But I'm so embittered right now that I blame Sylwin for not requesting some money for me. And I'm angry with the President, from whom I normally wouldn't accept a cent, for not having thought of taking care of my needs.

I'm so upset and panicky I shall take a sedative for the first time in my life.

September 15, 1930. When I opened my eyes this morning, I was surprised to see a dark man with a beard and a frightened hotel maid standing over me.

The dark man turned out to be a doctor who'd been summoned by the hotel when I neither opened the door nor made any reply to the knocking of the hotel employees. He examined my heart and picked up the empty box on my night table which had held sleeping pills. *"Vous avez de la chance, Mademoiselle, après avoir pris tout ça."* Marveling at my strong heart, he demanded one hundred francs for the call! That really woke me up. I told him I didn't know where my money was and would he please ask the clerk downstairs to pay him and bill me for the amount. I have a slight ringing in my ears, but I feel strangely rested and even glad to be alive. I'm hungry. I must figure out a way of getting some fun.

September 22, 1930. For the price of a ten-franc "coupe de vin," I had fun all night in Montparnasse. I danced and danced and danced and it didn't cost me a sou. I came to the conclusion this was a pleasant and inexpensive way to pass the time until Sylwin sends me some money. However, the money came sooner than I had expected, plenty of it — from Sylwin, from Father, and from Tadeusz — because today is my birthday. I'm rich now. I've paid my hotel bill and have set aside the amount I need for the trip back to Warsaw. But I shan't return yet. Paris is grand.

October 12, 1930. Still in Paris and enjoying it more and more. Nothing can equal Montparnasse for night life. They've come to know me a little in the whole section. Naturally my identity is a secret. They call me La Petite Dame. I drink very little but I give generous tips to the waiters and musicians who come to play at my table. I'm popular because I'm sociable, gay, well-dressed, and a good dancer. That's the only passport one needs here.

October 28, 1930. At long last I'm leaving Paris, resigned to the life of a straw widow.

Warsaw — February 16, 1931. Sylwin writes every day and so do I. In this way we know everything about each other and have no cause to worry. Sylwin's letters are so interesting, every one of them could be printed.

According to Sylwin, every concert is a greater triumph than the previous one. They stay in a private railroad car hired for the duration of the tour. An exception was made in Washington where Paderewski was invited by President Hoover to be a White House guest. He and Sylwin were treated just like members of the family.

Sylwin also sent me an autographed portrait of President Hoover to add to my collection.

I'm going on a trip in two days. I'm anxious to get to the Riviera and visit Mme. Paderewska, who is in Nice under Leniutka's care.

February 18, 1931. I left Warsaw for Paris at noon today on the new crack Nord-Express which arrives in Paris twenty-four hours later. It's quite a luxury to travel on this strictly first-class train. I'm really not in a hurry to get anywhere and I don't particularly like spending so much money. I splurged for the benefit of my acquaintances. I guess I'm wicked to show off like that, but I wanted them to see that a person close to Paderewski travels in style. Nobody leads the kind of life I do, that's one sure thing.

Thirty-two persons saw me off. Some of them were true, dear friends, the rest merely wanted to show that they at least know people who ride to Paris on the Nord-Express.

Paris — February 23, 1931. What a wonderful city Paris is. All I have to do is go out on the boulevards to enjoy myself. I like to step into l'Eglise de la Madeleine every day. To me it's the loveliest church in Paris. I thank God here for my rich life. This is the only place, too, where I confess how much I miss Sylwin. And my heart feels a little heavy whenever I leave Father and Anetka. I always say to them: I'll be back soon.

They welcomed me like an old friend in Montparnasse. Everybody remembered La Petite Dame. But somehow one doesn't enjoy a thing so much the second time.

Nice — March 16, 1931. Mme. Paderewska occupies a villa in Nice-Cimiez. She is cared for by Leniutka who is more than a daughter to her. There is also Soeur Paule to relieve Leniutka and there are *Mamcia* (Leniutka's mother) and old Fanny (for many years a cook at Riond Bosson). Quite a gyneceum.

I wanted to see Mme. Paderewska at least once, to be able to write to the President that I visited her and to tell him how she looked. The doctor forbids visitors because, although she recognizes no one, she makes an effort to recall whom she is talking to. I made arrangements, therefore, to wait until the ladies went for a drive. I slipped into the car next to the chauffeur without a word of greeting to Mme. Paderewska. After a while I quietly turned around toward her. Mme. Paderewska's still beautiful eyes looked at me with surprise and she suddenly asked: "Where is Sylwin?" I didn't answer because Leniutka had warned me not to, but I was profoundly moved. Nobody spoke a word until the end of the ride and Mme. Paderewska fell asleep.

In two days I'm moving on to Switzerland, to visit Mrs. Wilkonska.

Vienna — March 25, 1931. I remember Vienna from my childhood days. It was a gay city then and every visit to it made an indelible impression on me. The old Vienna is no more. Sad, impoverished, apathetic, it's not what it used to be.

Warsaw — March 30, 1931. Back home. I'm always glad to leave Warsaw but even more so to come back. Father is so happy to see me, and now that Anetka is getting older it will be more and more difficult to part with her.

May 2, 1931. In three days I'll be meeting Sylwin and the President at Le Havre. They're finally homeward bound. I'm taking the night train for Paris!

Hotel du Palais d'Orsay, Paris — May 5, 1931. I never realized how many emotions one experiences as one waits on the pier and watches a giant ocean liner slowly approach the shore. You try to make out a beloved face among the solid mass of humanity on deck. From a distance every man looks like Sylwin to me. But one could never mistake someone else for Paderewski. Regardless of the time of year, the

President is always dressed in the same outmoded manner. The black overcoat with velvet collar and the brown hat with its small round almost flat crown and turned-up brim that seems to be too small for his head, especially as a thick mane of graying golden-tinged hair flows from underneath the funny little brim. To keep this original piece of headgear from being carried off by the ocean wind, the President holds it in place with a characteristic gesture. Paderewski and his brown hat are inseparable. Only when he puts on formal clothes does he bow to the inevitable and don a black formal top hat.

The big ship docked and the President and Sylwin walked down the gangplank. We hastily boarded the waiting train and were soon speeding toward Paris in a luxurious drawing-room car. A table was drawn up and the President ordered tea and rolls. Pouring for the President, I took a good look at him. He looks remarkably well, not a trace of fatigue after his extensive concert tour. His facial expression is not triumphant but contented and more alive than when he left.

Sylwin, on the other hand, looks simply terrible. He's green-complexioned and haggard. But he kept smiling happily at me throughout the whole train trip. We never talk too much in front of the President.

Paris—May 8, 1931. Sylwin has been looking so bad and has been suffering so many dizzy spells that I asked Dr. Choussaud to have a look at him. The doctor came before nine in the morning, thinking he'd be able to examine Sylwin in peace at such an early hour. When Dr. Ch. came into the room, Sylwin was in the middle of a telephone call. Then a telegram came, followed by another phone call. Then some people came to see about the piano, the hotel manager dropped in, the telephone rang again, and reporters appeared on the scene. The door was constantly being opened and closed. Meanwhile, Dr. Ch. sat in a chair and impatiently waited for a chance to buttonhole Sylwin. Finally he could stand it no longer and exploded: "And then you wonder why you're sick. If I led the life you lead, I wouldn't be sick, I'd be dead. I don't need to examine you at all. This is a crazy existence!" There can be no other existence when one is with Paderewski.

A Symbol of Gratitude

Riond Bosson — May 14, 1931. We probably won't be here long. Sylwin and I hope that the President will finally go to Poland to attend the unveiling of Woodrow Wilson's statue in Poznan. He commissioned America's best sculptor, Gutzon Borglum, to make it and has presented it to the City of Poznan just as he presented the Grunwald monument to the City of Cracow many years ago. Paderewski wished the Wilson statue to symbolize Poland's gratitude for the Thirteenth Point which proclaimed her independence. The unveiling ceremonies are scheduled for the fourth of July.

June 16, 1931. Time drags on. It's already summer and my conscience bothers me that Anetka is still in Warsaw. But I couldn't leave because we kept hoping the President would go to Poznan. I was planning to pick Anetka up in Warsaw after the ceremonies and bring her back with me to Switzerland.

Something happened to make Paderewski change his mind and state that he definitely would not attend the dedicatory ceremonies. We were in bleak despair. Sylwin walked around in a daze but was still hopeful he could persuade the President to go to Poznan.

The arrival of an official invitation from Poland induced the President to give up the idea of going. Poznan sent telegram after telegram to Paderewski and Sylwin literally begged him to reconsider, but the President remained adamant. I finally learned that the invitation from Warsaw specified Paderewski must make an official call on the President of Poland and be the guest of the Castle while in Warsaw. The Polish Government made its participation in the unveiling ceremonies contingent upon Paderewski's visit at the Castle. Should Paderewski decline, the Polish Government would boycott the unveiling.

After Sylwin had exhausted all his arguments and was at his wits' end, we both went to the President. I had never offered my opinion on a political matter before, but this time I felt it my duty as a Pole to try to prevail upon him to return to the country which wanted to see him back.

We walked into his study. Sylwin pleaded some more and the President replied in his mild but determined voice! "I won't go because I can't."

Then I knelt beside the President, kissed his hand and looking him straight in the eye, entreated him: "Mr. President, please go to Poland. The whole nation loves you. All of Poznania is waiting."

The President spoke to us in that strangely quiet way of his. There was no anger in his words, no impatience, no reproach, only that everlasting determined mildness: "I can't go to Poznan if the Polish Government makes its presence at the unveiling conditional upon my visit at the Castle in Warsaw. President Moscicki's absence would create a dreadful scandal, would be an insult to America. The Polish Government must attend the ceremonies. And I will not go to the Castle because if I saw those people, I'd have to tell them what I think about their repressive measures and their treatment of my political friends."

Warsaw — July 9, 1931. Sylwin and I came alone to fetch Anetka.

Poznan — July 18, 1931. En route to Switzerland, we stopped here to see the Wilson monument and describe it to the President. It stands in a beautiful spot, surrounded by well-kept lawns and colorful flowers. Though it's an imposing piece of sculpture, we don't like it much better than when we saw the photograph of it.

Riond Bosson—July 19, 1931. Mrs. Wilkonska didn't receive Anetka and me with excessive cordiality. She's always a little afraid we might install ourselves here for good. But she quickly thawed out and in a few hours was perfectly wonderful toward us, especially when she learned that Anetka is already a student at Miss Plater's School and that we can't stay too long because the school year in Warsaw begins early in September.

Paderewski's Pupils

July 25, 1931. For the first time since Mme. Paderewska's illness life at Riond Bosson is gayer. I'm really enjoying my vacation. The exuberant atmosphere was introduced by Paderewski's Polish pupils. This isn't the first time they've been here, but I wasn't around before so that this has been my first chance to get better acquainted with them. Up to now I'd heard of them only through Mrs. Wilkonska, who had grumbled about the great burden assumed by the President and about the trouble the lessons entailed for her.

The lucky quintet consists of Aleksander Brachocki, Zygmunt Dygat, Stanislaw Szpinalski, Henryk Sztompka, and Albert Tadlewski. All five are exceptionally gifted pianists. They were recommended by Henryk Opienski. The President probably didn't wish to disappoint his old friend and agreed to have them come to Morges. Paderewski hates to give music lessons. If he were offered payment for it, the President would never give anybody a single lesson. That's why we're a little surprised that Mr. Opienski asked him for such an unusual favor. I can well remember the President's reaction whenever a letter came requesting an audition. He

would grimace or receive the plea in a gloomy silence, but
he rarely refused to listen to the aspiring pianist.

Paderewski's sessions with his Polish pupils are no
joke. The kind of lessons he offers can be given *only* free of
charge. And I don't think any other famous artist would ever
give so unstintingly of his time, effort, and labor to teach
five eager young men the secret of his art! His pupils do
slave, though, there's no denying it. They were quick to
grasp Paderewski's maxim that talent and even genius
does not suffice. Hard work is the basis of real achievement.
Realizing as they do that they are the most fortunate of young
men to be getting year after year of private instruction from
the world's greatest pianist, all of them work as they've
never worked before in their lives. Wherever you happen to
go in the vicinity of Riond Bosson, whether it's Morges or
Tolochenaz, morning or afternoon, day or night, you hear
thunderous piano-playing. They practise eight or nine hours
every single day in preparation for the great event of each
week—the Saturday lesson with Paderewski. They probably hope to play their assigned piece so perfectly as to win
the President's approval. Whether Paderewski praises any
of his students during the lesson, I don't know. At any rate,
after all these lessons, none of us has ever heard Paderewski
mention or confide to anybody whether this or another of his
pupils has greater talent, plays better, or is more musical.

The President's method of teaching is unique. All five
pupils arrive at three P.M. on Saturday and wait in the foyer
until we finish lunch. Then the President takes the group
upstairs to his study where there are two impossible, battered pianos, one an upright and the other a baby grand, on
which Paderewski does his own practising. The pair of
Steinway concert grand pianos in the drawing room are
seldom touched. Each of the pupils plays his assigned com-
position in the presence of the other four and all get the full
benefit of any critical remarks by the master.

Before each pupil plays his piece through to the satisfaction of the President it is often as late as ten o'clock, which means dinner is two hours late. This drives Mrs. Wilkonska to angry despair. She's very fond of company, children, us, and the pupils, but she'd like to have everything run like a clock. She'd be happy if the world conformed to the chef and the servants, of whom she is mortally afraid. The two hours of waiting for the President and his pupils—and we have to wait because we never know when the lesson will be over—pass in listening to Mrs. Wilkonska's lamenting. "Poor Ignace, I shall never forgive that Mr. Opienski. Why did he have to bring all those pupils here?"

The dinner bell rings and rings mournfully. After an eternity the music dies away and the characteristic slamming of the door to the President's study tells us dinner will start in a minute. We make a bee line for the dining room to wait for Paderewski.

Our pupils come downstairs limp, their coats soaking wet with perspiration. The President alone is fresh as a daisy, as if he'd spent the entire afternoon and evening resting. But there's nothing wrong with the boys' appetites. In no time they are relaxed. They're a happy, pleasant group, these artists. Sylwin adds his jokes to theirs and Mrs. Wilkonska is in seventh heaven—forgotten are her worries about dinner. By now she's so disarmed she gives each of the boys a motherly kiss, thrusts a bag of Riond Bosson fruit into each one's hand and invites them to come as often as they like: "Don't forget to be here early tomorrow."

They don't all leave after dinner, though. As far as the President is concerned, those pupils rate highest who play bridge, for he must have his bridge before retiring. So Mr. Dygat and Mr. Tadlewski remain, and, of course, Sylwin. Paderewski hates to play without Sylwin. Sometimes Sylwin tries to get out of playing, suggesting someone else, because he becomes bored with this daily bridge routine. Most people, however, regard the mere fact of being Paderewski's bridge partner as the height of good fortune.

July 31, 1931. At last I'm at Riond Bosson on the President's name day, that fabulous name-day celebration about which I've always heard so much, when hundreds of guests arrive from near and far and when all sorts of ingenious American schemes are cooked up to make the reception a truly gala and original affair. But this year the President is observing his name day without fanfare, because of Mme. Paderewska, who no longer leaves her quarters on the third floor and needs peace and quiet.

For many days before the great day, we all racked our brains to hit upon a suitable gift for Paderewski. Mrs. Wilkonska makes a tragedy even out of this: "What can I get that Ignace? He has everything already and whatever you buy him, he puts it aside and never looks at it again."

But I don't think that's true. The billiard table in the foyer was piled ceiling-high with presents, beautifully wrapped in colored tissue paper, daintily tied with ribbons, and accompanied by greeting cards. Shortly before lunch all the members of the household gathered in the foyer waiting for the President to come downstairs. The help and their families alone filled half of the foyer. And of course the Opienskis were present as usual. Residents of Morges, they are always welcome at Riond Bosson and spend all their free time here. Although he is advanced in years, Mr. Henryk Opienski is healthy-looking and spry, even-tempered, with the freedom from constraint that comes with high culture. He is also a bridge player, as is his wife, which partially explains the President's readiness to receive them at all times.

The slamming of the door upstairs heralded the President's imminent appearance. "It's about time," Mrs. Wilkonska heaved a deep sigh.

Mrs. Wilkonska was the first to convey her best wishes. Next came the children, followed by the rest of us, our turn depending on our age and rank. Then it was time for the inspection of the countless presents. Everything was there: gloves, scarfs, the woolen vests the President wears under-

neath his white vests—everybody tries to procure the thin-
nest but warmest available—handkerchiefs, wallets, books.
We unwrapped present after present for him. He examined
each one and learned whom it was from. But his greatest
interest was reserved for the amusing mechanical gadgets
he received. One package contained a sizable box made of
some sort of spotted wood. When the President pressed the
button at the bottom, it began to play a melody and the box
opened by itself. Several measures more and some cigarettes
rose to the top, paused for a few additional measures of music,
and then gradually receded. This musical cigarette box particularly appealed to Paderewski, so much so that he de-
lightedly repeated the performance.

Lunch was a repast consisting of everything the President
is fond of. Sylwin had managed to get some black caviar in
Lausanne. And there was beet soup with dumplings and the
President's favorite stuffed pike, Jewish style, and guinea
hens, and ice cream.

There will be more feasting tonight. We won't sit down
at table, because a great many guests are expected, although
we don't know how many. A cold and hot buffet will be
served.

Later. I counted around two hundred people at this quiet
and simple celebration tonight. The guests were headed by
Mr. and Mrs. Ernest Schelling, who own a magnificent
estate near Geneva and a hunting lodge on the lake. The
President is a frequent visitor at both of these places. He
feels at ease there and can play bridge to his heart's content
with excellent partners. As a matter of fact, the Schellings'
is the only home Paderewski goes to willingly, as well as
often. All his other devoted friends, of whom there are many,
and whom he is always glad to see, must come to Riond
Bosson.

An unusual feature of the buffet supper was the amazing
number of waiters. I don't believe this house has seen so
many since the day it was built. All the men, regardless of

age and nationality, came dressed as waiters, in dinner jackets and white trousers, with a white napkin over their arm. It was an entertaining and striking idea, which had naturally originated in the fertile brain of Mr. Schelling, who often plans Paderewski's parties.

September 1, 1931. The summer's over and we're going back to Warsaw today. School starts September 6th and Anetka is already attending Miss Plater's School for Girls in Warsaw. I really don't know when and how Anetka learned the three R's. She did it practically by herself. She's starting school very young. I want it that way. An only child, always surrounded by adults, she should have more friends her own age.

I'm bringing up my daughter quite differently than I was brought up. I've never spent a day in school. To be sure, during my girlhood under the Russian occupation, Russian was the language of instruction in all schools, so that anybody who could afford it secured private teachers for his children. Anyway, I was quite spoiled by my parents. When Mother died, Father demanded absolutely nothing of me. As a matter of fact, my parents didn't even bring me up. Their teaching was limited to setting an example of responsibility, good citizenship, and good breeding.

Warsaw — September 2, 1931. Thank heavens that trip is over. It's no pleasure to travel with Anetka. The poor child gets seasick whenever she boards a train and stays that way until the journey's over. It's agony for her and no relaxation for me.

More excitement at the Polish frontier. Our train stopped at Zbaszyn as usual for customs inspection. Ordinarily the passengers need not leave the train unless they have money to declare, and I'm always flat broke at the end of my travels.

Meanwhile the customs agent became interested in the crate of fruit which Mr. Dolezal, the gardener at Riond Bosson, had given us at parting. We had consumed only a fraction of the fruit during the train ride and I was planning to bring the rest to Warsaw. They're something to see, these plum-size black grapes and white muscatels, these apples that look like melons, these amazingly proportioned pears; but the customs official informed me I'd have to pay a high duty on such exceptional fruit, and without further ado, the customs gentlemen proceeded to cart my box away. I left the train, cautioning Anetka to stay put and watch our things. She took the adventure in her stride, but I was less unconcerned. I was afraid the train might leave with her while I'd be stranded at the border.

At the customs house they took the fruit out of the crate and placed it, piece by piece, on the scale. The duty I was supposed to pay grew with each pound. But I had different ideas on that score and decided to carry them out. "Gentlemen," I blithely began, "I'm not going to pay any duty because this fruit is Polish, even if it comes from abroad." They looked up to see if I was joking. "It's true this fruit grew in Switzerland, but it grew on truly Polish soil nonetheless. It comes from President Paderewski's orchard and it was raised by a Polish gardener, the brother of our Minister of Trade and Industry. I am Mrs. Strakacz, the wife of Paderewski's secretary, and I never pay duty on anything. I'm not going to sell this fruit. I'm merely bringing Polish fruit into Poland. Why don't you try some?" And I offered them some plums and grapes, which they didn't hesitate to accept. Nibbling these luscious delicacies, they put my fruit back in the crate. The subject of paying duty was no longer mentioned. Instead each of the customs men came up to me with a private appeal: "Please, I have a little garden around my house. Could you, would you the next time you pass this way from Switzerland bring a few shoots off the pear or apple trees in Mr. Paderewski's garden?" I gave them my solemn promise I wouldn't forget and returned to my train in a good mood.

Concert Tour in England

November 3, 1931. I can't seem to stay in Warsaw long. No one knows how happy I am. For the first time in my life I'm going to England and on a concert tour at that. The President will give a number of recitals in England and this will be my first tour with him.

I've heard him play so little. Often at Riond Bosson we'd station ourselves outside his study when we heard the sound of piano-playing, but it never worked out very satisfactorily. Even though Paderewski practises eight hours a day, he never plays anything to completion. He starts playing something, pauses over a chord and fusses around with it until he thinks it's perfect, then plays a few measures more, stops again, and strikes another chord over and over again. Only when he's absolutely satisfied with the way it sounds does he go on to the next measure. I don't think I've ever heard him play a single piece all the way through without interruption in all the summers I've spent at Riond Bosson.

I'm delighted to be going to England and I'm thrilled about the concerts, but it's getting more and more difficult to leave home. I've had to board Anetka out in her school because there's nobody to leave her with at home. Too bad I can't entrust her to Father. That would be something, if Father gave her the run of the house the way he did me. His theory of rearing children is to put on his eyeglasses, survey Anetka carefully and then remark: "Come a little closer, my dear. Let me have a look at you. Hm, you don't seem pretty enough to me. Oh well, don't worry, you'll grow up into a pretty young woman."

London — November 5, 1931. My journey was most pleasant. On boarding the ship, the first thing we all had to do was submit to passport and customs inspection. After viewing my documents, which were in order, I was asked how much money and how many English pounds I had with me. Declaring my hundred Belgian francs and my five pounds sterling, I was told I had to have at least forty pounds if I wanted to enter England. At this unforeseen development there was nothing I could do except explain in my very halting English that my husband was Paderewski's secretary, that they had passed through here only three days earlier, and that I was now on my way to them. Quick as a flash came the assurance that everything was all right!

I was met at the station in London by Mr. Sharpe, the President's old friend and impressario for England.

The Hotel Carlton, in which the President has put up, is dazzlingly sumptuous. Shortly after my arrival, Sylwin came to meet me, his face wreathed in smiles. The President popped in, too, and his first question was: "My dear children, are you sure your room is comfortable enough?" Hearing me go into raptures about it, the President smiled, said, "Well, that's fine," and went back into his sitting room. A moment later, piano music echoed all over the place — Paderewski was playing.

November 8, 1931. Mr. Ignacy Kollupajlo called us up unexpectedly yesterday morning. We asked him over to our hotel. Because he's an old friend of ours and a former colleague of Sylwin's on Paderewski's *Rzeczpospolita* [newspaper] in Warsaw, the President invited him for lunch. Fortunately, Mr. Kollupajlo fell to the President's liking and was asked to stay for dinner. When Paderewski learned last night that Mr. Kollupajlo is an expert at bridge, he forthwith invited him to every lunch and dinner during our stay here.

November 15, 1931. In a few minutes we shall leave for Paderewski's concert in Albert Hall which holds six thousand people. I thought this evening would never come. How different everything is on the day Paderewski is scheduled to play. Of course I haven't even seen him today, nobody has. There is no lunch, everyone eats on his own. We all know that the President suffers dreadfully from stagefright before every concert and never touches food until after the recital.

Today is a particularly important occasion. A London concert and in the largest hall in Europe to boot. I've caught the President's nervousness myself. It's silly to be scared about the way Paderewski will play, but I can't help it. I'm worried sick. I even went to church to offer a little prayer for the success of the concert.

Later. Well, it's all over. I couldn't even say what Albert Hall looks like. All my amazed eyes could make out was a sea of human heads—thousands upon thousands of them. The boxes were bulging with standees. When I looked for the stage, I couldn't find it; a second look located a small black dot—the piano. But how was the President to get to it? What was supposed to be the stage was so tightly packed with chairs seating part of the overflow audience that those closest to the piano could have reached out and touched it.

The lights dimmed and Paderewski walked in slowly as if trying to fit into the narrow passage that had been left for him. Everybody rose spontaneously and there was prolonged applause. Finally Paderewski sat down at the piano. He began to play only when the silence grew so deep you could have heard the buzzing of a fly.

It was so quiet I didn't dare look at my program to see what the President was playing for fear the paper would rustle. Gradually I fell under the spell of the music and no longer felt any need to consult the program. The unearthly beauty of that music transported me to another world where neither time nor space existed, and where everything was fine, noble, and sublime.

A lady fainted during the second part of the concert and was carried out without the slightest noise. It couldn't have taken more than a minute altogether. Still, after the concert the President asked me: "What happened during the concert, did someone faint?" It's beyond me how the President saw, heard, or sensed the incident because it occurred in an obscure corner of one of the balconies behind him. Sylwin says the President always notices everything that goes on while he is playing.

What a concert that was! The President gave eight encores.

Following the recital there was a tremendous supper for some twenty-odd guests in a private reception room of the Hotel Carlton. The President attacked the food with a healthy appetite. He was in excellent humor and very gallant toward the ladies.

The supper was fit for a king, deliberately so for the benefit of Jancio H., who has the reputation of being the greatest gourmet in Paris. Rumor has it that a chef at the Ritz fainted when he heard that Count H. was in the restaurant.

Paderewski showed no sign of strain or fatigue. On the contrary, he was bubbling over with fun.

Reading—November 17, 1931. The President is playing in Reading today. After the concert in Albert Hall, I shouldn't be nervous any more. After all, that was his most important engagement. But I can't help it. We're all in the same boat. Nobody can find a place for himself. Mr. Sharpe won't eat on the pretext that he ate in the morning, Sylwin tries to persuade me and I urge Sylwin to have a bite—but we can't seem to make up our minds to lunch without the President.

Later. Again the concert was a first-rate triumph. There wasn't a vacant seat in the house. And how he played! Afterwards there was another princely supper and more guests who'd come to Reading just to hear Paderewski.

Hastings—November 24, 1931. The President gave a concert at Hastings today. He was incomparable. He doesn't spare himself. There were eleven encores, each more beautiful than the previous one.

I can't think of anything more agreeable than accompanying the President on a concert tour. The President's personal success, the respect and worship which these cold-blooded aristocratic Englishmen show a Pole fill me with pride and give me a feeling of profound moral satisfaction. Even I have received countless proofs of friendship and hospitality from complete strangers merely because I am with Paderewski. Since I'm the only woman in Paderewski's retinue now that Mme. Paderewska is in retirement, I'm especially careful to keep in the background in order not to be accused of a desire to be important. Nevertheless, everybody knows that Paderewski's private secretary is married and these English people go out of their way to be nice to me.

Brighton — November 26, 1931. This is a magnificent town and the hotel is the last word in comfort. Just to live in the hotels we've been staying in is an experience to be remembered. Wherever we stop, the President's sitting room is chock-full of flowers. I hate to leave them behind but it's out of the question to take them along.

I've run out of adjectives to describe the ovations following each concert. Coming back to the hotel tonight, the President's car looked like a garden on wheels.

None of this tribute any longer makes any impression on the President. No wonder, his whole life has been a succession of triumphs. As for me, I'm living in a dream!

London — December 4, 1931. It's way past midnight. Nobody has gone to bed yet, so I'm still up, too, in the President's sitting room. We're leaving England tomorrow morning — with regret as far as I'm concerned. I'm enchanted with England and with the English. Their progressiveness coupled with their almost fanatical devotion to their English traditions impresses me. A combination like that can appear only in a country of great culture.

Four A.M. already. I wonder whether the President's final impression of England will be very merry. The poor man's been sitting here with us I don't know how many hours autographing his pictures. There's still a pile of portraits, albums, photographs, and programs waiting for his autograph or dedication.

The President rarely signs likenesses of himself that are sent in or brought to him. He doesn't care for any of them, makes a face when he sees them and usually rejects them. Then Sylwin hands the President a photograph from the supply made in America — the only photograph of himself the President really likes — which he signs in place of the others. A trunkful of these American-made pictures was brought to England for the concert tour.

Morning will soon be here and there is still plenty of John-Hancocking to do, but the President seems to be in no hurry. He can't find a fountain pen to suit him, though. One point is too soft, another too hard. I offered him the one with which I've been describing his autographing activity. He took it and tried it out, remarking, "This is a very good pen." I'm proud that Paderewski is signing his name with my pen and that I'm writing with his. It may be a state of mind, but I think the President's thick dark green pen writes more smoothly than my own.

Christmas at Riond Bosson

Riond Bosson — December 15, 1931. For the first time while on a visit to Riond Bosson, we're staying at the Hotel Mont Blanc in Morges rather than at the Paderewski villa. Mme. Paderewska's health is so bad she hardly ever takes an automobile ride any more. Consequently she needs more space upstairs. All the third-floor guest rooms have been turned into quarters for her. Only Mrs. Wilkonska, Mamcia, and

Leniutka, who is Mme. Paderewska's faithful companion and sleeps in the same room with her, and Mrs. O. with her son have remained on that floor.

To be perfectly frank, I'm rather glad we're staying at the hotel. It gives me more freedom and relieves me of the necessity of sharing the complicated upstairs arrangement at Riond Bosson. Between poor Mme. Paderewska, ever-complaining Mrs. Wilkonska, who scowls whenever she lays eyes on Mrs. O., and Mamcia's worried face, it's quite a merry-go-round. Mamcia is a wonderful person, good, kind, and tactful, but because she's deaf, she never knows what's going on. However, she does notice whenever something is wrong and cries until Leniutka or I tell her the cause of the misunderstanding. And so it goes on and on, day in and day out. Why these ladies get so worked up I don't know. The President gives them just about everything and they really should appreciate it more.

I shall spend my first Christmas at Riond Bosson, because we're going to Paris right after the holidays. The President and Sylwin are sailing for America again. This time the concert tour will be shorter. They'll be back in Europe late in May.

I'm unhappy and conscience-stricken about not going home to Father and Anetka for Christmas. Sylwin begged me to remain for his sake — we won't see each other for another five months — and for the President, who would be hurt if I left. I'm staying but my heart is in a turmoil.

Riond Bosson — December 24, 1931. This is the second Christmas Eve in my life that has been unbearably sad. The first was in 1913 soon after Mother died.

Tonight the supper table was graced by a small Christmas tree hung with Polish toys. All the traditional Polish courses were served too: a choice of mushroom soup or *barszcz*, three kinds of fish, noodles with poppy seeds, poppy-seed milk, sweets, fruits and nuts, poppy-seed cake. I kept swallowing my tears, but when we shared the wafer, they streamed down my face. Every time I looked at the President, sitting there dejectedly, mute, lost in his thoughts, my heart contracted more. The general mood was so funereal that even Sylwin didn't try to joke, and of course Mrs. Wilkonska reacts to depression by sinking into a deep gloominess herself. So we sat through the *Wigilia* [traditional Polish Christmas Eve supper], each thinking his own thoughts.

Paris — December 29, 1931. I am left alone again. Sylwin and the President sailed from Le Havre today. But I don't despair any more. I've gotten used to these frequent separations, to these solitary travels. Each situation has its flavor. I like solitude, I like freedom, I'm glad I'm going back to Warsaw, to Father and Anetka. I'm glad I'm in Paris. I can't complain that my life isn't rich and interesting.

Warsaw — January 10, 1932. I arrived in Warsaw today. The Christmas tree is still standing because Anetka wanted to show me what a lovely tree she had — and three times as many gifts as usual to make up for Mother being away! She doesn't seem the least bit disturbed by my absence.

After dinner Tadeusz made this surprising statement. "I wanted to tell you that I've joined Pilsudski's party. There's no sense being in the opposition all the time. If I'm not at peace with the government, I won't be able to do a blessed thing for industry in Poland."

I must admit I was amazed by Tadeusz's declaration, but I have such unlimited confidence in my brother, that I believe he had no other way out if he made this decision. Tadeusz represents Polish heavy industry in many European firms and concerns. He can really do a lot for Poland. I don't know whether he did the right thing, but I do know that my brother is considered one of the best brains in Polish industry, that he is a man of unblemished integrity and has a high sense of responsibility.

Now I have a husband close to Paderewski and a brother in the Pilsudski party!

Paris — May 31, 1932. Anetka and I have spent our name day in Paris. But we both forgot about the date and so did everybody else. We're all together again. Sylwin and the President are back from America.

La Baule, Bretagne — June 1932. We're at the seashore, Anetka and I. It's beautiful here but I'd prefer going to Brussels to hear the President play for Queen Elisabeth's charities.

Chopin Festival

Paris — June 1932. The President and Sylwin having returned from Brussels, Anetka and I left La Baule. Paris is brimming over with Poles who have come here in connection with the Chopin Festival. They all congregate at the Hotel du Palais d'Orsay anxious to see the President. The Chopin Festival is taking place in the Theatre des Champs Elysées, owned by Ganna Walska, internationally-known Polish beauty and artist. Queen Elisabeth of Belgium announced her intention of coming to Paris to attend the President's concert. There will be a reception for her at the Polish Embassy.

June 1932. Fortunately Leniutka is with us and, being a good sport, she takes Anetka around Paris. I'm so involved at the hotel, I can't budge.

Paderewski's pupils are all here. They've come especially for the concert. The President willingly invites them to join him at his meals, which are regularly served in a separate room because with so many guests a table the size of ours in the restaurant downstairs would look like a banquet.

After Sylwin had accompanied the President to a luncheon at the Royal residence at Laeken, he was awarded the Officer of the Belgian Crown decoration. He now parades around with two rosettes in his dinner coat lapel—one Belgian and the other the French Legion of Honor.

The Polish Embassy tendered a reception after the President's concert, and thereby hangs a tale. Because I knew that Queen Elisabeth is fond of Sylwin, addressing him *mon cher M. Strakacz*, I was afraid she might express a desire to meet me. There were several reasons why I wasn't too keen on being presented to her. In the first place, what does one say to a queen? And in the second, I'm so sun-tanned after my vacation at the beach that I look a fright. Even the President was shocked by my appearance. It may have looked attractive at the seashore, but hardly very chic when set off by a dressy hat and low-cut frock in elegant Paris. In the light of all this, I prudently put as much distance as I could between myself and the Queen and the President. But you can't fight against fate.

All of a sudden there was a slight commotion and I heard a murmur: *Où est Madame Strakacz?* Before I could gather my wits together, I was being told Queen Elisabeth wished me to be presented to her and I was being pulled through all the reception rooms to where the Queen was seated in a corner behind a table. Having deposited my confused person directly across the table from Her Majesty, the aide let go of my hand. All I had time to think was that I must remove my long blue glove from my right hand before I shook hands with royalty. Peeling the glove off, I was wondering how the dickens I could get close enough to the Queen to shake hands. She solved the problem herself by rising and extending her hand to me across the table. Squeezing mine cordially, she said: "I am glad to make your acquaintance because I like Mr. Strakacz for his devotion to our dear President Paderewski."

I curtsied low according to protocol, got up and replied with, "Merci, Votre Majesté," thinking the presentation was over and I could make a quick get-away. But the Queen did not let go of my hand and went on talking to me. I couldn't hear a word she said, partly out of excitement, but chiefly because of the conversational buzz all around me. I was getting panicky. If I didn't know what she was saying, how could I say something in reply? Meanwhile the Queen was making a little speech to me. At a complete loss, I curtsied again. But she had not finished talking. So I just went on punctuating her remarks with repeated curtseys until she had terminated the "conversation" and released my hand. Thanking her again, I made a hasty exit, close to tears and bearing a grudge against the whole world because I hadn't been briefed about the presentation, because the Queen had been placed behind the table so senselessly, because I had made a fool of myself. My friends laughingly consoled me that Her Majesty had doubtless appreciated my modesty, timidity, and embarrassment!

Summer in Switzerland

Riond Bosson—July 1, 1932. At the President's wish, Sylwin and I are going to Warsaw for the unveiling on July 4th of the Colonel House statue (by the Polish sculptor Franciszek Black) which Paderewski has had erected in payment of his last debt of gratitude to a great and noble American for Poland's independence. The President frequently told us that it was his friend Colonel House who had given him access to President Wilson so that he might present to him a clear picture of the Polish cause. The statue will stand in Skary-szewski Park.

Anetka will remain here with Leniutka, whom she calls her vice-mother. Leniutka will also be looking after the Paderewskis. As a matter of fact, Leniutka divides her life between Mme. Paderewska and Mamcia just as I divide mine between Father and Anetka on the one hand and the President and Sylwin on the other. Only Leniutka's situation is a little less complicated than mine because her mother is a resident of Riond Bosson, while I have to commute back and forth over half a continent.

I've often thought I shouldn't come to Switzerland so often. I'm absolutely useless here. Nobody expects anything of me. It's purely a pleasure trip as far as I'm concerned. Now that the President travels alone with Sylwin, I call myself "the fifth wheel of the cart." But the President waxes genuinely indignant whenever I refer to myself like that. I know that he prefers to have me around because he rests easier about Sylwin then. When I'm not here, he worries over Sylwin, realizing that willy-nilly he is disrupting our family life. In my absence the President watches over Sylwin like a father, checking up on him even late at night. But when we are together, and after finally bidding the President good night well after midnight, steal away to go dancing, he never checks up on us. I love him for being so good and kind to us and so solicitous of Sylwin when I'm away.

Riond Bosson — July 7, 1932. We're back in Switzerland. Mrs. Wilkonska greeted both of us cordially. She has come to like me at last because she sees I never pry into anything, never criticize, never make any demands and am always ready to agree with her. For the first time in a dozen years she said to me in all sincerity (Mrs. Wilkonska couldn't be hypocritical if her life depended on it), "It's a good thing you came along, Aniela. Ignace is so happy when you're with them." When Mrs. Wilkonska talks like that, you see how much she resembles the President.

Paderewski questioned us with great interest about the unveiling ceremonies. Was the monument well executed? We took turns telling him the details. We told him that beautiful, recently opened Skaryszewski Park in the Praga section of Warsaw had been renamed Paderewski Park, and that the statue, erected in a fine, clearly visible spot, was truly worthy of its surroundings. We did not tell him that the ceremony of the unveiling itself had been arranged without fanfare, that the only government official present was the District

Governor, W. Jaroszewicz, who made a very good impression on me, if only because he hadn't been afraid to come and because he was very courteous to us. Besides representatives of the U. S. Legation, most of the spectators were friends of the Paderewskis who held no government positions and could therefore afford to be independent. When we went to Paderewski Park the day after the unveiling to have another look at Colonel House's statue, more people were milling around Paderewski's gift than had attended the dedicatory exercises.

Mme. Paderewska still occupies the entire third floor. They found quarters for us in the tiny village of Tolochenaz, a five-minute walk from Riond Bosson.

The President grumbles about our separate quarters, insisting we can't be happy with such an arrangement, but we are equally insistent that everything is fine and that we're most comfortable.

August 8, 1932. Mr. Jozef Paderewski, the President's half-brother, was here for a few days. How very strange—I never knew the President had a half-brother! I had never heard about any relatives at all. The President hardly ever talks about his past, but he has said on many occasions: "Antosia and I have no family. There are just the two of us." In moments of depression, Mrs. Wilkonska mentions her little boy who died at the age of nine. She never has a kind word to say about her late husband, though the only thing she had against him was his advanced age at the time they married her to him. And she remembers her stepmother with frank hatred. Whenever Mrs. Wilkonska reminisces in this vein, the President unfailingly chides her: "Antosia was always tearful. Mr. Wilkonski was a very pleasant person and I don't know what Antosia has against our stepmother, she was always very good to us."

Mr. Jozef Paderewski has a most agreeable exterior, speaks little, and is rather unpretentious looking. Once you draw him out though, you realize he is an intelligent and educated man. He was hospitably and warmly received as are all visitors at Riond Bosson, but there were no intimate conversations of the kind you'd expect among members of the family.

The President's brother seemed to feel a little bewildered by the sudden change in his quiet, ordered life; Sylwin says he came to Riond Bosson at the President's specific invitation. The President had written to his half-brother several times offering him money — once he even sent some money outright — but Jozef had written back that he required neither money nor any other assistance from the President, that he earned enough to take care of his own needs.

It is my opinion that the President is so accustomed to having everyone who approaches him ask for a hand-out that an unassuming disinterested guest or relative who wants nothing from him only causes him embarrassment. The President likes to give and I would go so far as to say he must enjoy being taken advantage of. For I can't believe he doesn't know when he is being fleeced. He is perfectly aware of it, but he gives just the same, because he is generous, indulgent, and derives satisfaction from it.

A visitor like Jozef Paderewski — sweet, modest, never pushing himself forward and anxious only to return to his uneventful way of life — seems like someone from another planet. When her half-brother had left Riond Bosson, Mrs. Wilkonska sighed with admiration: "What a nice person that Jozef is!"

One of the few guests unreservedly welcome at Riond Bosson at all times is Count Pawel Morsztyn, a member of the Polish Delegation to the League of Nations, affectionately called Pawelek by everybody. Pawelek is a regular all-day Sunday guest, but he is *très correct*, so he never fails to telephone on Saturday to announce his Sunday visit. Early every Saturday morning Mrs. Wilkonska starts worrying that Pawelek might not come on Sunday, while not a single Saturday lunch goes by without the President inquiring: "Will Pawelek be here tomorrow?" This although Pawelek

never telephones before four P.M.! Even if there should be
a hundred guests invited for Sunday, Pawelek's presence is
the chief concern of both Mrs. Wilkonska and Paderewski.
Once he calls up to say he will come, they smile happily,
perfectly sure the Sunday reception will run smoothly.

I've always known Pawelek; he was a most popular and
sought-after young man in Warsaw. His unique position in
the Paderewski household is probably due to his great simplicity and intelligence. The President enjoys talking with
him and it's a real treat to listen to their glittering, witty
conversation.

August 1932. Among the guests installed for a vacation at
Riond Bosson is Miss Mary Lawton, an American. She came
from the United States to write Paderewski's memoirs, which
the President apparently agreed to dictate the last time he
was in America. I'm very glad because hitherto he'd always
refused. At last we'll have some reminiscences about his
past. We know so little about his early life from his own lips.

How rich and varied the President's life must have been
and how difficult to write down can be gleaned from a glimpse
of poor Miss Lawton directly after a session with the President. For all her keen intelligence and rugged good health,
Miss Lawton, who is a well-preserved forty, practically
tears her hair out. She emerges with glazed eyes and a half-
dead look and disbelievingly shakes her head. She wonders
despairingly whether she'll be able to stand the pace of a
dictation which she can't possibly keep up with. Miss Lawton
says she never came across such rapid-fire thinking before.
The President dictates purely from memory. Dates, names,
places, important and less important events—it all rolls off
his tongue in a swift torrent.

Miss Lawton has all my sympathy. I know exactly what
she's going through because I remember the time I played a
game of garibaldi with the President. He played each hand
with such uncanny speed that I lost my wits. When one stops

to think of it, the President must have a phenomenal memory. Nobody ever saw him jotting anything down, he never carries a pocket diary or memo pad, and yet he remembers every date, name, or appointment. The man is a walking chronicle. Whatever you ask him, he'll remember to the tiniest detail.

August, 1932. This has been the fourth and last summer for the Paderewski quintet of pupils. Strictly speaking there were quite a few more than five musicians here to get the benefit of Paderewski's instruction. There was a Mr. Bielicki from Poland; Felix Labunski, who is Kollupajlo's cousin and president of the Society of Young Musicians in Paris; and there was Alexander Sienkiewicz. The latter is from Poznan where Mr. Henryk Opienski met him. Mr. Opienski considers him a very gifted musician and a promising composer. Unfortunately Mr. Sienkiewicz comes from a poor family and in order to study music he had to try all kinds of odd jobs. He even was a dishwasher, until finally he had to give up serious music and take a job with a jazz band playing in night clubs. However, his real interest remained centered on classic music, and that, finally, brought him to Riond Bosson. The other pupils look at Mr. Sienkiewicz with a slight touch of resentment; not because he worked as a dishwasher, but because of his playing in night clubs, which they consider beneath the dignity of a real artist. The addition to the old team of pupils did not upset the established plan for their summer course; the new arrivals merely sit in on the lessons.

Life in Riond Bosson has been more than gay this season. The table in the dining room has been expanded to its maximum size because some of our musicians brought their families along. Italian Mrs. Tadlewska and their twin daughters and Mrs. Dygat and her two little girls have been here all summer. Mr. Brachocki's wife is in America—he's an American of Polish descent—and Mrs. Sztompka, who was here before, hasn't come this year.

The four years of lessons with the President were cli-

maxed by the quintet's gala concert in the drawing room before an audience of distinguished invited guests, Paderewski's
send-off gift to his pupils. For days before the affair the
pianists almost never left their keyboards, practising away
for dear life, fired by the ambition of giving the best possible
account of themselves. It's only natural that each should hope
to be regarded as Paderewski's star pupil. There has been
occasional friction among the pupils on this score, for which
the statements of incompetent "critics" anxious to play a
rôle in Paderewski's entourage have been responsible. But
none of these intrigues got beyond the door of the President's
study. If by some chance they happened to reach the President,
they vanished into thin air, because he never singled out any
one pupil for special praise. Treating them all alike, he gave
them equally of his titanic and inspiring artistic personality
and stood before them an unparalleled example of the super-
artist and super-man who is untouched by the minutiae of
life, who rises above all the petty personal problems that
poison the lives of ordinary men.

I'm sure none of the pupils will ever forget their recital
at Riond Bosson. The drawing room was packed. While the
President was in the drawing room with the guests, his
pupils cooled their heels in the card room, from which they
were to emerge one by one to play their concert pieces. The
poor things were so horribly nervous that, though I smiled
encouragingly at them, I was beginning to be afraid none of
them would be able to go out and play.

Aleksander Brachocki had turned waxen. Henryk
Sztompka, always pale and anemic, had acquired the trans-
parent look of someone about to faint. Stanislaw Szpinalski
and Albert Tadlewski, both husky, healthy-looking specimens, stood around like a couple of starry-eyed wooden
figures. And Zygmunt Dygat, with his sunny, inspired face,
had grown so tiny as to be almost invisible.

Paderewski must have sensed what his boys were going
through. He entered the card room, took the first victim by
the shoulders, shook him hard — but really hard — and literally

pushed him through the door into the drawing room. Then he went out after him. The same scene was repeated five times. If the lads were still frightened when they sat down at the piano, it didn't show in their performance. I don't know enough about music to judge the way they played, but it must have been fine, because the President looked very pleased. Neither praising nor criticizing, in fact making no comment at all, he embraced and kissed each of the performers. The brilliant international audience responded with real enthusiasm to the unique show, and apparently fell in with Paderewski's hard and fast rule of non-favoritism. The guests praised the boys en masse, expressed their delight at having been permitted to witness such an unusual spectacle — and stayed to dinner.

There will be no more lessons. The only pupils Paderewski ever had will go out into the world bearing the prized title of "Pupil of Paderewski." Everybody had heaped abuse on poor Henryk Opienski's head for burdening the President with all this extra work, but the world of Polish music certainly owes him a vote of gratitude. Thanks to him, at least these few Polish virtuosi have received the legacy of Paderewski's school and art.

Warsaw — September 3, 1932. Coming back to Poland from Riond Bosson this trip I had my crate of magnificent fruit as usual. But this time the customs officials at Zbaszyn did not subject me to inspection nor did they tell me to pay a duty on Polish fruits from Paderewski's orchard. They greeted me brightly and their faces broke into delighted grins when I got off the train to distribute the shoots I had promised them the year before. I doubt whether any train ever saw such unusual luggage as I crowded into my compartment on this trip. When I had related the customs incident of my Riond Bosson fruit to the President and had conveyed the request for offshoots to him, he had told me to bring the men as many of the finest specimens as I could manage. Kind-hearted Mr. Dolezal, the gardener, executed the President's wish to the letter, and dressed me up with an honest-to-goodness nursery. I carried whole trees wrapped up in straw, tissue paper, and bast.

A Concert for the Swiss

Riond Bosson — November 4, 1932. In Riond Bosson, in Morges, in Lausanne, even in our tiny hamlet of Tolochenaz, everybody is talking only of the President's November 9th concert in Vevey.

Vevey, Switzerland — November 9, 1932. The concert was so beautiful I don't see how anyone could ever play more enchantingly. Music like that gives you a holiday feeling all over. The atmosphere at the recital was that of a family reunion. One noticed so many nice Swiss, old friends of the Paderewskis and acquaintances from the neighboring estates — people whom we see rarely but who are true devoted friends of the President, regarding him as a sort of compatriot and proud of the fact that he has chosen their country for his residence. They wondered whether they'd be invited to a late supper in the Hotel des Trois Couronnes where we're staying overnight, but they needn't have. The President never forgets any of his old friends. It was the usual story: a sumptuous feast around a gigantic table amid laughter and gay chatter. The banquet lasted far into the night.

Music in Italy, France, and the United States

Riond Bosson — November 17, 1932. The President and Sylwin will leave today for a concert tour of Italy. Paderewski will play in Milan and Turin first and then go on to Florence.

Something very wonderful has happened to Leniutka and myself. Since neither of us has ever been to Italy before and since we wouldn't have much time for sightseeing if we went with the President (he leaves each town directly after his concert) he is sending us ahead to Florence, which is the most interesting of all the cities, to give us a chance to really become acquainted with it. But the main reason for this surprise trip are Riond Bosson's famous hothouse grapes. Every fall when they ripen, the President sends some to the world's great. The President remembers that when Pope Pius XI was papal nuncio in Poland at the time of Paderewski's premiership, he was particularly fond of these grapes.

The President is very anxious that the grapes be delivered to the Pope in perfect condition. Though Mr. Dolezal is a magician capable of keeping the picked grapes fresh up to Christmas, shipping them in crates by heated train is another matter. Leniutka and I will take the grapes with us to Florence. Right after Paderewski's concert there, we shall proceed to Rome to deliver the precious gift at the Vatican, for the President is scheduled to play in several other places before arriving in Rome.

Florence, Hotel Stella d' Italia — November 18, 1932. Neither of us expected we'd have so many complications with our grapes. We've brought sixteen boxes of them, eight bunches of black and eight of white. Each box contains one huge bunch of plum-size grapes intricately wrapped in tissue paper and sawdust. Wired together into two vertical rows, the boxes are light in weight but at least as tall as we. Depositing them delicately in the rack of our compartment, we thought we were all set for a peaceful trip.

That's what we thought! The unforeseen drama began at the Italian border. Neither Leniutka nor I speak Italian, but we were perspicacious enough to learn the Italian equivalent for "grapes" and "personal belongings," of which we don't have much to begin with, as all we have taken along is one suitcase apiece. The Italian customs official asked us what we had to declare and told us to bring out our luggage for inspection. Leniutka replied, *"Proprieta personale e uva."* Hearing the word *uva*, the official fiercely told us to open the boxes and simultaneously launched into a long and grim tirade, of which we naturally didn't understand a thing, except that he was constantly using the word *filoxera*. We had no idea what *filoxera* could mean, but we gathered it must be something serious if our offer to pay any duty they might levy had no effect upon the Italians. Five of them had already appeared on the scene, shouting *filoxera* increasingly often and threateningly. The one thing that got through to our consciousness was that they didn't want to let our grapes into Italy.

We were frantic. We had promised the President we'd get his grapes delivered to the Pope without mishap and now it looked as if we were going to make our journey purely a pleasure trip. Not knowing what arguments to use against the mystifying *filoxera*, Leniutka waved her hands about desperately crying *Il Paderewski! Il Papa!* I was enraptured! Following her example, I added my voice to hers. The Italians countered with *Filoxera* and we repeated our *Il Paderewski, il Papa*. And so we merrily strove to outshout each other. *Il Paderewski*, and we pointed to the grapes, then, our index fingers shifted in the general direction of Rome, *Il Papa!* Up against a stone wall of feminine intransigence, the Fascists finally shrugged their arms in an eloquent gesture of hopelessness, and departed. We closed our grape boxes before the customs officials might experience a change of heart and hastily retreated into our car. The train started.

Florence—November 19, 1932. The President has arrived. He enjoyed immensely our *filoxera* incident. [Filoxera is a disease of grapes.]

We shared Paderewski's box with a number of Poles. I don't know who they were, but they were compatriots and as we have no acquaintances in Florence, we filled the box with them.

I experienced some pretty anxious moments during the President's concert. The recital began as usual in the crowded hall. Suddenly, in the midst of his playing, as the audience sat motionless, all rapt attention, the President stopped and kept striking a single piano key with one finger. The surprised audience maintained a tense silence. Then, all of a sudden, Paderewski jumped up from the piano and left the platform. A good several minutes later, frightened-looking Mr. H., the piano tuner, appeared on stage, commenced tapping the keys, and to my horror started dismantling the piano. The thought flashed through my mind that if this took a long time, the impatient public would leave, and wouldn't that make a nice story! Every minute seemed a century. The tuning had been going on for twenty minutes already. I can't get over these hot-tempered impulsive Italians sitting quietly like so many lambs throughout this unplanned addition to the program. Nobody gave any sign of irritation, nobody so much as made a move to leave his seat. But when the tuner had reassembled the piano, he was rewarded by a storm of applause. The President returned, sat down at the piano, tried the offending key a few times, then leapt up again and hurried off the stage. The "piano doctor" reappeared, more dead than alive, and was greeted by the audience with gay laughter and even more marked applause. Fortunately this time he made only a minor correction which took but a moment. Paderewski came back and with all the calm in the world resumed his concert.

Rome — November 21, 1932. After our sad experience with a cheaper hotel in Florence, Leniutka and I registered directly at the Hotel Quirinal, where the President will put up. Without taking time out to change, we left our things in the hotel room, hailed a taxi and piled in with our grapes, determined to carry out our special mission to the Vatican with flying colors.

Passing through the gates of the Vatican and having our first look at the resplendent picture-book Swiss guardsmen, we drove into the deserted main courtyard. We got out of the taxi in front of one of the huge entrances, balancing our mountain of boxes. But we had no idea where to go. There wasn't anybody around to inquire of. Occasionally a cassock-attired figure darted from one entrance to another. But some moved so quickly that we could never hope to catch up with them, while others seemed so important — they all looked like cardinals to us — that we didn't quite dare accost them. We finally decided to enter the building anywhere at all and find out inside how and where we should deliver the grapes, that they might be eaten, before the President's arrival, by His Holiness and by no one else.

Walking in by the nearest and largest door, I seated myself on the marble steps, placed the two rows of boxes next to me and waited for Leniutka to come back from the office. She returned in a little while disconcerted by the fact that nobody understood her. No French spoken here, and no Italian spoken by Leniutka. We must have presented a strange sight — two be-jewelled, smartly dressed women carrying sixteen heavy-looking boxes unattractively wired together. It was the hardest thing in the world selling those Vatican priests the idea of fresh grapes for the Pope. Back and forth they sent us like a football. Two full hours later, we hit upon a French-speaking person who became interested in our plight and referred us to the proper department.

November 22, 1932. Two gentlemen, one an emissary from the Pope, the other from Mussolini, were waiting for the President in the sitting room of the suite reserved for him. As soon as Paderewski arrived, we found out from Sylwin that both the Pope and Il Duce wished to see him. It gave us a warm glow of pride that our President is important enough for His Holiness and Mussolini to be the first to approach him. Barely had Paderewski removed his coat, when he already had two appointments taken care of, following his concert of course, which is today. This time we're more thrilled about the prospective audiences with the heads of the Catholic world and of Italy than we are about the concert.

November 23, 1932. For once I envied Sylwin's accompanying the President without me on an official call upon the Pope. The audience was at nine A.M. so that by eight-thirty our two men were ready in cutaways, decorations, and top hats, looking very spruce and gala indeed. I pressed a dozen rosaries and holy medals into Sylwin's hands just before he left with strict orders that he bring them back blessed by the Pope. They'll be precious relics to our Warsaw friends, especially to Sylwin's parents who are both very devout Catholics.

Almost simultaneously, Leniutka left for the station to hurry back to Switzerland. Mme. Paderewska has been under only Soeur Paule's care for a week now. Three hours after Leniutka's departure and the return of Paderewski and Sylwin from the Vatican, I sent her a special delivery note that read: "The Pope received the grapes in time, his first words of greeting to the President being an expression of appreciation for them. He said they were delicious. His Holiness personally blessed all of our holy medals and rosaries."

November 24, 1932. The President talked with Mussolini for two and a half hours. All of that time Sylwin waited in the reception room. When the visit was over, Mussolini escorted the President to the door. Then Paderewski turned to his host and said: "Before I go, I'd like to present to you my friend and secretary, Sylwin Strakacz." Mussolini shook Sylwin's hand and commented "It is a great honor to serve President Paderewski." One thing I'm sorry about, though. Sylwin didn't get me the autographed photograph of Mussolini for my collection which I'd asked him to bring back. I do not dare ask him why, but I suppose he just didn't have the right opening.

November 25, 1932. A few hours before our slated departure for Naples, Mussolini's aide came around with a tremendous envelope. There were two very big photographs inside. One bore a dedication to Paderewski. The other had scrawled over it in a bold hand: "A Sylwin Strakacz. Benito Mussolini Roma 25–XI–1932." Hurray!

Same Day — Naples.

> *Oh, Naples, Naples, oh land of beauty!*
> *Who hasn't seen thee, has not seen heaven!*

I was brought up on the words of this popular song and it had been my most cherished girlhood dream to visit Naples. The city is lovely but it doesn't measure up to my expectations of something out of this world. The bay is striking and the sprawling city a gem, but all of Italy is so breathtakingly beautiful! Perhaps I should be ashamed of myself, but I've seen so many masterworks of nature that just now it's the Hotel Excelsior which captures my undiluted admiration. This hostelry tops every other I've been in, and I've stayed in plenty of them. If heaven is furnished, it must be something like our hotel.

When the President was told how I felt, he smilingly agreed the Excelsior was exceptionally beautiful and luxurious, but he added quickly that I shouldn't miss seeing the Neapolitan aquarium, which has no equal in the world. He proceeded to describe it in detail and to tell me exactly how to get there — just as if he'd been there yesterday. It's amazing when you think that nobody ever saw the President go anywhere except from the train to the hotel or to and from a concert. Sylwin also is seeing the world from train windows and hotels. I alone take advantage of every free moment and see whatever points of interest I can pack into my crowded day.

November 26, 1932. Never have I enjoyed myself as much at a concert as I did today. I went all alone because we don't know a soul here. And I was completely by myself in the box, which didn't bother me in the least. I had directly opposite me the Italian crown prince and his Belgian princess, who were occupying the royal box. "My" box, preceded by a sizable sitting room, could have accommodated at least twelve sitting or even reclining persons, for I was surprised to see love seats, armchairs, and divans in the box.

It amused me to be alone. At first I sat in the front to be able the better to cast discreet glances in the direction of the young royal couple. The public gazed fondly at the popular members of the royal house, but they also looked wonderingly at my solitary figure in the immense box on the other side of the stage. I felt like a queen too. It's fun being by oneself when the President plays. I moved back in the empty box, stretched out on the most comfortable divan with a pillow under my head, closed my eyes and listened to the music, which I now understand better and better. I wish I could always enjoy the President's concerts in solitude like that.

December 2, 1932. The day after his concert here Paderewski and Sylwin left for the north again. I stayed in Naples another week to get a better idea of Naples, Pompei, Herculaneum, and Capri. I love it here, but I don't feel very much at ease with growling Vesuvius nearby. A few days ago during a storm, the old rascal rumbled so he gave me the jitters. I'll do anything once, so I went up to the top of the volcano with a guide and waved my hand around in the giant crater. But I wouldn't live here permanently for all the gold in China—not even in my incomparable Hotel Excelsior.

Riond Bosson—December 10, 1932. Having been back in Switzerland for five days, I'm all set to leave today for the French Riviera with Mrs. Wilkonska. I'm supposed to look after her. This won't be a jaunt because I shan't have any freedom, but I've willingly agreed to accompany the President's sister. She's all on edge, embittered against everybody and terribly hurt that the President never asks her to go along on a trip with him. The President doesn't ask her simply because he knows she wouldn't go anyway, she hates to stir from Riond Bosson. But Mrs. Wilkonska isn't interested in going away. All she wants is to be asked. That's the crux of the misunderstanding. This trip to the Riviera is running true to form. When the President suggested she go, she accepted the idea with enthusiasm, then she grew frightened and now she's displeased about going, repeating over and over again: "If it weren't for Ignace's concert in Monte Carlo, I'd rather stay home." In the last analysis, she doesn't know whether to be happy or unhappy about it.

Nice—December 14, 1932. To my amazement Mrs. Wilkonska is actually contented, even happy. I suspect that the real reason for her newly found happiness, however, is that she's the person around whom everything revolves here, including me. The change in her is stupefying. She's a completely different individual—gay, sunny, extremely tactful, tender, just like the President. You'd never believe she's the same Mrs. Wilkonska who rules Riond Bosson in a perpetual mood of complaint and anger, with a chip-on-the-shoulder attitude toward the world.

December 15, 1932. Mrs. Wilkonska and I moved to the Hotel Riviera-Palace in Nice-Cimiez to be with Paderewski and Sylwin. The President accorded his sister a hearty welcome. It's really touching to see this pair of old people embrace fondly and then kiss each other's hand with respect.

December 16, 1932. The President's concert in Monte Carlo was this afternoon at three. I didn't derive complete satisfaction from this recital. It was a full house of course, but I didn't care for the audience—cold, indifferent, and above all, not music lovers. They were snobs who bought tickets for the concert just to be able to say they had heard Paderewski play. All they're interested in is *trente et quarante*, roulette, the Casino, and the baccarat room. I have no use for people like that. Furthermore, I don't think the President should give concerts in such an unwholesome locality. Doddering old ladies, tuckered out after a night of gambling, were nodding all over the place, while the men kept glancing at their watches to see whether the Casino had already opened so that they might return to it.

Riond Bosson — December 21, 1932. Today I go back to Warsaw. I feel terrible leaving Sylwin and the President, but I will not permit Father and Anetka to spend Christmas without me again. I wish I knew how to thank the President for that marvelous trip to Italy and the Riviera.

They're all a little peeved with me for going, especially since the President and Sylwin are departing for a new concert tour of the United States in the middle of January.

Paris — January 13, 1933. Well, I'm back in Paris to bid Sylwin and Paderewski bon voyage. I came a few hours before they arrived from Switzerland. By a miracle there were no callers waiting for the President. Apparently they hadn't learned he was expected today. So we went down to the restaurant for dinner. The President's traditional table was reserved for him in the corner. As it was rather late, there were few diners in the restaurant, but they all to a man got up and bowed to the President. If one didn't know, one would think they were acquaintances. A lot of people came up to our table to shake the President's hand, to recall themselves to his memory or simply to introduce themselves. Paderewski rose for each visitor and talked to all with the same courtesy.

The President himself ordered, hardly even asking us for our choice, because his amazing memory is such that he remembers what our individual preferences are. Then he selected the best wines "and we'll end up with champagne." I never have liked champagne, but since it's the President's favorite, I don't admit it. Many's the time I've drunk as many as three glasses of the stuff to please him.

At the conclusion of our meal the special chef assigned to Paderewski emerged from his behind-the-scenes realm, warmly shook the President's hand, asked if everything was to his liking, and inquired what delicacy he would care to have tomorrow.

Paderewski loves to eat and has a hearty appetite. Unfortunately he should cut down on his meals, especially in the evening. Dr. Choussaud keeps warning the President of his alarmingly high blood pressure. And here the President has another long, tedious *tournée* before him.

January 17, 1933. These few days before the President's departure for America are very busy. None of us ever goes out; there's no time for it. The wave of luncheon guests runs into the wave of evening visitors. Each reception surpasses the previous one, for the chef is making every effort to impress Paderewski with his culinary art. Dr. Choussaud, who is a steady visitor, growls all the time, but he can't resist the temptation to pitch into the fine food and drink good wines himself. He tells us it's good for every organism to eat and drink "like a coachman" once in a while.

This afternoon, Mrs. X., who came to Paris on purpose to audition before the President, played for him at the hotel. Paderewski maintains a death-like silence before and after such recitals. We never ask him any questions. One thing is sure, though: we can count on going to the movies. The cinema is followed by a game of bridge. It's all part of his program of relaxation after the distasteful experience of an audition.

January 18, 1933. I've returned from Cherbourg. Sylwin and the President sailed for New York on the *Olympic.*

Warsaw—May 1, 1933. These four months that Sylwin and the President have been in America flew by like a flash, though six weeks of it I spent in bed. This is how it happened: Tadeusz has three beautiful horses in the riding academy. I was riding one, a spirited Arab mare, who apparently disliked my nervous hand, for she swerved without warning and slipped. Instead of throwing me, she fell, bringing me down with her. Net result: one broken human leg. I didn't let on to Sylwin about my accident. In my daily letters to him I made up the most interesting stories of the wonderful time I was having. I didn't want him to suspect the truth for fear he'd worry and upset the President. Paderewski is amazingly sensitive. In one of his letters Sylwin relates how once, while the President was playing and couldn't possibly see what was going on back stage, he slipped out of the theatre for a few minutes to buy something. When he returned less than a quarter of an hour later, the President was still playing, yet, the first thing Paderewski asked Sylwin during the intermission was: "Did you go out anywhere?" Sylwin vowed he'd never leave in the middle of a performance again. But how could the President have known? He must have sensed Sylwin's absence.

Paris — May 6, 1933. The President looks grand after his American tour, but it's this too healthy look which disturbs Dr. Choussaud. His blood pressure is too high and will have to be lowered by a special reducing cure. The President is supposed to lose twenty-five pounds, which is a ticklish business at his age. But we have such faith in Dr. Choussaud's medical genius that Sylwin did not hesitate to use all his persuasion in trying to convince the President to accept the proposed cure.

Meanwhile the President's manner of living has not changed. Guests for lunch and dinner are an established institution. It's inconceivable that the President would ever eat less than his guests. So when we're among close acquaintances, we all agree beforehand to cut down on our eating and drinking. For instance, Sylwin pretends that he ate so many lobsters and so much mayonnaise in America he gets sick at the idea of looking at them. (Paderewski, who knows Sylwin only too well, stares at him with utter disbelief.) Or I complain of having been poisoned by something I ate the day before, whereupon, when the President lightly suggests a chocolate soufflé, Sylwin counters: "Let's save it for tomorrow when Aniela will be feeling better and can have it with us." As a result of all this conniving our menus are cut down to reason. The President does not protest, but he is clearly peeved, because he can see right through our bluffing.

Reducing on the Riviera

Riond Bosson — May 18, 1933. We leave for Warsaw today. As soon as Anetka's school year is over, we shall come back here, bringing her with us.

Warsaw — June, 1933. Sylwin, who has not been home for more than a year, has found a change in our house. Having served my parents for thirty-eight years, Andrzej is now retired; his successor is Franciszek Pajda, recommended by my brother's butler, Stanislaw. Both Stanislaw and Franciszek have the reputation of being the best servants in Warsaw.

Sylwin has taken a great liking to Franciszek. The other day he said: "Franciszek would be perfect for the President." I knew what he meant. Ever since Marcel Sentoll, a paragon of loyalty and devotion who had been with the President for forty-five years, passed on to his reward, Paderewski has relied on Mademoiselle Aline Fuchs, Mme. Paderewska's former maid. However, the President should have a man around him, not so much because he is demanding, but because not believing in class distinction and treating everyone alike, he hesitates to call on a woman for a variety of services.

But I have no desire to part with Franciszek. It gives me

a feeling of security to know that when I'm away, Father, the house, and Anetka are in his competent and solicitous hands.

Riond Bosson — June 26, 1933. We are back here, Anetka and I, but it looks as if I shall remain only a few days. I'm to help Leniutka find a quiet resort on the French Riviera where the President could stay a month or so. It has definitely been decided that the President will reduce. Dr. Choussaud is very insistent on this point, as the President's blood pressure refuses to go down. The President loves the Riviera. Besides, he is not too keen on staying in Riond Bosson a long time.

Finding a quiet secluded spot on the Riviera will not be easy, but I'm willing to try. I know from experience how reluctant everyone is to advise the President in anything. Dr. Choussaud said just recently that nobody is so neglected as are the world's great, precisely because everyone fears the responsibility of a wrong suggestion. The doctor himself is confident when it comes to medicine, but as for recommending a hotel, that's an entirely different story.

St. Raphael, French Riviera — July, 1933. We're happy because we've finally found something just right — a magnificent huge hotel on a hilltop overlooking the sea. Terraces, a large private park, pine trees and spruces, invigorating air, and no guests whatsoever. The owners, Mr. and Mrs. C., are a very distinguished looking elderly English couple. From the big autographed photographs in the hotel we gather that the King and Queen of England were guests here.

At first we were told the hotel was no longer open to the public. The C.'s were staying only for the summer until they wound up their affairs. So we inquired discreetly what the prices and terms had been in the past and when we found out all we wanted to know, we divulged our secret. We would like a suite of rooms for Paderewski for an extended stay, we said. Any chance of getting them? The reaction was immediate. Paderewski? Ah, in that case, why of course. They've

agreed to open up a whole floor for him. Leniutka and I selected the second floor because we know the President
doesn't like to live high up. The cuisine is none of our worry.
Dr. Choussaud will take care of that.

Riond Bosson — July, 1933. The President's departure for St.
Raphael has been set for July 19th. Dr. Choussaud is of
course coming along. I'm taking Anetka, too. The President
wants her to come.

Sylwin told me today that Franciszek will be here in a
few days. I was given this bit of information while cutting
roses for the house. "You know," Sylwin began sheepishly,
"I telephoned Franciszek to come here and work for the
President."

"What did Franciszek say to that?"

"First he said he'd have to think it over. So I told him
he had only one day to make up his mind because we were
going to France and the President needed a valet."

"And what did Franciszek say to that?"

"Well, he telephoned the next day that he had consulted
your father who told him there was nothing to think over —
a job like that was as good as catching God by the knees."

But Franciszek still wasn't satisfied. He went to ask my
brother's advice. Tadeusz wanted to know why he was still
hesitating: "Each of us would be glad to be Paderewski's
servant, if he'd only ask us." Franciszek hesitated no longer.

I can't say I'm pleased with this turn of events. I would
not give up Franciszek for the world, but since it's for the
President I only grinned foolishly, feigning satisfaction.

Riond Bosson — July 15, 1933. Franciszek's arrival in Riond
Bosson created quite a sensation. I think he made a very
favorable impression on everybody. In his thirties, tall,
slender, handsome, unhurried and dignified in his movements,
he really cuts a fine figure. We all, including the President
and Mrs. Wilkonska, marveled at the ease with which he got
here, knowing not a word of any save his own native tongue.

The servants in Riond Bosson, however, all of whom are
Swiss, are less cordial in their reception. It's obvious they
regard Franciszek as an intruder. Knowing Franciszek's
exceptional tact, I'm sure he will handle everybody and
everything very well.

St. Raphael, Grand Hotel Coirier—July 19, 1933. We were
not mistaken. The President approves our choice of place
and hotel. I must let Leniutka know. The poor girl had to
stay with Mme. Paderewska.

Our hosts like to tell how the King and Queen of England
spent their vacation here incognito three years ago.

July, 1933. Dr. Choussaud is in his element. At last he will
institute a regimen about which he'd only talked his head off
up to now, but which could not be tried at Riond Bosson or
during the President's travels and concert tours.

For the hundredth time Dr. Choussaud points out to us
that if one adheres rigidly to his precepts, he will lose 6.8
ounces daily. However all fatigue must be avoided so as not
to put a strain on the heart. Walking is taboo. Because
Sylwin is overweight too, he has decided to undergo the
reducing diet along with the President to keep him company
and spare him the unpleasantness of eating other foods than
the rest of us all by himself.

August, 1933. Dr. Choussaud reigns triumphant. Sylwin and
the President weigh themselves every evening and every
single evening they have lost exactly 6.8 ounces more.
Furthermore, they feel fine and have an excellent complexion.
The President raises no objections at all. He follows the
prescribed rules with an admirable singleness of purpose.
The Doctor sits at the table with the President, but he eats a
full lunch and dinner beforehand.

My brother Jan has come down to spend his vacation with
us. When a rare guest drops in, he sits at our table—we

rattle around in the tremendous empty dining room. Our table is sufficiently far away from the President to prevent his seeing what we are eating, for although our meals are nothing extraordinary, at least they are varied.

It's a unique diet our men are on, but it works. One day Sylwin left the President's table at lunchtime to come over to us for a minute. He swiped a potato from my plate. Another time he drank a glass of water at a meal. On both occasions he failed to lose the prescribed 6.8 ounces.

Since the President is not in the habit of taking an afternoon nap, which this diet calls for, we escort him upstairs in the elevator—Dr. Choussaud does not permit him to walk up even one story—and leave him to read his newspapers or a book on the beautiful terrace. At five Anetka and I bring the President a luscious peach. While I peel it for him, he says he isn't the least bit hungry, but he ends up by eating it—out of courtesy. Then we make our exit. The President makes no move to keep us. He is so steeped in his newspapers, he has no desire for conversation. But when Sylwin comes and suggests a game of cribbage, the President never refuses. They play until dinnertime.

Franciszek spends almost the entire day studying French. He has been dubbed "Professor" by the President and is always addressed thus by him.

The day after our arrival in St. Raphael, Franciszek surprised everybody by the amazing efficiency with which he had taken care of things without outside assistance. Had he used sign language or mental telepathy to get his messages across to the hotel people? We laughed when we discovered that of the two servants left in the Hotel Coirier to wait on the President, one is a Pole.

August 15, 1933. Tomorrow I'm taking Anetka back to Warsaw. The President, Sylwin, Dr. Choussaud, and Franciszek will remain on the Riviera until the President loses his twenty-five pounds. The Doctor continues to crow, particularly since the President's high blood pressure is falling while Sylwin's low pressure is rising. This means the metabolism of both men is becoming normal.

Warsaw — September 2, 1933. Though I pride myself on being such a true Warsovian, I didn't know there are in Warsaw itself such fine progressive convent schools offering a full secondary education. At Monsignor Kaczynski's recommendation I enrolled Anetka in the convent school of the Sisters of The Holy Family of Nazareth.

At first I must admit I was horrified by the idea. I had always regarded convent schools as the antithesis of progress. I thought they stressed prayer too much, taught little, and did not feed their pupils adequately. I had a notion that girls were graduated from these institutions with anemia and a propensity for gay living that was a reaction to the stuffy convent atmosphere.

Instead, the convent of the Sisters of Nazareth dazzled me with its modernity, cleanliness, and brightness.

A talk with the Mother Superior and the Sister Director made me decide to leave Anetka with the Sisters, who impressed me as intelligent, wise, and educated. When I told them how difficult and mischievous Anetka is, the Sister Director said: "Don't worry, we like girls like that because they grow up into real people."

But Anetka burst into tears and sobbingly protested: "Mother, how can you give your child to nuns! They never have children of their own, so how can they bring me up?" Anetka's logical assertion pleased the Sisters enormously.

Illness in Warsaw—Death in Switzerland

Paris, Hotel du Palais d'Orsay — October 6, 1933. I am again in Paris. Sylwin telephoned to Warsaw and induced me to come here directly. After his cure on the Riviera, the Presi-

dent did not go back to Riond Bosson for a long time. I think
that a prolonged stay at home in Switzerland tires and makes
the President nervous, even though he never shows it. So he
tries to get away as much as he can. You can't really blame
him. Everyone finds the atmosphere at Riond Bosson very
hard to endure. Upstairs there is Mme. Paderewska whose
grave, incurable illness is a real tragedy for the President.
Mme. Paderewska suffers no physical pain. She looks the
picture of health, but she is always dozing off, awaking only
to eat, just like a small child. She fails to recognize anyone
nor does she react when spoken to. Nevertheless, whenever
the President is at Riond Bosson, he never fails to go up to
see her before lunch. Leniutka told me that these meetings
of the Paderewskis are as terribly sad as they are touching.
Mme. Paderewska sits on a sofa in the library. On seeing the
President she stretches out her hands to him. The President seats himself beside her and they hold hands without
uttering a word until Mme. Paderewska falls asleep. It is
only then that the President leaves his wife. It's hard to tell
whether or not she recognizes him. Four years already and
there is no change in her condition. What a tragedy — worse
than death itself — it must be for the President.

Downstairs, too, Paderewski is confronted by a somewhat
tense atmosphere created by the constantly complaining Mrs.
Wilkonska, who is always upset by this or that.

Two members of the Riond Bosson household, Mrs. O.,
a half-sister of Mme. Paderewska, and young M. J., in spite
of many years spent under the same roof with Mrs. Wilkonska, could not find a common language with her or — especially in the case of Mrs. O. — appease mutual antipathy and
antagonism. Their very presence in Riond Bosson remains
for Mrs. Wilkonska an incessant source of irritation, which
hardly contributes to the harmony the President would like
to find in his home.

I've been observing the President. He has become much
slimmer; the white piqué vest which he wears all year round
regardless of the season, hangs straight and perhaps a bit

loosely, its former roundness having disappeared. His walk is a great deal lighter, his complexion wonderful, and the general impression he makes is that of a strong, healthy man. To my question about the state of his health, the President replied: "I feel fine." Glancing at Dr. Choussaud, he heartily clasped the Frenchman's hand and said feelingly: "Notre cher Docteur!" Our "cher Docteur" turned away to hide his emotion.

Paris — October, 1933. The crowd around the President is as large as ever. The elderly ladies never fail to be present. At times there are such multitudes of them that it's frightening. Often I feel the urge to cut my hair short and put on a pair of trousers merely to be one wench less, or at least to talk myself out of lunch to reduce the number of women at the table, but the President will not hear of it.

Dinners are somewhat more peaceful and the guests are rather adequately selected, but among them there must inevitably be at least two good bridge players. After dinner there is the usual card game. Non-participants either take their leave right from the dinner table or else remain and amuse themselves. After lunch, however, when there is no card playing, all the guests depart directly, since the President entertains his guests only at the table where much time is spent over black coffee. Immediately after lunch, the President retires to his room, while after dinner he goes directly to the bridge table, unless there are official guests, in which case black coffee is served in the drawing room where the President entertains his guests until their departure.

General Wladyslaw Sikorski is now in Paris, too. The President always greets the General cordially. He is very fond of General Sikorski and respects him highly. So, each time the General stays in Paris he is a constant, daily guest either at the luncheons or dinners. The great friendship between the President and the General dates back to the time of their first meeting in Paris. Paderewski never had occasion to meet Sikorski personally in Poland. Marjotka Mickiewicz, who judges every Pole primarily on the basis of whether he is pro-Pilsudski, and doubts his virtues and abilities if he is not, turns her angry eye on the General each time she sees him. The President, to tease her, related to her what Marshal Foch had told him about Sikorski — that he considered General Sikorski the outstanding militarist of the present day, adding that any army would be proud indeed to have such a leader.

Paris — Warsaw, Nord Express — October 24, 1933. I'm returning to Warsaw. About noon today, our friend and plenipotentiary, Andrzej M., telephoned that Anetka was stricken with appendicitis in the convent, and that the Sisters have brought her to the Red Cross hospital where she will be operated on tomorrow. I shall be in Warsaw by four in the afternoon, in time for the operation.

St. Joseph's — October 30, 1933. We are still in the clinic. I live with Anetka and to this day I have not left the hospital, not even for one moment to take a walk. Dr. Gout performed the operation splendidly. He even promises that in a few years the scar will be barely visible.

A letter from Switzerland addressed to Anetka was delivered today. No one even suspected whom it came from, but I immediately recognized the President's handwriting. "Look, Anetka, here is a letter for you from the President!" I exclaimed. Anetka, who by nature is quite lively and somewhat absent-minded yet rather prudent, replied: "Then be careful, Mother, not to tear the envelope when you open it." We read the letter together; I, greatly moved, and Anetka earnest and interested. The letter is a personal one written in longhand on two sheets of paper at the very top of which the initials "I. J. P." are discreetly embossed in white print. The President has written the note in such an adolescent style that one would think he was Anetka's playmate. He wishes her good health and expresses the hope that in spite of her serious illness and loss of time from school, she will, as soon as she is well again, catch up in her studies without losing the entire school year. It must have been difficult for the President to descend to this age level in writing and I am surprised that he felt the urge to actually write the letter, especially since I know how rarely he writes personal letters. I told Anetka this letter would be her most treasured memento. In reply she asked me to put it away for safekeeping.

Warsaw—November 6, 1933. Troubles and sorrows never seem to come alone but always together. They hit me so unexpectedly that I could easily go out of my mind, but somehow I don't, thank God! Yesterday at four in the afternoon I received a telephone call from Father's attorney, who told me he had "good and amusing news" for me. "Your father signed courtesy notes for over a million zlotys. He probably signed them for his friends at the Lourse Cafe as no one knew about it. Well, too bad they put one over on the old man, but now for his debts you are in danger of having your apartment auctioned off tomorrow. The creditors are preparing for it; they know what a fortune there is in your apartment and in your furnishings. So, if you don't want all your belongings plundered by your father's creditors you'll have to remove them from the apartment by ten o'clock tomorrow morning," the attorney informed me.

There was no time to hesitate, no time to lament. I didn't say a word to Father and let him continue his afternoon nap undisturbed.

Moving lasted all through the night. In our apartment at the Square of the Three Crosses where my father's family had lived over a hundred years, there remained only Father unconcernedly reading the newspapers in his bed.

Warsaw, 30 Swietokrzyska Street—January 16, 1934. At ten this morning Sylwin telephoned from Morges that today at seven Mme. Paderewska died of pneumonia after a three-day illness. I wanted to leave immediately for Switzerland, but Sylwin said I wouldn't get there in time, as Mme. Paderewska's body is being transported this afternoon to Paris, where she will be buried at the Montmorency cemetery to lie near Paderewski's son, Alfred. In view of this, I am going directly to Paris this evening.

[In 1880 Paderewski married Antonina Korsak, a student at the Warsaw Conservatory of Music. She died a year later, leaving him with a son, Alfred, who died of infantile paralysis in 1901. *S. S.*]

Paris — January 19, 1934. All of the closest friends of the Paderewski family came from Switzerland to Mme. Paderewska's funeral. Practically the entire floor in the Hotel du Palais d'Orsay was occupied by these funeral guests. Mrs. Wilkonska was surrounded by a multitude of old friends. Not one of those whom I've been meeting through the years at Paris or at Riond Bosson during vacation time seemed to be missing.

The funeral was scheduled for noon and was to proceed from the Church at Montmorency to the Montmorency cemetery. On leaving his room the President went directly to the corridor, avoiding the small sitting room where he would ordinarily stop to greet the assembled guests. Sylwin, Mrs. Wilkonska, Leniutka, and I were already dressed and awaiting the President there. All the remaining guests followed us in other cars belonging to the funeral cortege.

The President seemed lost in sad thought. Leniutka cried continuously. Probably more than any of us, she felt the tragedy of Mme. Paderewska's death. For five years up to the very moment of Mme. Paderewska's death, Leniutka had been like a devoted daughter to her.

I believe that for all of us, as well as for the President himself, Mme. Paderewska's death is merely a sad, accomplished fact. Her life actually ended five years ago when she lost her memory, her powers of recognizing people, and suffered a general lack of orientation. Sitting between the President and Mrs. Wilkonska, on the way to Montmorency, I thought that probably both Sylwin and myself were doomed

to a similar old age as a result of insufficient sleep. Who can
equal the President and his physical stamina? He invariably
goes to bed shortly before dawn and barely a few hours of
sleep suffice him. Mme. Paderewska always kept him company and never went to sleep before the President retired for
the night. Mme. Paderewska, too, had an inexhaustible supply of strength, even though she was four years older than
the President, but finally her endurance gave out. Neither
of us ever goes to bed before the President; we always wait
until he tells us good night.

After the burial the President ordered a dinner in one of
the larger salons of the Hotel Palais d'Orsay for the funeral
guests. There were over thirty people at the table. The
President, still in a gloomily pensive mood, remained silent,
and no one dared to address him. There was no general
conversation at the table. From time to time, people would
talk only with their neighbors in a very low tone. At the
conclusion of the dinner — delicious and abundant as always
at the Palais d'Orsay — everyone in turn came up to the
President to thank him for the invitation and to bid him farewell, as many of the guests were to leave Paris in the morning. The ladies with Mrs. Wilkonska were to return to
Riond Bosson.

Sylwin hurriedly escorted the President to the sitting
room to cheer him up a little by a two-handed game of cribbage. Well past midnight, Sylwin entered our room where I
was chatting with Leniutka. He told us that the President
was about to retire and that we should come to say good
night to him. The President asked Leniutka whether she
would stay with us in Paris. She'd be very glad to stay but
she couldn't let the helpless ladies, Mrs. Wilkonska and
Mamcia, travel alone in the care of the equally helpless Mrs.
O. The President took cordial leave of Leniutka. After bidding us good night, he said to me: "Thank you for coming to
my wife's funeral." I was greatly touched that the President
should thank me, especially me, who had so many times come
to Paris just for pleasure. How could I not come for Mme.

Paderewska's funeral? In tears, Leniutka and I left the President.

Mme. Paderewska was an unusual person. It would be insincere on my part to say that I loved her, but I was fond of her. In spite of her seemingly difficult character and certain severity, she had a heart of gold and was sensitive to human misery. She was a model of a loving, devoted wife whose ambition was to spur her husband—even the already great Paderewski—to new heights. This is why she never left him alone and constantly watched over everything and everybody in his immediate surroundings. She worked with him side by side, imbued with the same keen sense of duty, enthusiasm, and sacrifice, in the field of social work, and with the same full understanding and compassion for suffering humanity. She had absolutely nothing to do with politics, in spite of many false accusations to the contrary and antagonistic, intensive propaganda which was carried on against her in Poland.

Mme. Paderewska always impressed me as being rather bored with politics. She never showed any interest whatever in this direction. Her interests lay in an entirely different sphere, yet she could readily adapt them to Paderewski's mode of life. She was unfairly accused and criticized in Poland of butting into politics simply because she guarded the President (often quite indiscreetly) against the so-called "statesmen" who, wishing to save the country by one call on the President, took up a great deal of his much-needed valuable time. She was the only one in the Paderewski household to regulate the constant flow of people and bring order into their home. Sylwin, in those early years, was too young and inexperienced to select and retard the masses of people desiring to see the President. Poor control over her nerves, which may be justified by the irregular and abnormal kind of life she led, was chiefly responsible for her reputation of having an unpleasant character.

Like her husband, Mme. Paderewska was tireless in her endeavors. In culinary matters she was absolutely ignorant, although she never betrayed her lack of knowledge in this field. Anyway, she usually lived in a hotel. At Riond Bosson she never interfered in domestic affairs; here, Mrs. Wilkonska had full reign. If, however, she had had any experience in such matters, I'm sure there would have been misunderstandings galore on this score. Nevertheless, Mme. Paderewska often theoretically discussed matters pertaining to the kitchen with us, and, caring little about it, she frequently told us to remember that the way to a man's heart was only through his stomach. Although rather heavy, she ate very little; she placed infinitesimal portions of each course on her plate and claimed she did not know the meaning of hunger.

January 26, 1934. While going to lunch today through the long hotel corridor leading to the dining room, and accompanied by Marjotka and Irena Lewinska, Sylwin, holding the newspaper *Matin* in his hand, read that Poland had signed a ten-year non-aggression pact with Germany. This news impressed the President much less than it did Sylwin, and he said: "I cannot believe for one moment that the Germans will adhere to this pact for the full ten years, although I hope to God that I may be wrong. Anyway, it is a great diplomatic achievement for Mr. Beck, but it is purely his own, personal triumph."

January 27, 1934. We are still in Paris. Tomorrow I'm returning to Warsaw while the President and Sylwin are going to Riond Bosson. The President is himself again; he is no longer so silent and pensive. I think that the death of Mme. Paderewska was possibly a lesser blow to him than the mental suffering he endured for the five long years of her incurable ailment.

A Kaleidoscope of Visitors

Riond Bosson—June 19, 1934. We are again spending our vacation in Switzerland. Nothing has changed after the death of Mme. Paderewska. We've merely returned to our room upstairs. Anetka's room adjoins ours.

Since the death of Mme. Paderewska, Leniutka is even closer to us. Her affectionate and intelligent handling of Anetka has earned her the title of a "vice-mother." Indeed we all refer to her by that name. Whenever the President wants Leniutka he asks: "Where is the vice-mother?"

June 23, 1934. At the very beginning of our stay here there was a minor storm brought about by Anetka. It would have been quite trivial except that it prompted the President to tell us about an incident in his childhood to which Mrs. Wilkonska added her bit. This year, like almost any other, is a good year for cherries, and the orchard is so clustered with them that one can hardly eat or pick them fast enough, especially since it's hard to get labor in Switzerland. To help out, we pick basketfulls of them which are later sold, given away, or sent out. Those of inferior quality or of less attractive appearance are served at the Riond Bosson table, much to Sylwin's disgust. Only the President receives the specially picked, choice cherries, brought to his room on a separate plate. Every day it's the same story. The President does not even touch the cherries, and each noon Franciszek brings the plate of fruit to our room telling us the President had them sent to us. We naturally devour all the fruit. By supper time I try to reciprocate for the President's kindness by picking the finest-looking cherries and serving them as attractively as I possibly can. The President never refuses them and eats the whole prepared portion.

There is one tree, however, which the gardener forbids us to touch, claiming that it bears some special type of cherry for a special purpose. Of course Anetka got around to just this particular tree. It was heavy with great quantities of cherries, which would amply feed the entire household, but Mr. Dolezal complained that Anetka picked the whole tree clean. The attitude of all the residents here is motivated either by jealousy or hysteria, but to keep the peace I reprimanded Anetka, in the presence of the President, for being so gluttonous. Anetka, very much ashamed, cast sidelong glances at Mrs. Wilkonska and the President. Mrs. Wilkonska hates misunderstanding with which she is constantly surrounded in this heavily populated house, but she adores children and can never be angry at them.

The President looked at Anetka tenderly and said: "Once, when I was nine years old, I picked 180 cherries right from the tree and ate them—pits and all."

"Weren't you sick after that?" I asked.

"No, I wasn't," he replied.

Mrs. Wilkonska took up the story: "When Ignace was small, he always ate the cherries together with pits. He was quite a little glutton as a child," she continued. "Remember, Ignace, when you drank up all the cream just before the Bishop's visit?" We all turned our eyes to Mrs. Wilkonska: Anetka and the little son of Mrs. O. were so interested their mouths popped open. "Ignace was ten years old at the time. The Bishop was invited for supper by our father and stepmother. All that week our stepmother had gathered the heavy cream for coffee and placed full pipkins of it in the cooler where skin formed over their tops. When the Bishop came and our stepmother served coffee it was discovered that all the pipkins were empty. Ignace had used a straw to make holes in the skins so as not to leave a trace, and had drunk the whole cream right from the bottom of all the pipkins . . ."

"And that was one time I really got a tanning from my father," concluded the President.

July 15, 1934. Every vacation spent at Riond Bosson is a perpetual kaleidoscope of visitors. Not a day goes by but that there are guests either at dinner or at supper. This year General W. Sikorski, his wife, and daughter are spending the entire vacation with us, but they are staying at Lausanne at Mrs. Chelminska's. The President repeatedly requests their visits. He is very fond of the General, whose greatest fault is that he does not play bridge. In fact, he plays no cards at all. However, he is trying to learn. Sylwin is also urging me to learn how to play bridge. Sometimes I do look on while they play, but I've come to the conclusion that the game is too complicated for me. If I became a poor player I would merely make bridge enemies of Sylwin and the President, who are terribly critical of anyone who does not play the game well.

August 8, 1934. The President likes Mamcia and me to be his immediate neighbors at the table, since Mamcia is deaf and there is no need to converse with her and I try not to talk to him in order to spare him the necessity of entertaining one person more. Mamcia sits on his right, so when the principal guest happens to be a woman, Mamcia is shifted further down the line, since her seat heads the table. The President very seldom changes my seat, which is on his left.

The President is generally very gay; he enjoys a good joke although he seldom laughs and his eyes always have a rather sad expression. He so often is absorbed by deep thought. Nevertheless, he never misses an opportunity for some frivolity, as I have noticed sitting next to him. For instance, no matter how many guests there are, or how official they may be, each time Berthe (the spinsterish Swiss chambermaid who helps serve when there is a lot of company) comes around with a platter, he lowers his head and whispers to her in French: "I wish you a good husband and many, many children." Berthe invariably blushes while the President does not bat an eyelash and merely puts a vegetable on his plate. Aside from me, no one knows what is going on and everybody looks surprised at red-faced Berthe.

The atmosphere at the table is never stiff or formal. It

is only during our meals that we of his entourage truly have the benefit of the President's company; every lunch or dinner is like an interesting lecture on just about any subject. The President can discourse with the ease of an expert on any topic mentioned. Our conversation at the table is especially interesting when Miss Alma Tadema, daughter of the noted British painter, is there. Miss Tadema is supposed to be one of those ladies who never married because they were in love with the President. She became very friendly with Mme. Paderewska and for many years she made long visits at Riond Bosson. She is an unusual person: very eccentric but exceedingly pleasant, intelligent, and educated. She is very direct and simple in her manner but rather lacking in feminine charm. Mrs. Wilkonska tolerates her but cherishes no great love for her, primarily because, objecting to certain inconveniences in the guest rooms, Miss Tadema, at her own expense, had a closet made in the wall of her room at Riond Bosson, changed the wash basin, and, being a vegetarian, insists on a special menu; all this infuriates Mrs. Wilkonska and makes her consider the Englishwoman downright queer. The President likes her company but enjoys it only at the dinner table. I suspect Miss Tadema prepares herself beforehand for a discussion on unusual subjects, each from an entirely different field. But the President develops so extensively every topic brought forth by her that half an hour later Miss Tadema is forced to relinquish the floor to him. I was most impressed once when he gave us a virtual lecture about corals, mollusks, and marine life in general.

August 15, 1934. Tomorrow I am returning to Warsaw with Anetka. We leave Riond Bosson earlier than usual this year as we intend to visit my aunt at her Jablonna estate near Lublin before school starts.

The President asked me why we were leaving Riond Bosson so early. I told him that I wanted to show Anetka what the Polish countryside looks like. Up to now her trips have always been abroad. I also told him that Anetka can't tell the difference between a cabbage and a cauliflower, that pointing to a partridge in our Warsaw kitchen, she once asked me: "What kind of bird is that?" I added that many people in Warsaw wonder that, having a husband with Paderewski and therefore a splendid opportunity to educate Anetka abroad, I send her to school in Warsaw. The President told me that I was very wise to educate Anetka in Poland, and said that every child should go to school in his native country, for otherwise a child is ignorant of his country's history and geography. Only after completing his education in his native land should a person go abroad, especially to study languages, he asserted.

Tonight Paderewski entrusted me with the sad and unpleasant mission of distributing Mme. Paderewska's jewelry among her numerous relatives. He unfolded before me many brooches, charms, bracelets, and countless smaller items not so valuable intrinsically but precious as keepsakes and examples of fine workmanship. Mme. Paderewska did not possess much costly jewelry; probably neither of them had any special liking for it. But she did have countless dresses which she wore with complete disregard for the prevailing fashion.

The large diamonds which Mme. Paderewska always wore as earrings were given to Leniutka with the understanding that Mrs. Wilkonska will wear them as long as she lives. Mrs. Wilkonska wears them, but seems a bit hurt by the condition which deprives her of the right to dispose of them in any way she might see fit. Whenever the President is quite late for lunch and Mrs. Wilkonska is upset by the delay, she complains that she cannot make any decisions around here, not even pertaining to her diamonds. A long double necklace of real pearls, which was also constantly worn by Mme. Paderewska, and a beautiful mink coat, were received by her daughter-in-law. [Mrs. Waclaw Gorski.]

The President enumerated many ladies in Poland to whom I am to bring this jewelry and noticing my surprise at the strange names, he said: "These are all Helenka's first and distant cousins. I have no family." The President went into great detail as to which item is to go to which person; I carefully took notes so as not to make any errors. According to the President, these are all heirlooms which were given to Mme. Paderewska by her relations and which will now revert to their original owners, or in some cases, to their daughters or even granddaughters. It is amazing how the President remembers the history of every piece!

Warsaw — September 5, 1934. On my return from Switzerland in August, Warsaw was still deserted, so it was not until my home-coming from the country that I was able to carry out my mission of distributing the jewelry. With the exception of Mrs. Grabowska (whom I met previously in Switzerland on several occasions), who greeted me affectionately, I had to visit eight perfect strangers, all relatives of Mme. Paderewska. The visits were terrible! First, there was a look of complete surprise on the faces of my hosts. As I explained the purpose of my call, their puzzled expressions changed to one of contentment. Then, on presentation of the keepsake, again the expressions revealed utter disappointment. I prudently asked for a receipt with a full description of the article delivered by me. I sighed with relief at the conclusion of this most unpleasant mission.

We Visited the Cemetery

Paris — November 10, 1934. I am again in Paris — I don't know how many times this makes. I adore Paris and always feel wonderful here. Sylwin is happy that I came; he met me at the station. The President greeted me very warmly. "Our little sunbeam is with us again!" he exclaimed. I'm too happy for words that he said so, for I always worry that I impose on the President too often; especially when he's traveling only with Sylwin and Franciszek. I don't know why the President has come to Paris and I don't ask.

Right after my arrival, we went down to the restaurant for dinner. We had our usual table in the corner. Some of the patrons looked familiar; the men rose and bowed to the President, some came up to say a few words. The President couldn't sit down quietly to enjoy his meal. As soon as he'd be seated, he had to rise again, for he never speaks to anyone sitting down, not even to men.

For once there were no guests at our table. The President ordered everything for me without asking. He remembered that I always like sole frite, then lamb chops, Roman salad, then, naturally, a chocolate soufflé. But besides this, the President suggested fresh strawberry shortcake, as he was surprised to see it on the menu in November. Then, of course, sweet champagne, all in my honor! The President will never learn from me that I detest champagne!

After dinner, since we were alone and Sylwin had some important telephone calls to make, he suggested that I play cards with the President. I was quite taken aback, especially since I didn't know what game we were to play. I don't play much and only know garibaldi. Sylwin got the cards and the President decided on the latter. My hands shook from fright, but I laid out my cards quite confidently. Then something so extraordinary happened that I still become excited whenever I think of it! The President began playing with such lightning speed that I not only didn't have time to think, but became dizzy, and before I realized what was happening, the President had already played his hand and mine, too, in what must have been twenty or thirty seconds. The second hand was played in an identical manner. It seems that my rôle became limited to dealing the cards. By the time Sylwin returned, the game was long finished, for the President, evaluating my worth as a card player, had proposed solitaire. So I again laid out the cards for him — that's one thing I can do swiftly and skilfully — getting them all nice and straight. I had learned many kinds of solitaire by watching Mrs. Wilkonska

and Mamcia so many times in the dining room at Riond
Bosson while the President was playing bridge in the card
room. The President doesn't like to handle his own cards in
solitaire, only to dictate each move (but so fast I could hardly
keep up with him). I certainly had no time to use my head.
Of the eight games of solitaire played, six came out! But by
the time Sylwin returned, I was in a sweat from my hard
work. How wise Mme. Paderewska was never to play cards
with the President. Sylwin sat down to a game of cribbage
with the President and I fled, thoroughly ashamed.

November 15, 1934. The President wasn't in a good humor
today, hardly saying a word, listening to Miss Marjotka
Mickiewicz with her screechy voice telling for the hundredth
time the story of her deeds and popularity in Paris during the
war. To tell the truth, Sylwin purposely provoked her in
order to divert the President, for then the President didn't
have to listen or to talk.

On top of all this, a dreadful thing happened. Sylwin
planned today's menu. For Miss Marjotka's sake he included her favorite *oeufs à la gelée au jambon*, then, absent-
mindedly, a ham omelet for the second course! These two
ham-and-egg dishes served as two successive courses to
Sylwin's great consternation so amused the President that he
didn't even send the omelet back to the kitchen. We all ate
it with relish, happy that the President's mood was lightened.

It wasn't until after lunch that I learned the reason for
the President's gloom: at three P.M. somebody was to play
before him in order to have him give his opinion.

November 18, 1934. Today we visited the cemetery at
Montmorency where Mme. Paderewska is buried. Sylwin
asked whether I could go along, for we know that the President and Mme. Paderewska always used to go alone to the
grave of his son, Alfred. The President, however, consented
to my coming. A car had been rented for the occasion. As we
were getting in, the usual scene took place. I stood to one

side, so that the President could get in first, but he will never precede a woman. He made a gesture that was a command, so I got in first. I sat down at the left, but that didn't work either. He ordered me to sit on the right side. In the meantime, Sylwin was making gestures for me to hurry up and not keep the President waiting. Sylwin and Franciszek sat on the jump-seats. On the way, we stopped at a florist's where the President has traded for years. I stayed in the automobile while the President went in. Sylwin and Franciszek waited on the sidewalk. The only flowers the President himself picks out and buys are those for Alfred's grave and now for Mme. Paderewska's too. After some time he came out, followed by two clerks carrying unusually large bouquets wrapped in paper. Before getting into the car, the President drew from an inside pocket a used envelope with an address and stamp on it which evidently served as his wallet, and tipped the two boys; I didn't see how much but, judging from their expressions and their cries of *"Oh! Merci Monsieur,"* it must have equaled their monthly salaries! Sylwin excused himself and disappeared for a second, to return with another paper-wrapped bouquet.

When we stopped at the cemetery gate the President got out, took the flowers from Sylwin and Franciszek, and went into the cemetery alone. Sylwin, who knows all the President's habits, waited with me at the gate. Franciszek, as directed by Sylwin, slipped in through a side gate and crept along behind some other graves, in order to be at hand. Fortunately, the graves of Mme. Paderewska and Alfred are not far from the entrance. The President himself arranged the flowers on the graves and prayed, then he went to the nearby Mickiewicz family vault where he said another prayer and left more flowers. After he returned, he got into the car and we left him to Franciszek's care. Sylwin and I then went in with our modest bouquet of Parma violets, which Mme. Paderewska loved. Sylwin was in such haste he energetically crossed himself and wouldn't even let me finish my prayer. "Hurry up!" he ordered, "the President is waiting." On our way back everyone was silent out of respect for the sorrow of the musing President.

I'm quite surprised at the day's events because I recall that the President never handles flowers, not even on the concert stage, for fear that he might injure his fingers. Even if some very insistent lady forces him to accept flowers personally, the President always puts them down in the nearest possible place, particularly if they are roses. At the cemetery, the President himself decorated two graves and with roses at that!

November 20, 1934. Whenever we are in Paris, on the day before we leave the President makes a solitary pilgrimage; he never allows anyone whosoever to accompany him. We wouldn't even know where he goes if it weren't that during Mme. Paderewska's lifetime they always went together, also unaccompanied, and she once told Sylwin that they visited the church of Notre Dame de la Victoire. It is the one intimacy to which the President doesn't admit Sylwin. The whole time of his absence, Sylwin always feels ill at ease, and all three of us (with Franciszek) are terribly fearful that something might befall him before he returns to the hotel, from which no one of us dares to step out until we know he is back.

En route from Paris to Lausanne — November 21, 1934. Just going from the hotel to the waiting automobile is an endless trip in itself. In the first place, the President never hurries, and when it seems to be high time to leave for the station, he will dawdle in his room. What he does for so long, right up to the last possible moment, I don't know. Certainly he doesn't pack, for Franciszek takes care of all that down to the smallest item — wardrobe, music, everything, with the possible exception of the one small suitcase the President wants looked after specially, the contents of which have always been a mystery to us all, as no one has ever seen him put anything in it or take anything out. Franciszek, already fully dressed and holding the President's coat, hat, muffler, and gloves, was waiting in the sitting room to help him dress. Sylwin, jumpy, counted the usual endless pieces of luggage over and over. I grew more and more nervous each time I glanced at my watch. Finally, the President came out. Franciszek helped him with his things, as Sylwin and I simultaneously went into the President's room for that bag which either Sylwin or Franciszek never lets out of hand or sight. I don't know whether the President intended coming back or had just forgotten to close it; anyway, there it was, open for the first time. We looked from the open suitcase to each other and laughed. I immediately withdrew from the room while Sylwin quickly closed the bag in order not to be indiscreet; but we laughed, quite touched. That highly important, mysterious suitcase was almost empty. I couldn't help noticing its contents: a man's black garter, a handkerchief, a few letters, several fountain pens. How incredibly childish the President sometimes is in his personal, private life!

Then the leave-taking procedure began: one chambermaid, another, a valet, the shoeshine boy said good-bye and the President tipped them so generously that they all smiled happily — they were old-timers and the President shook hands with each one. All along the interminable corridor, doors opened; some of the hotel's guests bowed as the President passed, others shook hands and even spoke with him, while time grew shorter and shorter. But the President didn't hurry at all; he spoke to them all. Finally, we reached the restaurant where the waiters and the bus boys who waited on us and the maître d'hôtel stood in a row. The President pulled out his old envelope and distributed bills amongst them. Again there were handshakes, thanks, best wishes. At long last we got to the elevator, where again there was an army of elevator operators — the morning shift, the afternoon shift, and the night shift. In the lobby, the director's whole staff was waiting to say good-bye. I just couldn't stand it, surely we would miss our train. At the main entrance,

our car was surrounded by bellhops. The President didn't
skip a single person, he generously tipped each one personally.
"Doesn't the President have a wallet?" I asked Franciszek,
who became indignant at such a question. "The President has
a whole stack of them — he gets them as presents — but doesn't
want to use any of them," he replied. Finally, we got into
the car and I sighed with relief. But the doors had scarcely
been slammed shut, when Sylwin called *"Attendez! Attendez!"* to the chauffeur, and, turning to the President, said,
"Excuse me, but we've forgotten the poor telephone operator
who's put through so many calls for us." He jumped out and
ran into the hotel. He came back quickly and we were off
again. "We almost forgot the poor girl," the President
commented with feeling.

As we got out at the station, Sylwin asked the President
to go straight to the train with me while he and Franciszek
took care of the luggage, but the President did just the opposite. He stood and waited and followed the porters slowly
to the train. He no longer has his old springy step. We won't
make it, I kept thinking. The locomotive was already getting
up steam. Everybody stared at the President. Almost everyone bowed, all the men took off their hats. We reached our
coach at long, long last. In the compartment, the President
paid the porters who practically snapped in two trying to
thank him for the liberal tips. The train moved and we were
off. The President occupied, as usual, a whole first-class compartment. We traveled by day this time. The President,
surrounded by periodicals of all sorts, read them all in turn.
Then he and Sylwin played cards for a while. I brought some
fruit which I had peeled for them. The President keeps busy
every moment of the journey — he doesn't take daytime naps,
not even on long trips.

Riond Bosson — December 2, 1934. After Paris, where I don't
lead too gay a life when with the President, but still where I
always feel well and happy, Riond Bosson seems gloomy;
everyone has a long face and seems out of sorts with himself,

probably for imaginary reasons. Only Leniutka smooths everything and puts the ladies back into a good humor as best as she can. The President, too, loses his humor at Riond Bosson; he's always much gayer in Paris.

I'm remaining here until about the middle of the month, so that it won't look as if I'd come from Poland solely for the Paris trip. But I'm anxious to get back to Warsaw.

A Christmas Message

Warsaw — December 24, 1934. It was well after Christmas Eve supper, probably around 8 P.M., before Sylwin phoned from Switzerland. A few words of greeting and then he quickly said: "I'm giving the phone to the President who's standing here beside me." I was terribly touched and afraid I might not hear, but I had time to hush everyone in the room by saying "Paderewski is on the wire" before the President, speaking slowly, gave me his Christmas greetings as if he were reciting a verse or reading it off. I didn't have a chance to interrupt or say anything until he had finished. I tried once to break in, in order to thank him, but the President continuated speaking, beautifully and fluently, as if he were reciting. When he had finished, I gave him my best wishes for Christmas and thanked him for taking the trouble to speak to me. Then I told him not to stay at the phone any longer, because in Riond Bosson it is next to the pantry door where there's always a draft. Anyway, the President never talks over the phone. The only time I ever saw him go to the telephone was when he talked long distance with Grabski about the Spa Conference many years ago.

The Karszo-Siedlewski home in Warsaw, Square of the Three Crosses,
No. 3.

Aniela   Karszo-Siedlewska,
mother of Aniela Strakacz.

Tadeusz Karszo-Siedlewski receiving the Virtuti Militari
Cross from Marshal Pilsudski
during the Soviet invasion of
Poland in 1920.

Wladyslaw Karszo-Siedlewski, father of Aniela Strakacz.

Mme Paderewska in the uniform of the Polish White Cross, which she founded in the United States during World War I.

Above: *The Paderewski villa in Riond Bosson.* Below: *Paderewski's studio.*

In Riond Bosson. Seated, Lt. Gen. Tadeusz Rozwadowski, Mme Pade-
rewska, Paderewski, Mrs. Wilkonska; standing, Mr. and Mrs. Strakacz,
an American journalist Mr. Walter, Miss Kwapinska, and Capt.
Romaniezyn.

Paderewski and Syl-
win Strakacz arrive
for the first Assembly
Meeting of the
League of Nations
in Geneva (Nov.
1920).

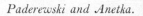
Paderewski and Anetka.

Paderewski in front of his private car during his American concert tour of 1930–1931.

At Riond Bosson: Paderewski, Ernest Schelling, Albert Tad lewski, Fritz Kreisler.

The Rt. Rev. Monsignor Anthony Tralka, pastor of Church of Our Lady of Mt. Carmel, Bayonne, N.J., with Paderewski and Mrs. Wilkonska at Riond Bosson.

On the terrace at Riond Bosson: Mrs. Wilkonska, Gen. Sikorski, Paderewski, Franciszek Black, the Polish sculptor of the Colonel House monument, and the Rt. Rev. Monsignor Kaczynski.

An informal luncheon at Riond Bosson. Aniela Strakacz and Anetka on Paderewski's left; Macius, the black cocker, awaits a juicy morsel.

Paderewski with Gen. Jozef Haller and Wincenty Witos, leaders of the Polish opposition, at Riond Bosson (1936).

At Riond Bosson (1936): Mr. and Mrs. Fritz Kreisler, Mr. and Mrs. Ernest Schelling, Paderewski, Mrs. Wilkonska, and members of the household. Aniela Strakacz and Anetka are at extreme right.

Sylwin Strakacz at the piano, at Riond Bosson.

Last Christmas Eve dinner with Paderewski (Buckingham Hotel, New York). Anetka, Miss Elizabeth Crafts, Mrs. Wilkonska, Paderewski, and Aniela Strakacz; and (standing) I. J. Kollupajlo, secretary to Paderewski.

Paderewski and Mrs. Franklin D. Roosevelt.

In the patio of the Stotesbury residence in Florida (1941). Gen. Sikorski, Paderewski, and Stanislaw Mikolajczyk.

Paderewski in Palm Beach, Florida (1941).

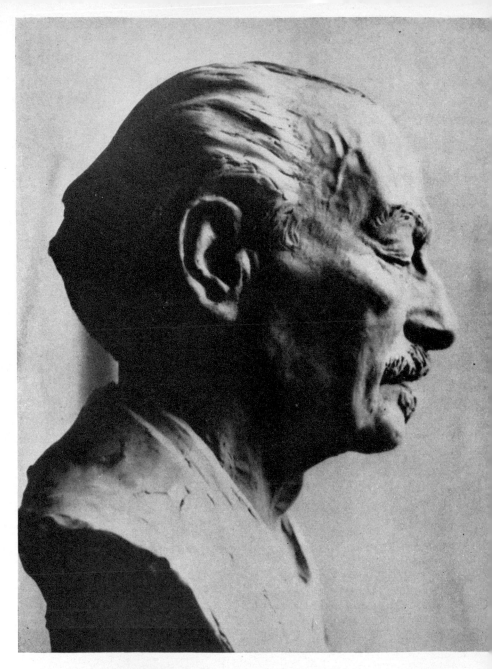

Death mask of Paderewski made by Malvina Hoffman in the mortuary of John Smolenski.

The Missing Telegrams

February, 1935. On February 1, 1935, I moved to a new apartment at 12 Father Skorupka Street. Unfortunately, I was unable to take my dear old father with me when I moved. He has had to leave his beloved Warsaw forever. He has moved to Otwock where the fresher air will perhaps help his asthma.

Everyone admires my new apartment, particularly the interesting way in which I've furnished it. The only thing with which I can please no one is the arrangement of my collection of autographed photographs of world-famous figures on my bedroom wall. Some say that Marshal Pilsudski should have precedence over Paderewski, others that General Haller should hang higher than General Dowbor-Musnicki, and still others that Marshal Foch was more important than Clemenceau. And why did Mme. Paderewska's photograph (with its beautiful dedication) hang beside her husband's when Colonel House really should be there instead? One entire wall of my bedroom is covered from ceiling to floor with these pictures. No one knew that I had hung most of the pictures according to the size of the frames, so that they would all fit and the whole collection would be well balanced.

March, 1935. Saturday night Anetka and I returned from the convent and found a beautiful black puppy, a Cocker spaniel, waiting for us. Our housekeeper informed us that my cousin Grodzinski had brought "Macius" for Anetka. I said that in my circumstances it was impossible to keep a dog, but Macius was so beautiful that I could not bring myself to give him away. I wrote to Sylwin about Macius, how much I worried about what I would do with him in the summer when we'd be going abroad. Sylwin replied that the President told him to tell me that when one has a dog, one does not part with it. So I have stopped worrying, so long as Macius is invited to Riond Bosson.

May 12, 1935. At 8:30 P.M. Michasia Borzecka telephoned me that Marshal Pilsudski was dying. That did not surprise me, for everyone has known for the past two years that Pilsudski was hopelessly ill and was kept alive only by artificial means. Fifteen minutes later Michasia called again to say that he had died.

May 13, 1935. I went out toward evening. The whole city was inundated with crape. There was literally not one display window that did not have a photograph of Pilsudski draped in mourning. I did not meet a single person without a mourning band.

May 15, 1935. I had an unbelievable visit today. At 3 P.M., the bell rang. My housekeeper announced that three unknown men had come. As it appeared, these "gentlemen" had come with a threat: "Why was there no telegram of condolence from Paderewski following the death of Marshal Pilsudski? If none came, then all unions and organizations throughout the country would react to such behavior . . ."

I was dumbfounded. After a long moment, I mastered my rage and replied as quietly as I could that *their* behavior surprised me greatly. "It seems to me that it is neither in your province nor mine to teach President Paderewski manners," I retorted. I continued that I did not know why they'd come to me in this matter, and that I was sorry but I was busy and had no time for further conversation with them. I saw them to the door myself in order to be rid as quickly as possible of my unwelcome guests.

A short while later I phoned to Switzerland and told Sylwin about the incident. He immediately dictated to me the wording of two telegrams which the President had sent two days ago to Mme. Pilsudska and President Moscicki, respectively. I went to the editor-in-chief of the Warsaw Courier, Mr. K. Olchowicz, and gave him copies of the telegrams. He promised to print them in the next edition. Other editors refused for lack of the originals; some wouldn't even

receive me, because they "didn't have time!" I have connections and friends even among Pilsudski followers, so I
made a fuss all over Warsaw that Paderewski's wires were
pigeonholed and had not yet been released to the press. In
the evening, Mr. Henry S. came in very upset. It seems that
he had a similar visit with the same accusations and threats.

Two Ugly Ducklings

May 18, 1935. Paderewski's telegrams have been found in
the Belvedere and given out to all the papers — they had been
held up five days. Those Pilsudski-ites even play politics in
times of death!

Riond Bosson — June 30, 1935. This is my first trip abroad
with Macius. When we drove up to Riond Bosson, Macius
was naturally the main attraction. Everyone wanted to pet
him, but Macius, taken off his leash, began to run all over the
house, so that neither Anetka nor Ignas O. behind her, could
catch him. He wouldn't let anyone come near him. Suddenly,
an unforeseen thing happened. While everyone stood about
staring with concern at Macius' crazy running, the President
appeared in the dining room door. At that moment, the dog
stopped before him and stood up on his hind legs! He begged
beautifully, something he's not yet been taught because he is
still too young. The President petted Macius on the head
and Macius rested his forelegs against the President's knee.
How had he known which of us was the President? Anetka and
I were really proud of our smart and elegant little dog.

July 5, 1935. I have never seen the President looking so mad.
He is so angry that he hasn't spoken to anyone. After luncheon
we all ran to Sylwin, and Mrs. Wilkonska was the first to
ask why Ignace is so angry and taciturn? We discovered from

Sylwin that someone recently sent the President a copy of Rom Landau's book about Paderewski. He has been reading it for three days and getting madder and madder—really, we'd never seen the President in such a humor.

According to the President, the book is full of errors and misstatements. No wonder, Mr. Landau has seen Mr. Paderewski only once during a luncheon at Riond Bosson. This short interview could hardly have given him enough authentic information to write a book about Paderewski.

In order to divert the President, Sylwin suggested a game of bridge. After the bridge game and tea, the President went for a ride, dropping Mr. Opienski, the fourth partner, at Morges on the way. Mrs. Wilkonska was already sitting in the car beside the chauffeur, which is her favorite place. As the President walked slowly toward the car, Macius dashed ahead of him and slipped into the car. When I ran after the dog and tried to pull him out, the President said, "Let Macius stay and take a ride with us." In the car Macius quietly lay down at the President's feet. It seems to me he'd put the President into a better humor. Paderewski thinks dogs are the best and truest of friends. I recall that once during some conversation, he said: "I'm not afraid of my enemies, only of false friends."

August 19, 1935. New trouble with guests! Actually not new, because it is constant, but today it is particularly bad. This morning we had two phone calls, one almost directly after the other, from the Hotel Mont Blanc in Morges. First Professor Turczynski, the pianist, announced his visit, and then Miss Dabrowska, the famous Polish miniature painter. Both had come from Warsaw. We knew very well what these two visits meant: Miss Dabrowska would want the President to pose for a miniature, while Professor Turczynski would want to play for him. The President detests both things, so Sylwin was worried, almost scared to tell the President about the two artists.

I went to the hotel to greet the guests, both of whom I know well from Warsaw. I soon discovered that Miss Dabrowska did not know of Professor Turczynski's arrival. She didn't even know him, although they'd come from Warsaw on the same train. After I had introduced them both, Miss Dabrowska said: "What will Paderewski say when he sees two ugly ducklings at once? Maybe he'll be frightened, or perhaps it will be better for him to see such an ugly pair at one time." Miss Dabrowska wasn't exaggerating. She is small, thin, legs as skinny as sticks, an egg-shaped head, eyes of an indeterminable color and small as two pinheads, very flushed from the hard work of painting miniatures in a strong light.

The very pale, tired face of Professor Turczynski is no beauty either! He, too, is small, emaciated, with tiny eyes which one can't see because he is so terribly nearsighted he has to squint. His face resembles a frog's. However, both of them are pleasant, gay, witty, intelligent, and when one talks to them, one forgets their ugliness. Anyway, both know how homely they are, so they make a show of it. Both are cultured artists and they understood one another immediately.

I warned both arrivals not to address Paderewski as "Master." The President has eccentricities in the matter of names. He hates to be called "Master," and is usually addressed as "Mr. President"; and he insists at all times upon being called by both his given names, *Ignacy Jan* Paderewski, and wants everyone to know that he always uses both names.

After talking with our artists for an hour, I phoned Riond Bosson and found that they were invited by Paderewski to lunch.

We waited a long time for the President to come down for lunch. When he came in through the open door from the hall, Miss Dabrowska took Professor Turczynski's arm; they both bowed before the President. Then she asked: "What do you think, Mr. President, of this pair of ugly monkeys who've come to Switzerland at the same time?" The President was so taken aback by the question that he didn't reply for a moment, looking first at the professor and then at the lady.

He laughed in embarrassment, but greeted them warmly and asked us all to be seated. Around the table, the conversation was general, gay, and witty. The President was really diverted and entertained by this pair.

After lunch, Miss Dabrowska accosted Sylwin and me: What to do? How to approach the President to get him to pose? She added quickly that she really didn't need more than fifteen minutes for a sketch (she always makes a pencil sketch first and paints her miniature from that). She went on to say that she wanted to make two miniatures: Paderewski the statesman, and Paderewski the artist.

In the meantime, we learned that Professor Turczynski plays bridge and loves it. We all smiled at that and Sylwin hit on a solution. "What we can do is play a game, which will give you time to make your sketch, if this is agreeable to you."

Miss Dabrowska was delighted. "That's wonderful. I'll sit in a corner and draw. The President needn't pose or even see me sketching."

Paderewski, Professor Turczynski, Sylwin, and Leniutka sat down to play in the card room. Mrs. Wilkonska, much interested, seated herself in an armchair by the window and sighed, while Miss Dabrowska pulled drawing paper out of her bag and took a chair in the right light for sketching. I sat down near her for company, but pretended to read a paper. The President didn't pay any attention to the rest of us, not changing his facial expression in the least, although I'm sure he knew Miss Dabrowska was going to draw him.

I peeped at Miss Dabrowska who was hard at work, in her ridiculously childish hand a pencil stub so small you couldn't even see it move over the drawing paper. I glanced at my watch, then at the artist. She drew continuously with short, almost lightning swift strokes. I began to read my paper. Mrs. Wilkonska stared straight ahead, lost in thought, sighing occasionally as is her custom. Suddenly, Miss Dabrowska jumped from her chair, holding the finished sketch in her outstretched hand. Sylwin rose, took the drawing and handed it to the President.

One glance at his face assured us that he was deeply satisfied. "An excellent portrait," he said. We all crowded around to see. It was really a life-like portrait of Paderewski, just as we know him, to the tiniest facial characteristic. The President must have been very pleased with it because he looked at it a long time and then kept glancing back to where it stood on a small table, propped against a lamp. Miss Dabrowska asked the President to autograph the sketch and then promised to give it to me as soon as she finishes the miniatures. She was very happy because the President thanked her for the wonderful likeness and personally invited her and Professor Turczynski to lunch tomorrow.

August 20, 1935. Our "handsome" pair came again today for luncheon. Encouraged by the goodness and kindness shown her and the recognition of her talent yesterday, Miss Dabrowska decided to figure out a way, without Sylwin's help or advice, of doing a sketch of Paderewski the artist.

We went to the card room from the dining room. Realizing that bridge was again in the offing, Miss Dabrowska went up to the President and asked him to sit at the piano for a moment with his hands on the keys. She leaned against a wall and began to sketch with her stub of a pencil. Looking at her hard at work, the President asked simply and sweetly: "Would you like me to play something for you?" While he played, Miss Dabrowska stood hunched into a little ball, sketching. Her face took on a rapt look. She controlled herself, looked, listened, and drew all at the same time.

The new sketch was superlative; it was a profile, with lowered eyes, and a look of concentration and inspiration. Nevertheless, the President preferred the first portrait. Miss Dabrowska expressed her sincere thanks to the President for playing and said: "When I was nine years old, I already played the violin. My parents couldn't decide whether I should study art or music, and finally decided on painting! I'll never forget how you played for me, Mr. President."

It seems to me that Professor Turczynski will be more of a problem. He has transcribed a "Fantasy" of Paderewski's, and wishes to play it for the President. He also wants to give concerts in Lausanne, Vevey, and other places. Naturally, he will have to have Paderewski's sponsorship, for he is unknown in Switzerland. Sylwin will have to take care of all that. It's lucky that Professor Turczynski is jolly, witty, and plays bridge, it makes him an easy guest.

Warsaw — September 14, 1935. Scarcely had Anetka, Macius and I returned from Switzerland, and visited my father in Otwock, than I found myself saddled with an exasperating commission. My brother Jan has come to Warsaw on a short vacation from Russia, after which he'll have to return to Moscow. Jan has been a Polish Embassy counsellor in Moscow since 1931 and at the same time Polish Consul General in Kharkov and later in Kiev. I can imagine how terrible living conditions there must be from the unbelievable list of things Jan has asked me to buy for the Embassy Staff. I have bought shoe laces, buttons, needles, thread, tape, safety pins, hooks and eyes, cotton, iodine, even several crates of eggs and other basic pantry supplies. These weren't too much trouble, but the list went on: a black felt hat with a small brim for a tall blonde with a long face; a small trimmed gray hat to suit a brown-haired woman with dark complexion and eyes; a navy sport dress with a red belt and a gray one to change off; black oxfords; stockings; night gowns; skirts; warm underclothing.

I asked Jan whether he'd read the list and what was the matter with the department stores in Moscow. He replied with irritation: "What department stores? There are none in Russia." Jan took a whole wagonload of only the most necessary things back with him. It looked as if he were going off to a desert island.

Paderewski: A Movie Actor

Paris—January 11, 1936. I arrived in Paris today to meet Sylwin, who came from Riond Bosson. We feel almost as if we were on our honeymoon. It is the first time since our wedding that we've traveled alone. That's why we've decided not to stop in the usual section of Paris, but at the Hotel de Paris on my beloved Boulevard Madeleine, close to all my favorite shops and department stores and near the Madeleine Church in which I like best to pray. Whenever I am in Paris, I always go daily to the Madeleine Church. To me, it seems the most beautiful church in the world.

We shall be in Paris a week. Sylwin has come for a special reason. For a long time now, he has secretly wished to have movies made of Paderewski playing the piano, to preserve his art for posterity. But the President hasn't been very willing, so Sylwin has tried to prepare the President gradually by talking him into it. Meanwhile, he has long tried to contact English film producers. Mr. Jan Horodyski, who lives in Paris, but has important connections in England, has been helping him in this. Now they're working hard at it. We hope that when they have something definite worked out, the President will consent to be filmed.

Riond Bosson—January 20, 1936. Our week's stay in Paris flew by all too quickly. Here in Riond Bosson we don't mention the movie. Apparently no one here has any idea of it.

January 26, 1936. My brother Tadeusz came here today on his way to Italy to attend an industrial convention. This is his first visit to Riond Bosson and probably the sole visit of a present Polish-regime man to Paderewski's home!

At the table, the President put Tadeusz at his left, instead of at Mrs. Wilkonska's right. They spoke of trade and in-

dustry in Poland and abroad and of commercial relations with
the rest of Europe. Tadeusz knows a lot about that subject, for
after all he is one of the captains of Polish industry. The
President listened carefully and spoke with such authority
one would think it his profession as well! He has an uncanny
memory for names, dates, and assorted facts. Paderewski always makes everyone wonder at his erudition. He certainly
surprised my brother.

Riond Bosson — June 23, 1936. Anetka and I are back at Riond
Bosson for the summer. Directly upon our arrival, Paderewski came down to greet us and to join us and the rest of the
household for tea. Mr. Lothar Mendes, an English film pro-
ducer, was introduced to me. Leniutka whispered in my ear
that the President will probably appear in an English film,
and that Mr. Mendes has come down from London to make
final arrangements.

June 26, 1936. Lothar Mendes left for England today taking
back with him Paderewski's consent to appear in a film. At
last we shall see the President on the screen. We're all happy
about it, that is, all except the President.

There certainly were plenty of obstacles to surmount. In
the first place, ever since Mme. Paderewska died two years
ago, the President, who spends long hours at the piano in
the privacy of his home, will not hear of public appearances.
Then, because he believes true art presupposes a direct contact between the artist and his audience, he is averse to the
use of mechanical intermediaries to bring him before the
public. But the greatest difficulty was the President's fear of
the powerful lights that will be turned on him during the
filming.

All his life Paderewski has been accustomed to giving
recitals in darkened concert halls because his eyes are so
sensitive to light. This time it will be just the reverse. To be
sure, Mr. Mendes did promise to do whatever he could
about this, but the President isn't convinced.

Once Paderewski's tentative consent to make a movie was obtained, scenario troubles set in. All the best writers were mobilized to write an appropriate story in which Paderewski would play himself. They handed in screen plays galore, but none did justice to the great stature of Paderewski.

Mr. Mendes finally selected two scripts, which he had brought with him to Riond Bosson. He let us read both of them. I liked one. Unfortunately, Mr. Mendes said the English producers feel that in it too much stress is placed on patriotic sentiment and that it is "too Polish." I am sorry, because the President would have been in his element and really played himself in that script.

The accepted scenario—I understand it was written by a Hungarian—is utterly banal. I don't think it's at all worthy of Paderewski; he is only an incidental figure in it. So instead of a film *about* Paderewski, the picture will be one *with* Paderewski.

But we don't take the screen-play's shortcomings too much to heart, because we think the most important thing is to have Paderewski's piano-playing immortalized on the screen for posterity.

We're all very elated over the fact that the President has at length agreed to resume his artistic career. But I do feel a little sorry for him. At his age and after such a long interruption, it won't be an easy matter to make a comeback, especially in a field new to him. I simply can't imagine Paderewski in the role of a movie actor!

Shooting of the film is scheduled to start on August 7th at Denham (Britain's Hollywood) near London.

Paris—August 3, 1936. Tomorrow Paderewski, Sylwin, Franciszek, and Dr. Masson are leaving for London. I'm glad the President took Sylwin's advice and invited his Swiss personal doctor to accompany him to Denham. Nobody knows how he will stand up under the strain, and we all will be at greater ease knowing that his devoted physician is within call.

August 6, 1936. Sylwin telephoned from London that the President decided against staying at Denham. He's stopping in London, at the Carlton, and will make the daily trip to the studio by car. In the light of this I am going to England. I'm beside myself with joy.

London — August 8, 1936. I was in Denham for the first time today. We left the Carlton Hotel right after lunch. The ride in a magnificent Rolls Royce took about forty-five minutes. Once we got out of the London traffic, we sped along the wonderful highway until we reached a point where we had to leave it. We passed several hamlets, a larger village, and finally came upon the film town of Denham situated away from any habitation. Clouds of heavy black smoke were billowing over some of the buildings. When we got closer I saw a pillar of fire shooting up. It turned out to be a perpetual bonfire fed with sets that had outlived their usefulness. Our car passed through the center gate and headed for the movie lot where *Moonlight Sonata* was being shot.

Just as soon as our car pulled to a stop, we were surrounded by a large crowd of actors and extras in the most fantastic assortment of costumes, as well as by mechanics and ordinary workers. They all wanted to see Paderewski. The crowd was so dense we were wondering how to get through. In the nick of time Mr. Mendes came out to welcome Paderewski and escort us to the studio.

A special dressing room in one part of the studio had been built for the President. Taking Franciszek with him, he went straight to it.

Paderewski's appearance in the film complicates matters for the director. Since every minute costs money in the filmmaking business, work begins at nine sharp in the morning. But the President has his own special work habits from which he never deviates, and it has been agreed that he will be at the studio every afternoon at three. In order not to waste precious time therefore, up to three o'clock they shoot scenes in which Paderewski does not appear and concentrate on him one hundred per cent after he arrives.

It was obvious from the start that everybody, from Mr. Mendes down to the extras, treated the President with the greatest deference, tinged with a touch of embarrassment. Paderewski was not called until all the other actors were in position and ready to begin. I was surprised to note that Paderewski was the only actor completely without make-up.

The President's "stand-in" struck me as quite funny. His function consisted of substituting for Paderewski while the lights were being adjusted and the cameras focused. He must have been chosen because he bears a slight resemblance to the President, but he's shorter and really looks like a caricature of Paderewski. This impression was heightened by the fact that, like all the other actors, he was heavily made up. Somebody told me Paderewski's "double" walked around in suspenders so as not to be mistaken for the President, but I think the terrific heat is a much more plausible explanation.

All of us—spectators and actors alike—were astounded by Paderewski's acting ability. From the very outset he moved so naturally that we could have sworn he had played the scene many times before! Besides, he's the only one of them all who not only knows his own part but the whole script into the bargain. He never muffs a line while the seasoned actors often spoil their scene by a slip of the tongue, necessitating a retake. It's pretty nerve-wracking to watch the same scene being shot over and over again. Paderewski took it all in his stride, maintaining his serenity, patience, and indulgence in spite of his exhaustion. He often relieved the general tension by a witticism.

Promptly at six, production came to a halt. Franciszek helped the President change, and fifteen minutes later we were on our way back to London.

August 9, 1936. Judging by the delicious and swanky lunch we had at the Hotel Carlton dining room today, Paderewski doesn't suffer from the slightest touch of stage fright. The eyes of the whole restaurant were turned on our table, which was swamped by a bevy of waiters constantly wheeling up such an array of hors d'oeuvres, appetizers, sauces, compotes and what-nots that I hardly knew where to begin. The President's interest in fine food was a sure sign that he was in a good mood. Dr. M. and Sylwin heaped their plates pyramid-high and fell to with a will. But Mr. Sharpe carefully inspected the contents of each rolling table and ended by ordering roast beef. A second later, a magnificent juicy roast beef was wheeled in. Paderewski kept encouraging us to try this and that dish and, since neither the Doctor nor I had ever tasted English ale, he suggested that we have some. Finally, so gorged that I yearned for a nap, we got into the Rolls Royce and started off for Denham.

Even though the limousine was spacious and comfortable, and nobody uttered a word in order not to tire the President, a nap was out of the question. Wedged in between the Doctor and Paderewski, I sat on the very edge of the seat, my legs growing numb. Ever since he had that serious attack of phlebitis, he seems to have a pathological fear of being kicked in the legs, and usually refuses to ride three in a seat. One time, however, when we were one too many passengers, not wanting me to ride separately, he told me to sit in the middle next to him. I wasn't the least bit comfortable, but I must have sat so carefully that I never stepped on his feet. Ever since, I'm the only passenger allowed "in the middle," but I always sit perched on the edge and in perpetual fear that I might hurt him.

On our arrival at Denham, Mr. Mendes first led us to the projection room to see yesterday's rushes. It was a lovely little room with marvelous red club chairs. The lights were turned out and I blissfully sank into my chair. If they had chairs like this in all cinemas, I'd see a film a day! The rushes were excellent. Paderewski seemed pleased and briskly went to his dressing room, followed by Franciszek.

The cameras resumed grinding. For some unaccountable

reason, the same scene was repeated over and over again at least a dozen times. "Camera stop" was called every few minutes, and the scene was reshot from the beginning. With bated breath I waited for the President to lose his patience. But without a word of complaint, like a conscientious pupil, he kept going through the same scene.

From Denham we rode directly to Bellini's, the President's favorite restaurant. (To avoid changing into evening clothes Paderewski never dines at the Carlton.) Bellini is our favorite too—we were introduced to it on our first trip to London. The President has eaten there for years, and there always is a private room with a burning fireplace ready for him. Remembering that I love roast duck with oranges, Paderewski ordered it for us all. Mr. Sharpe accepted the duck with enthusiasm and then asked for—roast beef. None of us could complain of lack of appetite. The President, too, was in excellent spirits, showing no trace of fatigue.

Work on *Moonlight Sonata* must be different from that on other films. Even though the studio has taken precautions to keep spectators away, there are still plenty like myself, Dr. Masson, and Mr. Sharpe, who are always present during the shooting. Another interested bystander is Mr. Mendes' lovely wife. There are many others peering out of every corner and every door or unobtrusively stationed against adjacent movie sets.

I'm becoming a little oriented in the intricacies of film making. Now I know that the afternoon session with Paderewski was a success, because there are three minutes of finished film to show for it.

August 11, 1936. The President did no acting today. Immediately after our arrival we stepped into the projection room to see the result of yesterday's work. As usual, the scenes were above reproach.

Then we went to a special studio where everything was in readiness for Paderewski to make his trial recording for the sound track. It was rather cool in the room and the President asked for a basin of hot water in which to soak his hands before playing. He does this before every concert and Franciszek always makes sure hot water is at hand, bringing it to the President in the silver basin that is invariably taken along for just this purpose. But since Paderewski wasn't going on a concert tour this time, Franciszek hadn't thought of bringing the special basin to England.

The odd request caused consternation. Everybody dispersed in search of a basin. Unfortunately, there wasn't a single one to be found. At last some hot water was procured from the studio's cafeteria and brought in in a battered old pitcher. Paderewski had to slip one hand in at a time, and had a hard time getting it through the narrow neck at that.

The President played superbly. Mr. Mendes is certain that the sound track recording will be even better than that of phonograph records.

August 12, 1936. Mr. Mendes' high expectations were not fulfilled. Excellent as all the spoken scenes have been thus far, the first attempt at recording Paderewski's piano-playing was a miserable failure. You didn't have to be an expert to know that the scratchy sounds issuing from the loudspeaker were a far cry from a Steinway grand piano's pure tone and Paderewski's incomparable music.

The President emerged from the projection room to make a second trial recording in an angry and gloomy mood. Mr. Mendes and the rest of us were thoroughly alarmed.

August 13, 1936. They've made Paderewski play the same piece of music over at least a dozen times. No sooner does he start playing than they shout "camera stop" and make him go back to the beginning. The minuet sequence, in which the girl runs away weeping from the piano and Paderewski plays in her stead, has for some incomprehensible reason been repeated so many times that I've lost count.

As I watched all this, I kept wondering when the President would lose his patience and chuck everything. It must be terribly nerve-wracking for him to have his playing interrupted every few seconds.

The longer I observe the proceedings the sorrier I am that the scenario is so commonplace and so unworthy of Paderewski.

August 18, 1936. The last few days I've been going to Denham at nine o'clock in the morning and spending the entire day in the company of screen stars, producers, and movie technicians.

Because I'm known all over Denham as a guest of the studio where Paderewski is making *Moonlight Sonata*, everybody is terribly nice to me. I'm free to roam wherever I please.

I find eating lunch with the actors in the cafeteria the most fun. At noon sharp, the bell rings and you'd think school was out, the way those actors dash for the cafeteria from all buildings to be first in the food line.

In no great hurry myself, I took the time to look around. It was truly a fantastic and unique sight. All actors without exception were eating their lunch in their costumes and make-up. My neighbor at the table was a queen or nymph with ankle-length flowing golden hair, while opposite me sat the picture of masculine beauty — an almost naked gentleman wearing an animal skin over one shoulder and a studded belt. At another table I recognized the great Emil Jannings whom I have admired in so many films. Never have I seen so many beautiful women and handsome men all at once!

But the greatest impression was made by the make-up man, who, moving from table to table with a bowl and a thick shaving brush, scrutinized each actor's face, and if he noticed that the thick layer of grayish-brown grease paint needed repair, without warning, mechanically but swiftly, he slapped some fresh goo on the hapless star's face. In the terrific heat, perspiration kept ruining the actors' make-up, and the face painter was very busy indeed. I wondered, not without a feeling of disgust, how the actors could eat when their faces and lips were so heavily made up.

Noticing my interest in the make-up artist's slap-and-run technique, my glamorous queen-or-nymph informed me that, according to studio gossip, when the make-up man saw Paderewski he was so afraid of being told to work on the President that he simply vanished, and could not be found.

August 22, 1936. For ten days now Paderewski has been playing the same thing over and over again. He must have done it at least a hundred times. Every day we've entered the projection room with hope in our hearts that this showing would at last turn out all right. But it's been the same old story all along—no improvement. The music sounds as impossible as ever.

We've all had our fingers crossed because we've been afraid the President would get discouraged and quit. Today the inevitable happened. After listening to the music, Paderewski lost his patience and told Mr. Mendes point-blank that he was giving up the idea of the film and returning to Switzerland tomorrow.

The poor director was at his wit's end. To halt production now would mean a world-wide scandal, not to mention the loss of the eighty thousand pounds the picture has already cost. The President must really be upset to make such a drastic decision.

For some time Sylwin had been after Mr. Mendes to hire a pianist for the experimental stages of the musical recording so as to relieve Paderewski of this tedious task. After all, this is the first attempt in British moving picture history to incorporate piano concert music into the sound track, and the engineers have had no experience in regulating the tone or in setting up the microphones. Sylwin warned Mr. Mendes that the President was worn out and that his nerves were near the breaking point, but the director had hoped against hope that the next sound recording would turn out perfect. Now he stood there helpless, while the elaborate structure he had taken such pains to erect seemed to crumble about him. We all shared his misery. Something had to be done, and quickly. In this calamitous situation Sylwin, evidently inspired by Providence, conceived an idea which saved the day, at least temporarily.

During yesterday's recording session, he had sat in the control room, where he'd listened to the music over the loudspeaker. He had noticed that the engineer zealously regulated Paderewski's playing the way he would regulate a dialogue. He softened forte passages and built up the piano ones, thereby destroying the quality of the music and reducing it to an unrecognizable evenly modulated series of notes. Furthermore, all experimenting with the microphone to date had consisted of shifting it in every direction, but it had never occurred to anyone to place it directly in front of the piano at about the spot where the audience sits during a concert.

When the President announced that he was through with the film, Sylwin made mention of his observations to Paderewski and succeeded in arousing his interest to such an extent that he agreed to make one final try.

Sylwin placed the microphone a short distance from the piano but in the exact center. The President followed these preparations with an amused smile.

When Paderewski sat down at the piano, Sylwin disappeared into the control room to make sure that an over-conscientious recording engineer did not wreck his experiment.

Tomorrow will tell whether Sylwin's idea had anything in it.

August 23, 1936. This morning I dropped into the National Gallery, but my heart wasn't in it. I couldn't get my mind off the film and kept thinking about the projection room, about Paderewski's last try, and about Sylwin's experiment. Sylwin is very musical all right, but what does he know about the technical end of film-making?

I was on pins and needles all morning. Coming out of the Gallery, I stepped into church next door—I don't even know what denomination it was—to say a prayer for the success of *Moonlight Sonata*.

Nobody said a word during the long drive to Denham. As we entered the projection room, I shivered with anticipation. Sylwin's cheek muscles were working furiously—a sure sign of nervous tension. Mr. Sharpe's excitement showed in the way he clicked his false teeth. Dr. Masson assumed a solemn, grave expression befitting a death-bed visit, and ensconced himself in a comfortable chair. Paderewski's face was a study in stony calm while Mr. Mendes kept throwing anxious looks at all of us.

The first sequences flashed on the screen were dialogue scenes, which were up to the usual high standard. Then the lights went on, for nothing would be shown on the screen while we listened to the music. From the very first measure it was obvious that the experiment of the day before had met with success. The piano sounded limpid and pure, and we were all brought under the spell of Paderewski's vibrant playing. The last notes of *Moonlight Sonata* were still vibrating in the air when everybody started talking at once. The mood was more than happy, it was festive.

August 26, 1936. Even though all technical difficulties have been taken care of, the shooting of the film is progressing very slowly. Each scene is repeated a number of times and yet this tiresome monotony has failed to exhaust Paderewski. We suspect he has not only become accustomed but has taken a liking to his new occupation.

I think the turning point in the President's attitude was the picture's concert scene, which proved a tremendous success in every way. That concert must have been the only one of its kind in the film world. When the news spread that Paderewski would give a recital for the benefit of the cameras, Mr. Mendes was literally swamped with letters from notables in British society requesting permission to attend the concert as extras, just so that they might hear the music and be part of a Paderewski moving picture. Despite the fact that an invitation to amateurs to participate as spectators would have meant a considerable saving to the studio, Mr. Mendes feared the scene might not turn out as it should and hired at least a thousand professional extras, paying them something like two and one-half pounds per person. By way of exception, a handful of prominent individuals were permitted to join the extras. The improvised concert hall was constructed in an unusual modern style and with imagination. For the concert scene it was filled to overflowing with elegantly attired ladies and gentlemen who did not have a difficult part to play. All they had to do was listen to the music and burst into enthusiastic applause at the conclusion of the recital, a kind of behavior that always comes naturally to a Paderewski audience.

But the part that wasn't in the picture and won't appear on the screen was the deluge of flowers awaiting Paderewski in his dressing room. The extras presented him with countless bouquets and wreaths as an expression of homage and, I suppose, gratitude for having been privileged to enjoy such a rare treat.

I thought the President played divinely. It was so beautiful it made me feel prickly all over. And the way his fingers traveled up and down the keyboard! When the virtuosos of the world see the agility of those hands on the screen, they will have to admit there is no one quite like Paderewski.

During the program, Mr. Sharpe, Dr. Masson, and I had good seats from the acoustical standpoint, but we were not within the camera's range. I feel a little disappointed that I wasn't in the scene. Nobody thought of it and, to tell the truth, neither did I until it was too late. Had I worn an evening dress and asked Mr. Mendes if I could sit among the concert audience, I'm sure he wouldn't have refused me. But I'm glad that Sylwin is appearing in a scene with Paderewski —the one in the club room where the President starts narrating an incident in his artistic career. Mr. Mendes gave

Sylwin this bit part because he knew how much pleasure Sylwin would derive from it.

Sylwin has also received a lovely gold cigarette case inscribed: "To Mr. Sylwin Strakacz to 'record' his invaluable help and assistance. Lothar Mendes."

Meanwhile, my stay in London is about over. School in Warsaw begins in a few days, so I have to leave for Switzerland tomorrow to pick up Anetka and return to Warsaw. If I weren't ashamed to, I'd cry because I must leave.

Denham has given me one of the richest and most beautiful memories of my life. I've had all the pleasures and none of the tribulations of a film star's existence in this "British Hollywood."

I'm going back with a feeling of security about Paderewski. To be sure, he did say at Bellini's the other night: "I'll surely lose my eyesight because of those lights and spotlights. My eyes keep hurting me more and more and I don't see so well now." But I think this was said to arouse Dr. Masson's and our sympathy at having been forced to submit to the battery of lights he's hated so all his life.

Paris — November 21, 1936. It's a long time since I've really "lived" in Warsaw. More and more I seem unable to settle down. Though I'm extremely fond of my Warsaw apartment, I don't use it very much. I must constantly be on the move, between Anetka at the convent and my father who's taken up permanent residence in Otwock. It certainly tires me out. Actually, I'm keeping my apartment more for my furniture than for myself. I've become so used to traveling that I feel best while on trains. Railroad cars are my real home; in reality a train is the only place where I can lead my own life. All the customs officials and conductors know me by now. As soon as they spot me, they inquire about Paderewski. Even the Germans have ceased bothering me with customs inspection and have become used to my baggage, which, instead of my wardrobe, consists mostly of hares, partridges, sausages, doughnuts, cream babkas—everything that the President likes best in Polish delicacies.

November 24, 1936. The game which I brought is now resting safely in the hotel refrigerators. It will remain there until we leave for Switzerland. Unfortunately, we won't be able to stay in Paris long this time. The President is probably exhausted after the filming of *Moonlight Sonata*, although he doesn't show it a bit. He's in good humor, looks hale, and lately hasn't even complained of his eyesight or of eye aches which he thought the film might bring on. He only makes a face when anybody mentions klieg lights or reflectors.

Today, Sylwin had an amusing conversation with the President on the subject of jazz music. One can speak freely about jazz to Paderewski, inasmuch as he doesn't consider it music. Sylwin has composed many light pieces of music for dancing and for jazz bands, but ever since he's been Paderewski's secretary, he's had to give it up for lack of time. Today when he defended modern music, the President replied: "Jazz bands! They're the Bolsheviks of music!" Then Sylwin very bravely proposed to play for the President and "convince him that jazz is nice music." The President agreed out of politeness, or perhaps out of curiosity to see how Sylwin plays. Sitting down at the magnificent Steinway, Sylwin played a good many jazz pieces. The President listened with interest, and when Sylwin finished, he said: "It is horrible stuff, but I must admit that you do it well."

Christmas in Otwock

Riond Bosson—December 2, 1936. I've been in Riond Bosson since November 28th, but must leave tomorrow for Warsaw. How many years is it since Sylwin and I have spent Christmas together? However, I wouldn't stay here for anything, and anyway no one urges me to, for they all know I always spend Christmas with Father and Anetka, just as Sylwin wouldn't leave the President during the holidays. The President knows that he is the most important person in the world to Sylwin and that everybody else, even his own family, comes second. That's why he bestows more than a father's affection on Sylwin.

Otwock, Poland — December 26, 1936. Father has settled in Otwock for good. Since he's been living here, he hasn't had a single attack of asthma. When he once came to Warsaw for a day, he began to choke up after two hours in the city air. Since then he's been so terribly afraid of a new attack that there's no question of his again going to Warsaw. Otwock, which is only eleven miles from Warsaw, has an entirely different climate; so different that it's hard to believe the town lies in Poland.

We're spending the entire holiday season here. (I must admit that I haven't felt as well anywhere since we left California. Sometimes on our frequent walks in the fragrant pine woods, Anetka and I come upon dirty, neglected little houses. I often think to myself how I would re-plan Otwock if I had the money. How poor Poland is. With such a climate, if Otwock were in some other country, it would be a famous spa to which people would flock from all corners of the world. Instead, there are only a few tuberculosis hospitals and a new casino which stands empty; there isn't a single decent hotel or boarding house where one could live comfortably.) As usual, Sylwin telephoned to us from Switzerland on Christmas Eve, and then the President talked to me over the phone. The President hasn't changed his old ways. He only comes to the phone once a year, to give us his best wishes at Christmas.

The Favored Guests

Riond Bosson—June 25, 1937. Anetka, Macius, and I are again vacationing in Switzerland. Everyone greeted us with real joy and friendliness. Macius now feels at home in Riond Bosson. At present, besides Macius there are also a parrot, whose cage always hangs in the dining room near the window leading out to the terrace, and two exotic gray birds which Monsignor Kaczynski brought Anetka from Spain. Since I was horrified at the thought of traveling with them, he gave them to Mrs. Wilkonska, who was very surprised at such a gift and merely shrugged her shoulders when the Monsignor wasn't looking. Anetka felt a bit disappointed.

July, 1937. So many guests have come to spend their vacation with the President. There are Paderewski's pupils, with their wives and children; General Sikorski with his wife and daughter, Mrs. Deschamps of Paris, Dr. Fronczak of Buffalo, and Miss Elizabeth Crafts of New York, who comes to Switzerland every summer. Miss Crafts is "Elzbietka" to us all ever since the President gave her the Polish nickname. Everyone in the President's household considers her one more member of his adopted family. Elzbietka is a great bridge enthusiast. Besides this, her truly deep feeling for Poland and for the President has endeared her to us all. To please the President she's learning Polish by reading and studying Mickiewicz's "Pan Tadeusz." She already knows a good bit of the language, and that is quite an accomplishment when one reflects that the epic poem she chose for her textbook contains some of the most beautiful but most difficult Polish.

Mrs. Wilkonska's regular Sunday receptions are more and more heavily attended.

During the week, we usually try to avoid guests to spare the President, but we seldom succeed because old friends and important persons show up who can't be turned away. The President, to say nothing of Mrs. Wilkonska, grimaces whenever he learns of all these impending visits. But once the guest has arrived, the President is such a wonderful host that no one wants to leave. Sometimes the President personally invites a guest to come again, but such privileged individuals are few. Usually Sylwin has to ask the President and sometimes must wait until he can catch him in a good mood before he'll invite some guest he doesn't particularly want to see. Actually, only the Opienskis can come whenever and as often as they wish, for they're such old friends that the President doesn't have to be formal with them. The Ernest Schellings seldom come on Sunday, for they live near-by and prefer to visit and receive the President in smaller company. And, of course, Elzbietka who besides Sunday, comes twice a week for luncheon or dinner.

Warsaw — September 3, 1937. Vacation is over. I'll be happy when Anetka finishes school, so that we can travel abroad and return home whenever we wish.

Paderewski's Last Pupil

Riond Bosson — November 17, 1937. This is the first time I've ever dared talk about music to the President. I didn't even dream that my musical criticism of young Witold Malcuzynski would bring the President another pupil. I'm certainly grateful to him for his goodness to me and his understanding.

During my last stay in Warsaw, an international Chopin competition was held with first, second, and third prizes. Young pianists from all over Europe entered it. Anetka attended many of the concerts and was so thrilled by them that she wanted me to go with her. Finally, Mr. and Mrs. Marjan Borzecki insisted that I go especially to hear Witold Malcuzynski, who was one of the contestants favored for the first prize. I didn't much feel like going. After having heard Paderewski play so many times, no other pianist seems worth the trouble. However, the Borzeckis, both great patrons of music and young musicians, at last prevailed, and I agreed to go.

Malcuzynski's playing impressed me strongly. Although I'm not especially musical and even less a judge, I thought Malcuzynski played beautifully, so beautifully that I dared speak of him to the President. Besides, the Borzeckis had begged me to do so. And I added that Malcuzynski's dream was to play before the President.

Malcuzynski had won the second prize at the Chopin Contest. The first was awarded a Russian, Uninski, who also played beautifully, but everyone in Warsaw claimed that the jury had been unfair and that Malcuzynski should have won first prize. According to rumor, he received second prize because he is a native of Warsaw, and it didn't seem in good taste to have a local boy win first prize in an international competition.

The President listened to all this carefully and then very quietly gave his reply (which I at first took as a joke.) "Since *you* (with emphasis) think he is so good, let him come to Riond Bosson so I can hear him myself." I couldn't believe my ears. I hadn't even had a chance to ask that, but the President had divined my intention. Here Sylwin and I are supposed to protect the President from just such requests which pile in from everywhere.

"Can Malcuzynski *really* come and play for you, Mr. President?" I gasped with pleasure.

"Of course he may," Paderewski replied.

How good the President is to me (for I know he did this for me, perhaps because this is the first time I've ever asked him for anything).

Sylwin sent a wire to the Borzeckis at once, telling them that Malcuzynski was to come without delay, for we will soon be leaving for Paris. Malcuzynski will probably get a passport quickly. After all Borzecki is the mayor of Warsaw.

November 21, 1937. Malcuzynski has arrived and will play before the President. I imagine he's scared to death. I'm not, though, for I'm certain that the President will see his talent.

November 22, 1937. Malcuzynski is slender and very pale. When he came out after his audition with the President he looked like death itself. I asked him (the first time in my life that I've ever asked anyone such a question, but isn't he my protegé?), "Well, what did the President say?"

"He insisted that I learn English, but," he added with a look of utter despair, "he gave me so much to do for to-morrow." And he pointed to a stack of music he held in his arm. "This is impossible. I'm supposed to have all this ready by 4 P.M. tomorrow. I'll never be able to do it!"

I was delighted. The President had told him to come a second time and had assigned him a lesson! That means Malcuzynski has real talent. If he were only average, he wouldn't be told to come back except for luncheon or dinner. If the President assigned him so much, it means that he is really interested in the young man.

"Don't worry," I told him, "it's wonderful that the President told you to come back and gave you so much to do. You'll probably have to play all night, but you must prepare everything Paderewski gave you."

"I will have to sit up all night, but even so, I won't be able to do it all," he said, not very convinced.

November 23, 1937. Malcuzynski came out after a second lesson that lasted several hours, exhausted and pale but quite calm. He had prepared everything Paderewski gave him, and has received as much more to prepare by 4 P.M. tomorrow. Malcuzynski has stopped despairing; he is young, but has understood from the beginning that it isn't enough merely to have talent or to work at it a little. A genius like Paderewski plays *no less than nine hours* a day when he's preparing for a tour.

My Heart Contracted

Riond Bosson — March 9, 1938. Although I haven't seen the President since last December, I am struck by the big change in his appearance. He has aged considerably. I got a shock when I saw him shuffle into the dining room leaning heavily on his cane. That thick light-colored malacca cane is something new and Paderewski will not take a step without it. It's really Sylwin's, he bought it when Warsaw fashion decreed walking sticks for men.

The President's hair is also much thinner. True, Franciszek keeps it perfectly groomed, cutting it shorter than he used to, but it is utterly gray with hardly a trace of its former golden gleam. All in all, I felt I was looking at an old man and my heart contracted at the sight.

Paris — March 25, 1938. As usual, we began our stay in Paris with Dr. Choussaud. The doctor is touchingly devoted to the President. In spite of his extensive practice, he always manages to find the time, sometimes twice a day, to visit the President.

When we asked the doctor why the President walks with such difficulty, he replied in no uncertain words that it was the fault of us all. By trying to anticipate the President's every wish, we deprive him of the possibility of executing normal movements. "If you go on waiting on Paderewski the way you do, he'll completely forget how to move. He reaches for the sugar — you push the sugar bowl up to him. He looks for his cane — you jump up to hand it to him. He wants the newspaper — you put it on his knees. For heaven's sakes, let the man enjoy a little freedom! His mind is what it was, his memory is phenomenal; what he needs is a little exercise. Tomorrow I'll teach him how to walk instead of dragging his feet along."

April 8, 1938. Though he walks so feebly and slowly, the President made his solitary pilgrimage to Notre Dame de la Victoire. He went alone and returned without mishap, but we promised ourselves this was the last time we'd let him go alone. The President just doesn't realize how infirm he is when it comes to moving about.

Another English Tour

Warsaw — October 23, 1938. I haven't made an entry in my diary in ages. I'm always pressed for time and feel as if I were on a merry-go-round. I try to visit Father as often as I can. He's old and lonely and misses me. Anetka needs me too. Sylwin writes over and over again: "Come, the President and Mrs. Wilkonska keep asking for you." It's bewildering to say the least.

And now I'm going to England. The President has agreed to a small concert tour. Because Paderewski is very weak and does not feel well, Sylwin is afraid to have only himself and Franciszek around. I shall meet Paderewski and Sylwin in Paris.

Paris — October 29, 1938. I'm here alone. The President, Sylwin, and Franciszek have already left for London. Dr. Choussaud and I will follow on November 1st. It was no easy matter to get the Doctor invited. When Sylwin first suggested it, the President announced: "I'm healthy and I don't need a doctor." So Sylwin began a new attack. The President would do the Doctor a great kindness by inviting him to England. To maintain the fiction that Dr. Choussaud is not accompanying the President, but is being summoned to London to examine and treat Miss Alma Tadema, who has suffered an attack of phlebitis, we are leaving a few days later.

London — November 2, 1938. We arrived here last night. Dr. Choussaud is proud as punch because he wasn't sick.

The President grew truly angry when he heard that Miss Alma Tadema, upon being informed that Paderewski had sent for the famous phlebitis specialist to help her, replied that she would receive no doctors, that she didn't believe in doctors, and that she was getting along fine on her own course of treatment — camomile brew.

Brighton — November 5, 1938. Paderewski's initial recital took place in "The Dome" today. The concert hall was filled to capacity. Our hotel, too, is crowded with guests who have come to Brighton especially for the concert. Kind-hearted, elderly impresario L. G. Sharpe is with us, just as in the old days. So are the Adlingtons and their daughter Mabel, Scottish friends of the President.

What a day this was! We suffered terrible stage fright for the President because we were afraid that a recital at his age and in his physical condition would be too much for him. Time has completely ceased to exist for the President; he gets up very late and with difficulty, he even dozes off during the day, an unheard-of thing in the past. That Paderewski always manages to be on time is a tribute to Franciszek's remarkable ability to arrange things around the President.

But our fears were needless! The President walked onto the stage slowly but confidently, gracefully acknowledging the long applause of the audience which had risen in greeting. His playing was very different from that of several years ago; in the place of his old dynamism had come a spiritual quality that gave one the impression that Paderewski's very soul was speaking.

Southampton — November 10, 1938. Today's concert was at three in the afternoon. The President was not feeling well. When he finally appeared on the stage, the metamorphosis in him was unbelievable. Head high, step firm, he looked capable of playing for hours.

He sat down and I settled myself back in the third row orchestra to listen. Suddenly, to my consternation, Paderewski stopped in the middle of his playing, looked around the hall, and left the stage. My heart stood still. Nobody knew what had happened. After a long pause Paderewski returned to the piano and looked up toward the ceiling. I turned around to follow his glance. Somewhere in the peanut gallery a door closed and a light went out. Only then did Paderewski resume his playing.

Sylwin later told me an illuminated sign reading Exit had bothered the President. They put the light out, but had to replace the sign marking the emergency fire exit with a policeman.

At supper today the President said to me with a touch of reproach: "You certainly were dressed like a nun at my concert." To be sure, I had worn a black dress with a gold rope belt. I never wear black except to concerts where I am sure the President will not see me—how did he notice me today?

Eastbourne—November 12, 1938. The entire concert tour has been an unqualified success. Here in Eastbourne, too, there was standing room only. Crowds, ovations, and flowers everywhere. Nevertheless, we shall be relieved when the tour is over. There will be only one more recital, a private one.

Between concerts things haven't changed much. The President sits in his room surrounded by flowers of all description, newspapers, and a stack of photographs and programs to be autographed. He asked me to open some of the envelopes accompanying the tokens of tribute and read the messages. There were five of them, some in French, some in English. They were all from elderly ladies whom the President had not heard from nor seen in the last thirty or forty years, yet he remembered each one individually; as I read off the name he would tell me whether she was pretty or clever, where and when he met her, what her maiden name had been, and how many husbands she had had. What a fantastic memory he has.

I drew the President's attention to one extraordinarily beautiful basket, which looks as if it held all the flowers of England arranged in a magnificent color gradation. It must have cost a fortune. But for once the President shocked me. The floral basket from a faithful old admirer did not please him. He even made a face at it—the President doesn't like anything modern in style.

London—November 15, 1938. The private recital at the Lady's residence—I wish I could remember her name—was a great success. I know so only from Franciszek. The President seldom relates his impressions and Sylwin is always too busy. Franciszek came back delighted and in a talkative mood. He insists he drank champagne with some royalty who smiled at him, that the President played divinely, and that all the guests looked upon the President as on a real king!

Paris—November 16, 1938. I was sorry to leave England. I was all the more sad because I'm convinced this was Paderewski's last concert tour. In any event I have taken away with me a beautiful memory of true and sincere friends.

Our departure was a memorable one. Arriving at Victoria Station we learned that in order to get to the track from which the Dover train was to leave we'd have to cross several platforms. The President walked with obvious difficulty. A railroad official must have noticed this because suddenly out of nowhere appeared a porter pushing a wheelchair. When it dawned on the President that this vehicle was intended for him, he gave the porter such a terrible look that the poor fellow disappeared as quickly as he had come.

A moment later someone came up to us to suggest that the President shorten the distance by crossing directly over the tracks. Before we could answer, the stationmaster himself appeared. He asked the President not to go any further, but to wait where he was. He would have the train switched so that

it might pick us up at this platform. Sure enough, the Dover
train pulled in on our track.

Even Paderewski, who by now has become accustomed to
special treatment, was surprised by this unusual courtesy on
the part of the English railroad official.

Will There Be War?

Warsaw — December 8, 1938. Crossing the border at Zbaszyn
on my way to Warsaw I had an experience that I won't forget
in a hurry. The whole thing happened so quickly I sometimes think maybe it was a dream.

Settling my passport formalities with record speed, the
customs officials vied with each other in telling about the sensation of Zbaszyn: Jews, Polish citizens whom Hitler de-
ported from Germany, had been ejected from their homes
and had not been allowed to take anything with them. Loaded
onto cattle cars, they were sent to the Polish border town of
Zbaszyn. The Polish authorities and the local population
took them under their wing, but the tiny community simply
was not equipped to take care of so many unexpected arrivals.

"If you could only see what Hitler did to our Jews," said
one of the officials. "It's so inhuman and savage, you wouldn't
believe it."

Whereupon another cut in: "But you're with Paderewski.
You really should see it to tell him about it."

"How far is it from here?" I asked, interested.

"Oh, about ten minutes by bicycle," they answered.

"I can ride a bicycle very well," I boasted, never dream-
ing I would immediately be offered the loan of a bicycle and
the services of a customs official who would act as my guide.

"Are you sure you pedal well?" one of the men wanted to
know. And he painted a disheartening picture of a road filled
with puddles of half-melted snow. But I wasn't going to

back out now. I left the station and was handed a bicycle, at the sight of which I quaked in my boots. It was a huge man's bike, with a saddle raised up. My chances of landing in the mud along with the bicycle before I even got started were pretty good. With help I managed to climb up on the impressive conveyance. We were off, pedaling along a slushy sidewalk. Between my fear of falling into the puddles and my apprehension about getting back to the train too late, the ride was a nightmare. At length, the sidewalk ended and my companion halted. I followed his example and plunged one leg ankle-deep in the cold mud.

Looking up, I saw a picture of such tragic implications that I instantly forgot my discomfort. A middle-aged woman, clad in a beautiful lace-trimmed pink housecoat and a silver fox neckpiece, held a sewing basket in her hand. Next to her stood another one in her nightgown, judging from the red bedroom slippers that protruded from beneath the Scotch plaid blanket with which she had wrapped herself. An old wrinkled woman in a man's coat and a befeathered hat was cradling a dog, swathed in a towel.

They milled about like so many apparitions, these victims of Hitler's. From time to time my eye caught sight of a figure holding a pillow or a blanket or a basket, picked up at the very last minute and without any more logic than one might show in fleeing from a burning house. A little further off a small heap of luggage stood in the melting snow: a few suitcases, bags, bundles and a bird cage with a canary inside.

I can still see the frightened helpless faces of these men, women, and children wandering about aimlessly. I can still see them though I remained but a moment at this center of human misery. Mounting my bicycle I pedaled as fast as I could to return to the train on time. When I sank back in my compartment, my guide said to me: "You know, you really didn't see the worst of it. A lot of them have already found shelter in our homes. We try to feed all the refugees but we simply can't put them all up in our homes. Because this is the border area, there isn't another settlement within

miles of here. So they have to stay out in the open until somebody figures out a way of solving the problem. Anyway, you
saw enough to tell Paderewski what Hitler did to the Jews,
and I'm sure this is only the beginning."

Warsaw — February 6, 1939. I leave for Switzerland today.
The President has signed a contract for a four-month concert
tour in America. I'm going to Riond Bosson to say good-bye
to Sylwin, but this time I shall stay away only a very short
time. I'm in an awful dilemma: with all the war talk in
Warsaw, I'm afraid to leave Anetka and Father alone. But
Father, always an optimist, says we won't have war for a
while yet. If it does come, he doesn't think it will be before
the fall. The young people, especially those in the army,
predict its outbreak in the very near future.

Warsaw is tense these days. We can all feel the storm
clouds gathering over our heads. Wherever you go you run
into the same topic of conversation: Will there be war, and
when?

On the Train — February 7, 1939. I was curious to hear what
the customs officials in Zbaszyn would have to say about the
Jewish deportees. Had the border town succeeded in its feeding and housing program? When I asked one of them whether
the Jews were still in Zbaszyn, he replied: "You'd never
recognize the town. Our women have to go to the neighboring towns to do their shopping because prices have sky-
rocketed so; we'd never be able to make ends meet on our
government salaries." I looked at him in genuine surprise,
uncomprehending. He explained hurriedly: "You have no
idea how Jews stick together. If we Poles could only be like
that! Why, just about ten days after they came here and our
authorities were trying to take care of their needs, Jewish
organizations in America sent them such huge sums of
money that they were able to buy practically everything they
needed. Now the Jews are buying out the town. Things have
become so expensive we can only afford to buy bread."

Riond Bosson — February 8, 1939. There is plenty of war talk in Switzerland, too, but things are calmer here because the Swiss expect to remain neutral the way they did in 1914.

As far as I'm concerned, a greater cause for worry than the threat of war is the President's lamentable appearance. Paderewski looks so feeble and moves about with such difficulty that I simply don't see how he can contemplate a concert tour of the United States, of all places. None of us believes he can see it through and we're deeply disturbed by his decision. Sylwin is in a quandary because he feels he should dissuade the President from making the tour, knowing, as he does, how badly the President needs the money. On the other hand, how can you tell a seventy-nine-year-old man he should give up the idea of further recitals because it's too much for him? That would be tantamount to telling Paderewski he's finished.

Meanwhile, the President plays the piano from morning to night. One can only marvel at the stamina and will power which enable him to practise eight or nine hours daily. He can't be in need of so much practising, yet he will not relax his demanding schedule of work. How strange that the hands and brain of the otherwise decrepit President should have remained nimble. How on earth will the President walk on the stage during his recitals? Surely not with the support of his cane, which he uses to get from room to room!

Though anxiety clutches at our hearts, we try to be gay and unconcerned. Sylwin jokes his way through every meal. He plays the fool, which annoys me no end, but the President evidently enjoys it. Sylwin makes a special effort to be entertaining, in spite of his heavy heart, to counteract Mrs. Wilkonska's lack of self-control. She keeps casting at her brother such lugubrious glances that they could drive even a healthy person into a fit of melancholy.

A Cancelled Concert

Paris—February 12, 1939. Even though the President is terribly weak and walks so slowly one doesn't know what to do with one's feet when one accompanies him, he made his regular trip to the Montmorency cemetery and today he went on his customary solitary pilgrimage to Notre Dame de la Victoire.

Upon his return Franciszek excitedly told us all about it. Sensing that the President was thinking of going to church, Franciszek had discreetly asked whether the President was not planning to go into town and whether he could accompany him. Paderewski replied that he was not interested in going out and that Franciszek should go and have his lunch.

Franciszek obeyed, but he felt uneasy and came right back. Not finding the President in, he ran downstairs and saw Paderewski entering a taxi. Franciszek lost him on the way and when he walked into the church was very disturbed to find no sign of the President. "I hurried outside and saw the President approaching with a taper almost as long as himself. So I hid behind a pillar and when the President came out, I bowed to him on the street and asked: 'May I accompany you back, Mr. President?'

"The President said: 'All right, please do!' "

February 15, 1939. Tomorrow morning Paderewski, Sylwin, and Franciszek are sailing on the *Ile de France* for New York. I didn't even go to Le Havre with them. We parted at the Gare St. Lazare, our hearts filled with misgiving and worry about the President. Sylwin is very uneasy about what will happen to Anetka and me in the event of war, but we didn't speak of it. God's will be done! My bags were packed. I'm going back to Warsaw tomorrow.

Seven in the evening. I've just put down the receiver. Sylwin called from Le Havre. It's not certain yet whether they'll go to New York. Crossing the railroad tracks at Le Havre, the President tripped and fell. He was only slightly bruised, but the awful thing is that he lost consciousness for a while.

Paris — February 16, 1939. Sylwin telephoned at three o'clock in the morning to say they would sail in an hour. The President declared he felt fine and would not hear of canceling his trip.

I can't wait to get back to Anetka and Father. Paris suddenly strikes me as the saddest city in the world. For some reason, I'm reminded of my last conversation with one of our French friends, or rather of his prediction that France would collapse if war should come, because morality has sunk to a new low among the French people. Father, who was brought up in France, always says she's such a rich country, she'll withstand everything.

Warsaw — March 1, 1939. All the papers reported that Paderewski has fallen ill and that his concerts have been called off. A detailed letter from Sylwin confirms this tragic news. I can imagine what Sylwin must be going through. What a calamity! Just about the worst thing that could have happened has befallen the President — his hand is so swollen he can't play. The President practised so strenuously for his public appearances that his organism rebelled. The doctors are helpless. They can't diagnose the swelling and don't know how to treat it.

March 15, 1939. Sylwin writes that the President's hand was in bad shape for two weeks. Absolutely nothing seemed to help until it occurred to Sylwin to apply Dr. Choussaud's phlebitis liniment, which Paderewski always carries with him. Working on the theory that what's good for the legs cannot harm the hands, Sylwin had Franciszek apply a compress of that truly miraculous fluid to the sore hand. Three days later the swelling subsided and the hand stopped hurting! Most important of all, just as soon as the President recovered, he announced he would fulfill his recital commitments. Sylwin adds despairingly that Paderewski has blithely resumed his practising in preparation for his concerts. He's afraid the President will not be able to stand the strain of his heavy schedule. I'm worried myself.

April 6, 1939. I get a letter from Sylwin practically every day. America must be war-conscious, too, because Sylwin keeps suggesting that I take Anetka and go to France, to be nearer him in case of war. I won't even consider it. It seems to me that if there is a war, I should either stay home in Poland or be with Sylwin and the President, not stranded in France, among strangers, midway between Sylwin and Poland.

I'm trying to persuade Sylwin to keep the President in America in the event of war. He'd be safer there. It would be wonderful if Anetka and I could go to New York.

May 30, 1939. Anetka has passed her maturity examination at the Convent and graduated with honors. She's only sixteen, but quite a young lady.

Tomorrow is our name day. I didn't feel like arranging a party when we're going to Paris to meet Sylwin and Paderewski in only five days. But so many of our friends have been insisting on a farewell get-together, that I finally gave in to Anetka's plea. Let her have a pleasant memory of the home in which she spent so little time.

As a rule, I like guests and entertaining, but this time I'm pretty handicapped. The practise air-raid alarms and compulsory blackouts cramp my style. Besides I'm constantly uneasy about the President. The concert which was to have been given in New York's enormous Madison Square Garden was called off at the very last minute.

[The concert of May 25, 1939, in Madison Square Garden was canceled when Paderewski was stricken with a heart attack. Dr. Theodore Dunham, a dear friend of Paderewski, who was present in the audience, was hastily summoned, and he decided that Mr.

Paderewski should not play. Mr. Paderewski, accompanied by
Dr. Dunham, returned to his private car, and five days later sailed
for Europe. *S. S.*]

June 1, 1939. What a party that was! To give the more than
hundred people who came enough space to move around in,
we had to take our furniture out into the yard. People I
hadn't seen in years dropped in.

Of course it wouldn't have been a Polish affair without
politics. Some of my guests, having different political beliefs,
launched into a friendly albeit not very concordant discussion.

A few of the guests mentioned that I shouldn't have invited M. Borzecki. He's a defeatist, they said, and a kill-joy.
He goes around telling everybody that we won't have the
arms to defend ourselves with and that we're utterly unpre-
pared for war. To back up his Cassandra-like predictions,
he cites how few bombers we have, how little antiaircraft defense, how we're deficient in this and absolutely lacking in
that. Only a few share his opinion. The others are convinced
we would defeat Germany if she should declare war on us.
And we'll get East Prussia into the bargain. Even the movie
houses run a trailer every day that proclaims: "We are strong,
united, ready."

Paris—June 5, 1939. Anetka, Leniutka, who came from
Riond Bosson to be on hand, and I met the *Normandie* at Le
Havre today. The President shuffled along very slowly.
Sylwin, next to him, and Franciszek, a few steps behind,
patiently adjusted their speed to his. All three looked very
tired. Paderewski greeted us warmly, his face lighting up
when he saw us. He's in good health, only he looks frightfully
old.

June 10, 1939. We're staying in Paris longer than we had
expected. The President is undergoing a completely new and
very risky cure: Jaworski's rejuvenating treatment! Dr.
Jaworski is a Pole who has been living in France over thirty

years. He's famous because of his inventions in the medical field. He has also hit upon a rejuvenating substance. However, although Dr. Jaworski had cited Parisian great names as references, Sylwin was reluctant to introduce him to the President until Dr. Choussaud gave his blessing to the experiment. Even then, he insisted on receiving an injection of the rejuvenating fluid before it was administered to the President.

In the meantime, Paderewski practises at his piano for hours. You'd think he was getting ready to start a new tour.

June 22, 1939. The President has completed the first series of injections. We're going back to Switzerland.

A Night-and-Day Vigil

Riond Bosson — August 7, 1939. The telephone rang at eight this morning. We wondered who could be calling so early. The operator said it was Warsaw. What happened?

Father had a stroke yesterday at Otwock. In a few hours, Sylwin, Anetka, and I will be on our way to him.

Otwock, Poland — August 9, 1939. I'm with Father every minute and I won't leave him until the end. He's conscious and constantly smiling at us with pleasure at our arrival. There may be a chance for his recovery, although his entire left side and hand are paralyzed.

August 14, 1939. Father's condition is unchanged.

Everybody is talking war these days. I was afraid Sylwin might be cut off from the President, so I persuaded him to take Anetka and go back to Riond Bosson. They left today.

August 22, 1939. Father is growing weaker. At times he sinks into a coma, but when he comes to, his eyes follow me around. I force myself to look cheerful.

August 24, 1939. War is just around the corner. I keep a night-and-day vigil at Father's bedside. I'm terrified at the thought of being cut off from Sylwin and Anetka, but I can't abandon my dying father. I know it's a mortal sin, but I pray to God to take Father in time for me to rejoin my husband and daughter.

A Crushing Burden

On the train between Warsaw and Berlin—August 26, 1939. I left Warsaw at 9:20 this morning. I'm the only passenger in the whole car. Nobody but me seems to be getting out of Poland. Tadeusz and Mr. Moszczynski drove me to the station, and then the train started. After that I don't know what happened. When I came to, my face was wet with the cold water dashed on it by the conductor. Every once in a while the conductor steps in to inquire how I feel. He's very solicitous. I'm trying hard not to cry. Maybe if I write it all down, I'll experience some relief from my crushing burden.

Last night at eleven, Sylwin telephoned from Switzerland. The whole house was already fast asleep. Only the nurse, the attendant, and I were still sitting up with Father. Sylwin asked me to leave at once because the war was expected to start any moment. I replied that he was exaggerating, that it wasn't certain at all, and that anyway Father was on his deathbed so I couldn't leave him. Sylwin insisted that Father can live at most only a few days, while I have no right to risk being separated from Anetka and him by the war. When he failed to convince me, Anetka came up to the telephone and sobbed into it: "Mother, please come right away. Don't leave us alone; please, Mother." That was too much for me. I told her I'd leave on the first train I could get.

I put down the receiver. Then I was overcome with such an attack of despair that I had to run out into the garden, not to awaken the guests with my weeping.

Never have I suffered such anguish before. What have you done? I kept asking myself. Are you going to leave your dying father because your husband and child summon you? Toward whom is your responsibility greater? I reasoned with myself that my husband and child come first, that Father will be gone in just a few days. But I knew that I was rationalizing this way because I was suddenly seized with an even more stabbing fear that I might be separated from Sylwin and Anetka, that I might not be able to get out in time.

I walked into Father's room. He opened his eyes and recognized me. It seemed to me there was anxiety in the look he gave me. He'd been unable to speak for several days but he communicated with me by means of his eyes. Putting on a smile, I quietly told him everything was all right and that he should go back to sleep, but Father continued to watch me anxiously. Kneeling at his bedside, I prayed silently in an agony of fear and despair. Dear God, please take Father away, I want to go before it is too late. Father's glance rested on me a few moments more and then he fell into a coma again. I kissed his hands, tore myself away from the bed, and ran out of the room. The nurse and the attendant escorted me into the drawing room. I was sobbing wildly.

It was midnight when I telephoned Tadeusz to drive down for me. Will God forgive me my terrible sin? I should confess it and ask absolution. At least let it be entrusted to my diary. Nothing will ever wipe out the guilt I feel at having deserted my father. As long as I live that scar will remain a part of me.

East Prussia Will Be Ours!

Berlin, much later. I'm writing this in the Anhalter Bahnhof restaurant, waiting for the train to Switzerland. For lack of anything better to do in this swastika-bedecked station, I'm setting down my impressions of the trip across Germany.

At Zbaszyn on the Polish-German frontier it developed that I was the sole woman not only in the car, but on the whole train. Soon the compartment was filled with frontier officials, who had nothing to do in the empty train and were glad of an opportunity to chat with me while the train stood in the station its allotted time. "You see, Mrs. Strakacz," one of them said, "absolutely no one is going out of Poland. The war will break out any minute. This may be the last train to have left Warsaw for Berlin."

"We can understand your departure," another chimed in, "after all you should be with your husband."

"Tell Paderewski we're prepared for war. We'll show the Germans! That we will!"

"Oh, yes," the others took him up, "we'll get East Prussia, too. Just tell that to Paderewski. Give him our regards, won't you, and tell him to come back after the war. We love him, we'll welcome him here at Zbaszyn."

I started crying in earnest, listening to these good western Poles. They consoled me, kissing my hands and shedding tears along with me like big children. "Don't cry, we understand you, it's not your fault that you have to leave Poland. Your place is with your husband, with Paderewski. East Prussia will be ours now," they repeated stubbornly. The train slowly left the station. I ran to the washroom, dashed cold water on my face, put on some powder and sat calmly waiting for German Neu Bentschen.

In spite of myself I felt a light shiver go through me when a fat burly German in uniform walked into my compartment. He recognized me, saying, "Ah, you are here again? You are going to Switzerland, to Paderewski?" I was flabbergasted. Never had I told anybody at a German frontier that I had anything to do with Paderewski.

The Friedrich Strasse depot in Berlin was hung from ceiling to floor with tremendous swastika banners. There was such a mob, mostly army men with swastika armbands, in the huge station that I could barely follow the porter.

Having seen Berlin today, I'm one hundred per cent sure

war will come. The streets are jammed with lorries transporting soldiers, and the Anhalter station is just as packed with the military. Civilians are a rare sight indeed. Waitresses have replaced the waiters in the restaurant here. The city is fairly seething with feverish excitement. Every few steps you can hear enthusiastic cries of self-confidence: "In Danzig for Christmas!" "See you in Danzig!"

While in Poland it was "East Prussia will be ours. . . ."

Riond Bosson—August 28, 1939. A telegram came from Warsaw: Father died yesterday, Sunday, at 10 P.M.

3

War

This Sore Trial

Riond Bosson — September 1, 1939. War! Germany has attacked Poland! That was the first thing we heard over the radio this morning. Although we'd been expecting war to break out for the past several days, it was a terrific shock just the same. In spite of the early hour, Sylwin hurried to the President to convey the bad tidings. He came back in a dither, and dashed upstairs again to listen to further broadcasts. We followed him to Leniutka's room, which has the only radio set in the house, as Paderewski never listens to the radio.

Somebody suggested that Leniutka bring the radio downstairs. Since we spend the better part of the day in the dining room, we'd be able to listen to the communiques without interruption. When the President came down for luncheon, Sylwin asked whether we could plug the radio into the dining room so that we might listen to the news flashes. The President's unhesitating reply was a terse "Very well."

We lunched in silence. We still couldn't believe that the grim tragedy of war is stalking our country and that while we were listlessly consuming our noonday meal in the quiet of this Swiss home, Warsaw and so many other Polish cities were being leveled by enemy bombs. My throat tightened when I heard a radio announcer mention towns, villages, and airfields that had suffered bombardment.

Paderewski listened attentively to the radio, offering no comment. When the afternoon mail was brought in, he eagerly plunged into it, as if relieved that he wouldn't have to hear the radio's heartbreaking announcements for at least a little while.

All day we listened to the tragic news bulletins, and as we listened, our hearts sank. For the first time since I've known Paderewski, there was no bridge after dinner. It didn't even occur to anyone to suggest it. Sylwin only laid out one game of solitaire after another in front of the President to take his mind off the horrible news pouring in over the radio.

Late at night the President rose from the table and slowly made his way into the card room where there are photographs of Mme. Paderewska and his son Alfred. It was a long time before he came out. We knew he was praying amidst the likenesses of those nearest to him, seeking in prayer the strength to withstand this sore trial which Providence has visited upon him.

September 4, 1939. England declared war on Germany at 11 A.M. yesterday, while France entered the conflict at 4 P.M. This news gave us a lift. If England and France have come to Poland's assistance, Germany must lose the war.

Here in Switzerland everybody is calm because the people are convinced Switzerland will remain neutral the way she did during the last war. Nonetheless, Switzerland declared a general mobilization the day after the Germans invaded Poland.

The day mobilization was announced, Anetka had gone to Lausanne as usual to attend the lectures at the University. She did not show up for lunch. The President, generally the first to worry when one of us is late, reassured us, blaming her absence on the great mobilization activity. Switzerland, he said, is a country in which mobilization produces immediate results. Each reserve officer and soldier keeps his uniform as well as his side-arms at home. As soon as mobilization is announced, the Swiss men of military age stop whatever they happen to be doing, go home, don their uniforms and proceed to the nearest railroad station in full military regalia. This radically changes the appearance and spirit of the whole country. But, the President added, only a highly developed democracy like Switzerland and a nation so completely trustworthy as the Swiss can afford to maintain such a unique system.

The Swiss government's foresight is surprising. This highly industrialized country has always had to import vast quantities of foodstuffs. The war and its attendant dislocations in the neighboring countries will naturally interfere with further imports. Hence, the federal government appealed to the population to buy and hoard for a rainy day at least a two-month supply of imperishable food. Those unable to meet the cost of these unplanned-for purchases were promised a government loan repayable when the supplies begin to be consumed. Thanks to this novel decree, space is being made in the shops for new stocks, which are hurriedly being brought in from abroad.

September 8, 1939. Switzerland's mobilization of horses lasted several days. The park of Riond Bosson was selected as the canton of Vaud's headquarters for this quadruped mobilization.

Our dining room windows command a full view of the park, which must be one of the largest private parks in Switzerland. Its inviting lawn completely disappeared from sight under the army of horses brought here from the entire canton.

Hundreds upon hundreds of strangers have passed through the park, and yet I didn't see a single broken branch in the orchard where the trees hang heavy with ripe fruit. I don't think any of the visitors even reached for these enticing apples and pears. The maturity of a society shows best in times of great crises. It's pretty evident that Swiss civilization rests on firm ground even in the face of the threat of invasion of this beautiful land. Never until today have I appreciated the rare degree of culture and respect for the rights of others which characterize the Swiss nation.

September 17, 1939. We had become somewhat accustomed to the tragic reports brought daily by the radio, but today's news hit us with the force of a thunderbolt. Was it possible? After all, Poland had a nonaggression pact with Russia, and we should never have to expect an attack from this quarter. Recovering from the impact of the first German blow, the Polish army had been regrouped, and there was hope that the German steam-roller would be halted in Eastern Poland long enough to permit the Western allies to invade Germany and compel her to withdraw part of her forces from Poland. Now, Russia has struck a bleeding Poland in the back and hope has been dashed.

We have a big radio in the house now. The President acceded to Sylwin's plea to have one installed in the dining room. We take turns listening to the news broadcasts, hoping against hope a joyous flash will inform us that the tide of ill fortune has been stemmed. Instead, each hour brings fresh tales of defeat. Contact with Poland is scanty; we hear reports of bloody battles in various parts of the country and we are told the government has left Warsaw and is somewhere near the Roumanian frontier.

You would think the President barely tolerates the radio, engrossed as he is in the newspapers all day, but we discovered he hears everything anyhow. Talking with Elizabeth Crafts at dinner today, he surprised us by repeating several news items which had not yet been reported in the papers and which he consequently must have heard over the radio. Dear Elzbietka often comes over from Lausanne to share our worries. Today she mentioned that the United States government has urged all American citizens to go home.

September 24, 1939. Three days ago when the telephone rang during dinner, a ray of hope filtered through the deluge of grim news. It was General Sikorski calling from the Lausanne railroad station. We pushed our chairs back in a flurry of excitement. Even the President forgot the cane upon which he has come to depend. A few minutes later we were driving to Lausanne to pick up the General.

The meeting of the President and the General moved us deeply. To see these two great Poles face each other with the realization that their lifework lay in ruin, to see them so choked up by emotion that they could not utter a word of greeting to each other, was an unbearably painful thing.

On the way back to Riond Bosson, the General launched into an account of his recent experiences. Owing to political intrigues, General Sikorski, relieved of his command, failed to receive a new assignment. As war drove on, he tried in vain to report to the Commander-in-Chief, Marshal Rydz-Smigly. Trying to catch up with the Marshal, General Sikorski made his way from burning Warsaw to Lwow and then on to the Roumanian border, which he crossed on the seventeenth. It is his belief that following the Soviet stab in the back, military resistance on Polish soil will soon crumble. But he doesn't think that should be the end of the fight. He's for assuring the legal continuity of the Polish government outside the frontiers of the occupied country and for organizing an armed force abroad to battle for Poland's freedom. France seems to him the natural base for these operations and one of the first things he said was that he would proceed to Paris just as soon as he made sure of Paderewski's support. The President has now again become a figure of the highest authority not only to Poles but to our allies as well. Road-weary and physically exhausted though he was, the General radiated optimism and energy.

Sikorski was here only three days because he was anxious to get to Paris and start work at once. There was no need for the two statesmen to harmonize their views; their close friendship and co-operation within the last few years resulted in a complete unanimity of outlook. Paderewski assured the General of his wholehearted support in all the latter's endeavors. His poor health precludes his going to Paris just now to head the new work, but he appointed Sylwin his liaison man and plenipotentiary in dealing with the General. Sylwin is supposed to leave for Paris the day after tomorrow.

Not until Sikorski was departing did I muster the courage to inquire about Mrs. Sikorska and their daughter, Zosia. He answered briefly that the last time he'd heard from them, they had still been in Warsaw.

September 27, 1939. We live through some very difficult moments when we listen to the broadcasts of Warsaw's radio station, which is still functioning in the besieged city. Nobody here deludes himself into thinking the capital can still be saved. We can only pray for the lives of those who are now defending not so much the soil of Poland as her honor. Battles are still raging on the Hel Peninsula and in southern Poland, but Hitler evidently knows that our western allies cannot undertake an offensive, because he continues to use his entire army and air force in liquidating what's left of the dog-tired Polish army.

Riond Bosson has become a mecca for the human flotsam cast adrift by the catastrophic events in Poland. There is a steady stream of arrivals from Poland who managed to cross over into Hungary and Roumania and are now headed west. Professor S. Stronski (a former editor of *Rzeczpospolita* and a member of Parliament), Professor S. Kot of the Jagiellonian University, and Strasburger, a former cabinet member, all stopped here in transit. We've also played host to several diplomats who'd been accredited to the Polish government. They all expect to keep their posts if a new Polish government is organized in France.

The President is indefatigable. He sees everybody in spite of his obvious exhaustion and fatigue.

September 29, 1939. The Germans are entering Warsaw today. I doubt whether we shall ever forget the nightmare of this past week. The voice of Warsaw's Mayor Starzynski, exhorting the population to hold out and at the same time calling for relief of the burning city, echoed throughout the dining room in which we sat with Paderewski, following with bated breath the final act of this horribly tragic yet heroic defense of Warsaw.

An even more terrifying impression was made upon us by the unemotional voices of the radio announcers giving factual communiques on the fighting in the various sectors of un-yielding Warsaw. We found it hard to believe that at a time when the encircled and blazing capital was being subjected to the furious pounding of Germany's concentrated heavy artillery, the broadcasting staff of Warsaw's radio station carried on with its peacetime efficiency and calm. Increasingly often the programs ended with the playing of the Polish national anthem. It was as if Warsaw sensed that a long time would elapse before this anthem would again be heard over Polish air waves.

And then came the fateful day when the announcer informed his radio listeners that he was interrupting his broadcast because the Germans were already storming the building and would take over the station any minute. The strains of *Poland Is Not Yet Lost* followed, to be abruptly broken off in the middle. We don't know whether the brutal hand of the enemy pulled the switch or whether the station was hit by a German shell. In the deafening silence that fell upon our ears, we sat mute and immobile. Only the President nervously raised his hand as if wishing to hide the two tears that slowly coursed down his cheeks. We sat there staring at the radio and none of us could bring himself to get up and shut off the current. No one wanted to throw the first handful of earth into the open grave.

In vain my mind tries to pierce this black curtain of silence. What happened to my dear brother Tadeusz? What about all my relatives and friends? Is my house among the burning buildings of my martyred, beloved Warsaw?

Poland Shall Not Die

October 1, 1939. Paderewski's September 23rd appeal to the civilized world, protesting against the invasion of Poland, has made a profound impression everywhere. But the President has not limited himself to this public action. He is busy contacting his powerful and influential friends. Letters and telegrams are pouring out of Riond Bosson to the far corners of the earth. I can only marvel at the inexhaustible store of energy and initiative which the President seems to have at his command. In his desire to see Poland get justice, he would like to stir up the whole world.

A few days ago lunch was two and a half hours late, but even Mrs. Wilkonska stopped complaining when she found out what it was all about. The President was writing a long telegram to Gandhi in India. Paderewski and Gandhi have never met, but they are both national leaders who stand above their governments and need no diplomatic envoys to exchange messages.

October 4, 1939. The war news is changing from bad to worse, depressing not only everybody at Riond Bosson but also our friends in Switzerland. The American colony here is winding up its affairs and returning to the United States. Elzbietka is one of the last to leave. Even though her family had been insisting that she come back, she'd remained because her affection for the President and her friendship for us prompted her to stay with us in our hour of sorrow. Today, however, she came to tell us that she has finally given in to the urgent pleas of her relatives and with a heavy heart will sail for New York on October 10th. Elzbietka consoles us and herself that the President will surely come to America.

October 5, 1939. Sylwin returned today after a week's stay in Paris. He brought back a lot of interesting details about the formation of the new Polish government there. When Sylwin arrived in the French capital, he found the list of members of the forthcoming Polish Cabinet had already been drawn up. Professor Stanislaw Stronski was slated to become Prime Minister, while General Sikorski was to receive the posts of Minister of War and Commander-in-Chief of the Polish Armed Forces. Even though Sikorski had established with Paderewski that he would assume the premiership, he later yielded to his colleagues' argument that should he, a military man, become head of the government, such a step might be construed in Poland and abroad as an undemocratic militarization of the new regime. Fears were expressed that England and, particularly, France might react unfavorably to such an appointment.

Arriving at the Hotel du Danube where all discussions linked with the formation of the government had taken place, Sylwin found the group of future Cabinet members awaiting the return of General Sikorski, who had gone to President Raczkiewicz to present the prepared Cabinet list for approval. Acting on instructions from Paderewski, Sylwin told them he could not convey Paderewski's acceptance of the Cabinet as constituted in Paris. It was, he said, a violation of the understanding concluded between Paderewski and the General at Riond Bosson. Paderewski has nothing personal against Professor Stronski, but he feels that in the present crisis, Sikorski is irreplaceable as Prime Minister. Sylwin's declaration naturally evoked consternation.

Stronski himself found a way out of the delicate situation by unhesitatingly withdrawing his candidacy in favor of Sikorski. Just then Sikorski entered the room, having, of course, no idea as to what had transpired a few minutes earlier. He announced that President Raczkiewicz had approved the entire Cabinet list and that the new ministers would be sworn in two hours later. When the new circumstances were explained to him, he was clearly taken aback, but he was touched by Paderewski's confidence in him. However, Sikorski preferred not to participate in solving the unexpected dilemma, and all further talks were held without him. Because of Stronski's good will and patriotic stand, it was not too difficult to settle the issue. Stronski became vice-premier and Sikorski was made premier. There were no shifts in the rest of the Cabinet. Professor Stronski was entrusted with the task of going to President Raczkiewicz to tell him about the change and obtain his consent to it. Everything went off smoothly and the new government was sworn in that same day, with only a slight delay occasioned by the preparation of a new nominating decree.

It later developed that this solution had pleased everyone. There can be no doubt that Sikorski is the best man to unite all camps and get the backing of his compatriots in Poland and outside the country. Paderewski's prestige makes it pretty certain that no voices of protest will be raised against a government which enjoys his absolute support.

Simultaneously with the formation of a new Polish Government, President Raczkiewicz, General Sikorski, and Paderewski entered into an agreement of close co-operation. All basic decisions regarding the reconstruction of Poland's independence and the general policy of the government are to be passed upon first by this highest triumvirate.

Paderewski listened to Sylwin's report with unconcealed satisfaction and congratulated him on the success of his mission.

I also learned that Sikorski offered Sylwin the post of Under-Secretary of State in the Presidium of the Cabinet, which would have given Paderewski the opportunity of direct participation in the government's work, but Sylwin couldn't accept the flattering proposition because he regards his service at Paderewski's side as his primary duty. Sikorski saw the reasonableness of his arguments, but stressed that he counted on Sylwin's co-operation in some capacity which would enable him to remain with Paderewski.

October 17, 1939. Sylwin is back from Paris again. He now spends the better part of each week there. Sikorski placed a room at the Hotel Regina at his permanent disposal, where he resides and where the headquarters of the Government and the Supreme Command are located. He surprised us all by returning a "Minister Plenipotentiary and Government Delegate to the League of Nations." Sikorski kept his word and named Sylwin to a post which he can accept without leaving Paderewski. Sylwin's constant trips to Paris will now be augmented by excursions to Geneva. Mrs. Wilkonska's frightened comment was: "Won't Sylwin ever be home any more?"

The President was especially pleased by the appointment because he held the same post for a year after he left Poland in 1920.

October, 1939. My own tragedy has been added to that of my country. I learned that on September 24th on Jasna Street in Warsaw, my brother, Senator Tadeusz Karszo-Siedlewski, was wounded in the abdomen by a fragment of a German grenade and that he died in St. Roch's Hospital on September 26th. He was buried in a public square on Krakowskie Przedmiescie. This happened during the heaviest bombardment of the city, when the dead were no longer being buried in the cemeteries but in squares and streets of the city itself.

November 4, 1949. I received a postcard which created quite a stir because it brought us our first news from a German war-prisoner camp. Mr. K., whom I knew from Warsaw, reports he is a prisoner of war and asks for ski boots, socks, sport shirts, chocolate, coffee, tea, etc. When I showed the card to the President, he read it carefully and said: "We must send him a package at once." After lunch Leniutka and I rode into town, bought everything that might be of use to Mr. K. and made it up into an impressive package. Tomorrow we will mail it.

Paris — November 22, 1939. Sylwin goes to Paris just about every week to confer with General Sikorski on behalf of the President. This time I came along because I have some things to take care of. Riond Bosson has become a regular Polish relay post office. Everybody in Poland knew Paderewski's address and when postal service between the warring countries was suspended, friends and strangers alike began to write in care of the President, requesting him to trace their relatives and deliver the message. Leniutka and I have taken over this work and we had to start a filing system to keep from getting lost in this avalanche of letters. I expect to come across a great many Polish refugees in Paris about whose fate I'll be able to notify their families in Poland.

I've already met many people I knew in the good old days. They all ask the same questions: How is Paderewski? Is he still vigorous? When will he come to Paris?

November 29, 1939. I've settled the matter of greatest importance to me. The Polish Red Cross has agreed to help us locate those persons in France about whom we receive inquiries.

Riond Bosson — December 10, 1939. Today the President gave a luncheon for the Polish delegation to the League of Nations Assembly. Mr. Gralinski, Vice-Minister of Foreign Affairs and head of the delegation (Sylwin in his capacity of permanent government delegate to the League is his deputy), Mr. Gwiazdoski, and Mr. Wszelaki all came. The President receives a daily report of the League's deliberations from Sylwin. Once he even went to Geneva himself and heard Mr. Gralinski speak.

Back from Geneva, Paderewski shared his impressions with us. His criticism was scathing. The President complained bitterly that the spirit of the ideals of President Wilson had obviously abandoned the magnificent palace of the League of Nations. The League has become a marketplace for political horsetrading, a passive tool in the hands of the great states. Her decisions are influenced by the pressure of temporary expediency and the selfish interests of the great powers. Under such circumstances it is even difficult to talk of any moral authority exerted by the League. The smaller nations have completely lost hope that with such a perversion of the League's rôle they will find in her a defender of or a fighter for international justice. According to Paderewski, the present Assembly offers the most glaring proof of the League's complete decline and of her surrender of those ideals which her founders had set for her.

Here, said Paderewski, the League of Nations was meeting at the moment of Soviet Russia's aggression against defenseless Finland. At the same time she was faced with a recent similar aggression against Poland by Hitler, an international crime in which Stalin was a partner. Now, the League of Nations, or to be exact, the government delegates making up the League's Assembly, use every available means of exerting pressure upon the Polish delegation, including the threat of denying it the right to be heard, to keep the League from condemning Hitler's aggression against Poland and incurring the wrath and vengeance of the "powerful" dictator. Their fear is so great that they forced Minister Gralinski to submit to censorship the speech he was supposed to make! He may criticize the Soviet Union all he pleases, but Hitler may not even be mentioned.

Paderewski spoke of this as a man who after co-operating in the building of a temple of world peace was now seeing the edifice crumble under his very eyes:

"I can understand the anxiety of small states that border on Germany," he said. "They are afraid to give Hitler even the shadow of a pretext for a new aggression. What naïveté! Hitler will not need a pretext if his plans call for further expansion. But what I cannot understand," here Paderewski made a characteristic gesture with his hand, "is the stand of England and France, who are at war with Germany. Should they, too, fear Hitler?" Paderewski bowed his head in thought and added: "How fortunate for him that President Wilson has not lived to see this ignominy."

Paderewski summed up our discussion of the League today by unexpectedly uttering a sentence in English: "The League of Nations—dishonorably discharged!"

December 24, 1939. Christmas—sadder than ever this year. Each of us is inwardly in mourning, the tortured thoughts of each go out to his loved ones back home. What will Christmas be like in occupied Poland?

Still, because of the President and Mrs. Wilkonska, we try to keep up appearances. A Christmas tree, the usual ex-

change of gifts, and the Christmas Eve meal with the traditional hay underneath the snowy tablecloth—none of these
was skipped.

Saddled with political burdens and responsibilities though
the President has become, he didn't deviate one whit from
custom, remembering everything and everybody. One week
before the holidays, he made his regular visit to his old friend
Jacques Schwob's jewelry store in Lausanne to get presents
for all of us—costly ones at that. In previous years he was
wont to run these errands "in great secrecy." This time,
however, braving the President's dissatisfaction, Sylwin
walked in with him to try to prevail upon Paderewski to
select less expensive gifts in view of his difficult financial
situation. Sylwin's good intentions were just that.

Our Christmas Eve supper wasn't a very joyful affair,
though we all exerted ourselves to cheer the President up.

Paris—January 21, 1940. This time quite a group of us came
to Paris. The President is accompanied by Sylwin, Franciszek,
and myself, as well as by Mrs. Wilkonska and Leniutka. We
came here to witness the inaugural session of the Polish National Council. It's a foregone conclusion that Paderewski
will be elected president of the National Council.

How different from those in peacetime was our departure
from Riond Bosson! The President, who had always enjoyed
the prospect of going on a trip, this time left without enthusiasm, motivated solely by his sense of duty. Moreover,
he was exceptionally tired because he had spent several
nights in a row writing his address. Since the National
Council is our Parliament-in-exile, Paderewski's speech is
supposed to express the feelings and aims of the whole Polish
nation, condemned to silence as a result of the country's
occupation by the enemies.

Whenever I approached Paris, the city of light, in bygone
years, I could always tell we were near our journey's end by
the powerful glow of a million lights reflected against the
evening sky. Now as our train sped through the outskirts of

the French capital, there was only inky darkness outside. Parisian taxi drivers performed miracles of skill, passing each other by sheer instinct in the pitch-dark streets.

Even though all the windows in our hotel are blacked out, there is a dim-out inside. Here and there a single lamp swathed in a heavy blue material burns feebly. It was strangely cheerless and cold when we came in—the central heating system was turned off. The President, always sensitive to the cold, sat down in his drawing room in his fur coat, with no apparent intention of taking it off. In the meantime, Sylwin and Franciszek scouted around for some wood to build a fire in the fireplace. They soon showed up with an armful of laths and in a few minutes the President had some warmth in his room.

Paris—January 22, 1940. Thank God today is over. The telephone has been ringing without interruption since early morning. Everybody has been asking for the President, everybody wants to be presented to him. This is, of course, impossible, so Sylwin has had to make excuses with particular care not to offend anyone. General Sikorski came only for lunch while Wladyslaw Raczkiewicz, President of the Republic of Poland, called upon Paderewski in the afternoon.

January 23, 1940. How can I ever forget this day? So many things happened, I don't know where to begin.

Sylwin ran such a high temperature, he hardly slept a wink. Good Dr. Jaworski was waiting for him at the crack of dawn. He'd noticed how sick Sylwin looked upon our arrival in Paris, but he had not had a chance to examine him before because Sylwin was so busy. This morning Dr. Jaworski made a diagnosis of pneumonia and while Sylwin was hurriedly shaving in the bathroom, he administered an injection of "avistil," an anti-pneumonia serum of his own invention.

My deep uneasiness was somewhat allayed by Dr. Jaworski's solemn assurance that the serum would really work.

The session of the National Council was a memorable one in every respect. In the festively decorated ballroom of the Polish Embassy, two armchairs were placed at one end for President Raczkiewicz and General Sikorski. Behind them sat the members of the government. At the opposite end of the room stood an armchair for Paderewski; in front of the armchair was a small table and next to it a chair for Sylwin. Running down both sides of the room were armchairs seating the members of the National Council, and closing the rectangle. Outside the rectangle, under each wall, stood rows of chairs for the chosen few who had received an invitation to attend this historic ceremony.

When we arrived at the Embassy, the huge room was already full. It's hard to describe the enthusiasm with which the entrance a few minutes later of President Raczkiewicz, General Sikorski, and Paderewski was greeted. Everybody rose and it was a long time before the Bravos and hand-clapping subsided.

President Raczkiewicz spoke first. Then Paderewski was called upon to speak. In a spontaneous gesture all those present got up from their seats and watched the venerable figure on whom his painful experiences and the labor of these last few months have left their mark. He rose from his armchair with obvious effort, leaning heavily against the table, and started to speak in a rather quiet voice. My heart contracted for fear he might not have the strength to get to the end.

But as Paderewski spoke, as his audience responded to virtually every sentence he uttered with a storm of applause, the President's voice began to grow stronger and acquire volume and power. At such dramatic moments, the tension in the hall was almost unbearable. Paderewski sensed it and drew his strength from it.

All of a sudden, Paderewski's voice half-broke, as if he had run out of breath, and only a stifled sob rent the air — he was talking to Poland now. Over the heads of the assembled, his voice caught the vibrations of our hearts and traveled on to those who have not succumbed to their enemies, who are still fighting for freedom and for a joint victory:

"I turn to you, our beloved Brethren. Across the trench lines, across the land of our foes, my voice speeds on toward you, bringing you a steadfast faith in our strength, faith in the inflexibility of our sacred rights to our land, faith in ultimate victory. That voice cannot be silenced by the violence of the barbarous oppressor because it lives in the soul of each one of you. That profound faith in God and in Poland gives you the strength to survive the period of bondage and will permit you to live to see the day of our ultimate joint triumph.

"Poland shall not die, our martyred Brethren, she shall not die. She shall live for all eternity mighty and glorious — for you, for us and for all mankind!"

Paderewski spoke as one inspired. His spirit had fled somewhere into space, it had torn itself away from the reality of the hall and that distinguished audience. Paderewski was indeed talking to all Poland across the trench lines and the land of our foes. . . .

His listeners were aware of the exceptional character of this scene. As soon as the first words of this appeal to our country fell on their ears, they jumped up and remained standing with bowed heads in silent prayer.

Paderewski had finished. For a minute a deathly silence settled over the room. Then a tempest of applause broke the mood of lofty concentration. Thoroughly exhausted, Paderewski sank heavily into his armchair.

General Sikorski was the last speaker. He presented before the National Council the Government's proposed program of work. In his address Sikorski paid tribute to Paderewski, saying he "personified not only a deep political sense, but also the noblest things brought forth by the earth — an unequaled spirit of sacrifice and the purest love of country."

Riond Bosson — January 31, 1940. We got back from Paris yesterday. The President is well, but completely worn out.

Sylwin, whose life Dr. Jaworski saved by means of his miraculous injection, has caught another cold. I do hope it's not pneumonia again. Leniutka and myself are fagged out; we are bundles of nerves but have to hold on to ourselves to maintain an atmosphere of good cheer around the President.

Paderewski spent the entire week following the National Council session in conversations with the members of the government and the representatives of the parties in the National Council.

Dr. Jaworski also took advantage of the President's presence to administer a further series of injections which are doing the President a world of good. But there was one scene — a brief one — which saddened me. One evening as we were all relaxing in the sitting room, the President remarked that Paris makes him feel depressed. To that I replied that the war will end some day and Paris will regain its luster. And the President responded: "Yes, but I won't see that Paris any more."

Our departure from Paris also made a deep impression on me. As we rode down the blacked-out streets, the President kept looking through the car window as if anxious to fix in his mind the beautiful historic buildings along the Seine River. When we passed the Cathedral of Notre Dame, he even turned around in his seat and peered through the back window until the cathedral faded out of sight. It occurred to me that the President's remark about never seeing Paris again had not been an idle one, but expressed his real conviction.

Our train was standing on a remote track and the long walk tired the President. We finally settled ourselves in our compartment. Only Sylwin remained outside on the darkened platform chatting with a group of close friends who had come to bid the President good-bye. Suddenly Sylwin came in to tell the President that some twenty Polish officers had just arrived on the platform out of breath. They'd been misdirected to another track, but they'd give anything to see Paderewski. The President said he simply didn't have the strength to go outside again. At that Sylwin opened the window in our compartment. A mighty cheer rent the air: Long live Poland! Long live President Paderewski! The effect on the President was electric. He jumped up from his seat and replied with a cheer of his own: Long live the Polish Army! As if at a given command, the officers drew themselves up and saluted. Just then the train slowly started moving. The President leaned out of the window and stretched his hand toward them in a gesture of benediction. We all had tears in our eyes.

Gandhi's Reply

February 3, 1940. The President came down for lunch today in an exceptionally good mood. You could see he was very pleased about something. During the meal he told us he'd received a reply from Gandhi. He had appealed to the Mahatma to take a stand in the matter of the aggression against Poland and he had asked his moral support of the Poles' struggle for freedom. Gandhi's stand unreservedly condemned the attack on Poland and expressed the hope that justice would triumph and Poland would recover her just rights.

[The following statement was issued by Mahatma Gandhi on September 9, 1939, in response to an appeal made by Mr. Paderewski. *S. S.*

"Of course my whole heart is with the Poles in the unequal struggle in which they are engaged for the sake of saving their freedom. But I am painfully conscious of the fact that my word carries no power with it. I wish I had the power to stop this mad destruction that is going on in Europe. I belong to a country that has lost its independence and is struggling to be free from the yoke of the greatest Imperialist Power on earth. It has adopted the unique method of non-violence to regain its lost freedom. Though the method has proved its efficacy to an extent, the goal seems far off. All that I can, therefore, send to the brave Poles is my heartfelt prayer for the early termination of their fearful trial and for the grant of the required strength to bear the suffering whose very contemplation makes one shudder.

"Their cause is just and their victory certain.

For God is always the upholder of justice."]

I didn't quite understand what far away India had to do with the Polish cause, or how her stand could affect the fate of Poland. So I screwed up my courage and asked the President about it. His explanation enlightened me concerning the importance of the question. It seems that some doubt had existed regarding India's attitude in this war. Its animosity toward England, which German propaganda has been seeking to exploit for its own ends, had aroused fear that in this conflict of two worlds, India's sympathies might be transferred to the camp of our enemies. India's co-operation in this war is of the utmost importance to the British Empire and by the same token, to us. Moreover, Soviet propaganda has been tremendously active in India. Russia, as Hitler's ally, not only has been backing his plans with the force of her propaganda, but she has, in the case of Poland, had her own ulterior motive, having signed the pact of partition and plunder of Polish territory with Hitler. Hence, India has been exposed to a double-edged anti-Polish pressure. That's why it was so important to keep India from succumbing to that pressure. Gandhi's stand settles the problem in Poland's favor and will permit England to count on the loyal aid of this very valuable member of the Empire.

A Miracle Has Taken Place

March 8, 1940. One thing I learned in Paris was that a rumor was being circulated among the Polish colony regarding the escape of Mr. K. from a German prison camp to England, thanks to the pair of shoes he received from Mrs. Strakacz.

March 10, 1940. It's incredible! A telegram came from Monsignor Kaczynski today advising us that the prelate would be in Morges in two days! How did he get out of Poland? Meanwhile we're glad to know he's alive. We hadn't heard of him since the war began.

March 16, 1940. The Monsignor stopped at Riond Bosson only two days. It's difficult to describe our emotions at the sight of the prelate. A shadow of his former self, he's just skin and bones. The President was deeply moved. He clasped Monsignor K.'s hands in a long and hearty handshake. Monsignor told us he'd been wounded in the head and spine on September 21st during the fiercest German air raid on Warsaw. Because he was bedridden, the Germans hadn't arrested him and he was able to leave the hospital secretly. Along with others he plunged right into underground activity against the occupants. That's when the first secret civilian and military authority was set up. After the congress of the political parties, which formed the underground movement, was held in Cracow on March 4, 1940, Monsignor K. was delegated to go to Paris and communicate to General Sikorski's government the decisions of the congress and the program for future activity inside Poland.

The prelate stopped at Riond Bosson to visit the President and to give him the latest information. Mrs. Wilkonska is very proud and happy because when she asked him how he'd managed to get out of Poland, he told her he had her to thank. Twice he bribed the Gestapo — once with a bottle of the renowned Riond Bosson "white Kirsch," and another time with a can of Nescafc. Both of these articles had been presented to the Monsignor by Mrs. Wilkonska, before the war, the last time he had visited Switzerland.

When Sylwin notified General Sikorski about Monsignor K.'s arrival in Switzerland, a telegram came posthaste instructing the prelate to proceed to Paris immediately.

Sorrowfully we took leave of the man who, aside from being our friend, was to us a particle of Warsaw. . . .

A Back-Breaking Job

March 25, 1940. I'm snowed under by the mail I have to handle. Day and night I write, write, write until I feel like a human writing machine. This past month I've penned more than eight hundred letters. It's a back-breaking job, but I've become so practised I can write letters while entertaining guests or even at table. I scribble between courses, writing on my knees. The President noticed it today and remarked: "You certainly write without let-up, on the table and under the table. You're amazing!" It was very agreeable to be be praised by the President for my work. I have to cudgel my brain for new ideas all the time. Polish servicemen in France, most of whom are complete strangers to me, ask me to write to Poland in their name. They're afraid to write themselves for fear of exposing their families to arrest or deportation to concentration camps by the Germans. This compels me to think up all sorts of between-the-lines formulations to avoid stating outright that the father, son, husband, or brother in question is in the Polish army in France, especially since the letters are supposedly written by them from Switzerland.

This intermediation of mine isn't foolproof. I probably exercise too much caution, particularly in the case of one airman (I know neither him nor his wife), for I received the following reply from the wife after I'd written her a few letters: "Darling Zuzi: When, oh, when will you stop sending me those idiotic letters? When will you finally write yourself?" We had a good laugh over this compliment! The lady evidently doesn't believe that discretion is the better part of valor if she pays so little regard to German censorship.

I've learned how to change my handwriting so the letters won't look as if the same person had written all of them. This record correspondence isn't my only occupation. Leniutka and I have formed a regular Committee on Parcels.

Whenever we get a letter with a new war-prisoner-camp address, we make up packages and send them to the Oflags and Stalags where Polish prisoners are held. It's no longer against regulations to send these packages. The President has earmarked an unlimited sum of money for this purpose. I write to each prisoner informing him of the forthcoming gift. The one thing that hurts me is that I can't write them the identity of our anonymous parcel committee. Will ever the day come when I will be able to tell each of these boys that all these packages from Switzerland came not from a committee but from a single individual — Paderewski!

Nobody has the faintest notion of how much good the President is doing, and of what vast sums he spends to salvage the remnants of the Polish army, those countless Polish fighters whose one goal is to get to France, to Sikorski's army, and resume the battle. Paderewski not only uses his contacts in the political field but also pulls every string he can privately, sending money through various channels, trying to help the Poles wherever the war has brought them. He used his connections at one of the consulates here to dispatch sufficient funds for thirty Polish officers to get out of the country where they had been held up, board a ship, and proceed to France, where all of them are already serving in the army.

How many heart-stirring letters of appreciation come to Morges from these lads! Here's a fragment of one: "Please tell Paderewski that we fought without sparing our young lives, but we had nothing to fight with. With our bare hands we charged tanks and the enemy." The President listened to this with a deeply furrowed brow.

I can't possibly do justice to Paderewski's activities in this diary. I'd have to give up my letter-writing and my parcel-packing if I wanted to write up the President as he deserves. There should be a chronicler here who would keep a day-by-day record of everything that goes on at Riond Bosson. Unfortunately, neither Sylwin nor Leniutka nor I have the time for it.

Tomorrow Sylwin and I are going to Paris again. I'm taking well over a thousand letters from Poland to our army men in France.

A New Army

Back at Riond Bosson — April 3, 1940. We got back from Paris yesterday full of wonder at General Sikorski's prodigious and tireless activity. Under his leadership a new Polish army is rising phoenix-like from its ashes. It's simply unbelievable that so many large groups of Polish officers and soldiers could have surmounted the thousand and one obstacles on their way and have reached France to report for further military duty. I've talked with many of these new arrivals and listened to their harrowing tales of escape from Roumania or Hungary on foot, in the most fantastic disguises, always one jump ahead of the Gestapo agents. The news that General Sikorski had grasped the banner of embattled Poland was the lodestar that guided them along their uncharted journey. They didn't all begin their odyssey from Roumanian or Hungarian internment camps. Many had been taken prisoners by the Russians or Germans. Very many paid for their attempted flight with their lives. Others fell by the wayside in their trek over snow-covered mountains. Still others were felled by the bullets of frontier guards. But those who have succeeded in getting through to France evoke universal admiration by virtue of their great inner strength.

Your blood congeals at the stony calm with which they enumerate their tragedies, without a word of complaint but with an almost inhuman resolve to pay their enemies back.

Another amazing development is the patriotic fervor of the Polish prewar emigrants in France. Thousands of volunteers are queuing up at recruiting centers, not only young men of draft age, but oldsters as well, longtime residents of

France. Dr. Ludwik Gout, the Warsaw surgeon who operated on Anetka and who is now on the medical board at one of the centers, told me of the tragedies that occur daily when overage or physically unfit volunteers vehemently protest against their disqualification.

If you look at it objectively, you might say a miracle has taken place. The Polish nation, attacked by both Germany and Russia and defeated in the unequal struggle, has not lost its spirit. Instead, it is continuing its fight with redoubled energy from the foreign, though friendly, soil of France. Thousands of Poland's finest men have arrived there emaciated and in rags, the horror of their experiences and contempt for death mirrored in their eyes. They have lost everything except their faith. Each keeps a holy picture, cross, or a medal bearing the image of the Virgin Mary hidden on his person, perfectly certain that the Holy Queen of the Polish Crown will lead him back safely to a free Poland. They also have unassailable faith in General Sikorski's ability to conduct them to victory and they believe Paderewski, recognized as the symbol of Poland by the world, will help President Raczkiewicz and the Polish Government-in-Exile through his mighty connections.

"What's Finessing?"

April 7, 1940. Busy as I am, I've had to take on an additional assignment, something which I've been avoiding all my life: cards! Now that we do so little entertaining, the traditional fourth at bridge is usually lacking and I have to pitch in virtually every day! I do it in order not to disrupt the President's routine and deprive him of his only means of relaxation. Of course I really don't know how to play bridge. I play against all the rules, relying more on my intuition than on reason. By standing agreement, the President and I are al-

ways partners. I do my own bidding, which the President and
Sylwin concede isn't too bad. If the President is the highest
bidder, I'm happy, because all I have to do is put out my
cards and sit tight. If my bid has won out, I don't have to
worry either, because the President examines my cards for a
few seconds, hands them back to me, and without consulting
them anymore dictates each move of mine. I still haven't
become accustomed to the President's uncanny memory. Not
once has he called the wrong card. If our opponents are
declarers, I'm in pretty much of a pickle because I often don't
know what to discard. But my intuition generally helps me
out, as witness the following amusing incident which evoked
the consternation of the President, Sylwin, and Leniutka:
Especially pleased with one particular hand of mine, the
President praised me: "You finessed beautifully that time!"
Whereupon, I asked in all innocence: "What's finessing?"

More Than Poland

April, 1940. Nobody realizes, and even I learn only later,
how ceaselessly the President is working for Poland. His
tireless political activity, designed above all to insure aid for
Poland, goes beyond national considerations. Somebody once
called Paderewski "a citizen of the world." This strikes me
as a very apt description, because Paderewski not only firmly
believes that a happy era of the brotherhood of nations will
dawn some day, that Christ's teachings of brotherly love will
triumph, and that mankind will eventually replace war and
mutual destruction by peaceful collaboration for the common
good, but he does everything in his power to bring that
moment closer. It must be this goodness of Paderewski's,
this love he feels for all humanity, which radiates from his
person, that accounts for the legion of his devoted friends
and admirers the world over. The President feels at home

in Switzerland, Italy, France, England, or the United States, because he is regarded as one of them by the peoples of these countries.

These reflections occur to me in connection with the mysterious strictly secret visit of the Italian Consul General at Lausanne, who arrived in Riond Bosson for a conversation with Paderewski. I've just found out from Sylwin that as far back as October, 1939, the President dispatched a letter to Mussolini, which Sylwin had kept secret even from me. The letter was prompted by Mussolini's speech in which Il Duce, seemingly arguing for peace, declared that "since the Polish question has been definitely settled, nothing any longer stands in the way of the conclusion of an honorable peace among the belligerents."

I remember how the President was upset and exasperated by that speech. He had been friendly with Mussolini in former days, calling upon the Italian dictator whenever he was in Rome. One of Mussolini's collaborators, Senator San Martino, President of St. Cecilia's Academy in Rome, was an old and close friend of Paderewski's. Similar ties of friendship linked Paderewski with the royal family. Until recently a portrait of Queen Elena with a dedication to the President occupied a place of honor in the Riond Bosson drawing room. These ties were strengthened by Crown Prince Umberto's marriage to Princess Marie José, daughter of the King and Queen of Belgium, whom Paderewski had known from childhood. In the light of all this, Mussolini's declaration that the partition and enslavement of Poland by Hitler and Stalin constituted a "settlement of the Polish question" was, as Paderewski expressed himself at the time, "a nail driven into Poland's coffin." What I didn't know, though, was that the President had written a letter to Mussolini.

Sylwin tells me that in his letter Paderewski categorically protested against Mussolini's statement that the German and Soviet conquest of Poland settled the Polish issue. He cited his own conviction that a world war had just begun, and that Poland's military defeat was simply a temporary set-back which did not rule out the advent of ultimate victory. Then he went on to express his faith in divine justice and his confidence that the war would end in the complete defeat of Hitler and Germany. Paderewski was aware that because of the political situation this was probably the last letter he'd be able to write directly to Mussolini. So, in the second part of the letter, mindful of the persistent rumors that Italy would enter the war on Germany's side, the President formulated the following warning:

It is rumored that Mussolini is being subjected to strong pressure from Hitler to have Italy enter the war. Paderewski warns Mussolini that Germany will lose the war. He is positive the United States will not permit Great Britain to be routed and, if the need arises, will actively come to England's defense. Ruin awaits Italy, should she suffer defeat along with Hitler. But even if Hitler were to win the war, Italy's future would not look any rosier, for a victory-drunk Hitler would not stop halfway and would most certainly reach out for the Italian regions in the north which Italy recovered from Austria after the last war. He would not rest content until Trieste became a German outlet to the Mediterranean. And he would doubtless strive to reduce what would be left of Italy to a vassal state.

By linking her fate with Hitler, Italy would ally herself with an aggressor, participating in an aggression violating all sense of justice and morality, and such a compromise with the honor of the Italian nation can only bring disaster upon her. It can never prove of the slightest advantage to the Italian people. Her history, tradition, and culture link Italy with the West and not with Germanic barbarism, to which ancient Rome succumbed. This letter is not motivated solely by Paderewski's concern for Poland. After the war a free Poland will return to the family of civilized nations and states. Paderewski is deeply anxious about the future of Italy, for which he cherishes real affection and respect as the cradle of our civilization.

The President concluded his letter with an expression of his hope that Mussolini would not break the ties of so many centuries of friendship and cultural interaction which had traditionally bound Poland and Italy.

Now, six months later, Mussolini has replied to Paderewski's letter. But he apparently feared to put his answer down in writing because the reply was verbal and limited to a few sentences which the Italian consul general read to Paderewski from a slip of paper:

Il Duce is grateful to Mr. Paderewski for the letter which he received and took under advisement. Il Duce requests Mr. Paderewski to take into consideration the difficult political situation in which Italy finds herself as a result of a war that is being waged at her doorstep. Il Duce's sentiments toward Poland and the Polish nation have not changed. Il Duce believes the war will end soon in a German victory. Italy must make sure she will have a voice when the terms of the future peace, affecting the fate of many countries, are discussed. Il Duce believes he will then be in a position to render many a service to the Polish nation, and assures the Polish people they can always count on his friendship and help. Il Duce asks Mr. Paderewski not to judge him by his words, which are often dictated by circumstances beyond his control, but by his acts, which will ever remain friendly toward Poland.

The conversation terminated with the consul's request that Paderewski treat Mussolini's statement as strictly confidential. I have jotted it down just as Sylwin, who was present at the meeting, told it to me. Sylwin also says that the President now considers Mussolini's entry into the war a certainty. Paderewski remarked sadly that Mussolini will destroy by his own hand everything he has done for the development of Italy and which in part might have atoned for the suffering that Fascism had imposed upon the Italian people. Italy will again be faced with chaos and bolshevism, she will revert to the state in which Mussolini found her at the time of his march on Rome. "I think with fear and horror that the old prophecy might come true, that no stone will be left standing in Rome and the Pope will flee from the burning Vatican over the bodies of his cardinals." The President was apparently referring to a prophecy, supposed to have been written in the Middle Ages by an anonymous monk, which had been discovered in Poland about a hundred years ago.

Painful Reality

June 6, 1940. The Swiss press is filled with stories about the heroic evacuation of British troops from Dunkirk that sounds like something out of Dante. Paderewski shares the unanimous admiration for the wonderful spirit of the British, but he's more disturbed by the realization that the abandonment of the European continent by the English presages the fall of France. Too bad Sylwin is in Paris. We didn't have any luck in cheering up the President at lunch. We couldn't even get his mind off the subject. He just sat there gloomily, saying hardly a word to anybody.

June 10, 1940. Sylwin came back from Paris today. He didn't bring much good news with him. Together with my brother Jan he watched from the balcony of our Embassy an air raid on the French capital. The President followed every word of Sylwin's report with profound interest. The battle front is now so close to Paris that the cannonade can be heard even in the daytime. It must have been decided to give Paris up without a struggle, for the streets of the capital are congested with trucks taking everything removable out of the city. Everyone who has a car and has managed to get some gasoline is fleeing Paris before the Germans. Strapped to each automobile roof is the family bedding, partially because it represents a priceless possession to people who don't know where they will make their bed tomorrow and partially to serve as additional protection against the attacks of German fliers who strafe with impunity the long lines of automobiles along French roads. Except for this feverish evacuation, Paris has become a kind of dead city. Sylwin says the people simply wander about aimlessly, looking with envy upon those fortunate enough to be leaving. Around the railroad station the jammed mass of refugees stage royal battles for each coveted foot of space on the outgoing trains. Sylwin left Paris late in the evening in the midst of a complete blackout. On the horizon he saw flash upon flash of exploding shells. Along the way many stations were in flames or a smoking heap of rubble.

Paderewski was still under the spell of this alarming news when the radio announced Mussolini's declaration of war against France. "Verily it would seem that hell has conspired to destroy mankind," said the President. And then, to my surprise, he added: "I'm sorry for Italy. The Italian nation will pay dearly for Mussolini's mistake. Apparently the cup of Fascist sins has run over and God will now mete out his punishment."

In the face of Paderewski's unshaken belief that our side will ultimately win, I felt reassured. But I must confess there is plenty of cause to plunge a person into the abyss of darkest despair.

June 17, 1940. More bad news came over the radio in a report that Marshal Petain had appealed to Hitler as "soldier to soldier" for an armistice, which is tantamount to capitulation. Paderewski was thunderstruck. Although since Sylwin's last return, following the fall of Paris, the war news had been getting progressively worse, the President's love of France, his respect for her great tradition, his faith that the threat of catastrophe would bring out the intrepid French spirit—all this had buoyed Paderewski's hope that everything was not yet lost, that France would be roused from her lethargy before it was too late, and that the French army would be reorganized along some new line of defense to fight on for its honor and its native land.

Painful reality dashed the President's hopes. I must admit, though, that I was amazed by the swiftness with which Paderewski got over his disappointment. We were all sunk in a gloomy silence when the President, without further regretful comment, began to appraise the new situation confronting the Polish Army in France. His great concern is to prevent the Polish troops from being destroyed in the French debacle and to enable them to go on fighting Hitler.

"Our boys will not surrender," he said, "they will not lay down their arms before the Germans, they will fight until the end, but the French campaign is really over. It would be folly for them to remain in France. They must be gotten out at all cost. Maybe someone in Algiers will raise aloft the banner of France which now hangs limp in mourning, maybe the French will continue the fight from North Africa. Their navy is untouched. If it could only muster up the courage for an act of defiance, it could still save the situation by evacuating the French army and our divisions. The French navy is strong enough to ward off a German invasion of North Africa for a long time." Paderewski paused. None of us dared break the silence.

A moment later, as if thinking out loud, the President asked himself a question: "What's happening to the Polish Government? Where is General Sikorski? He was at the front, but he couldn't have been caught by the Germans, could he?" It was not in our power to relieve the President's anxiety on this score.

To take his mind off these distressing questions, Mrs. Wilkonska, for the first time in her life, suggested we turn on the radio to see if there were any new developments. Sylwin began looking for a French station. He came upon the guttural voice of a German broadcasting gloatingly from

Paris. Finally we got the Lyons station. The announcer's sober voice was acquainting the French nation with the facts, calling upon the people to be calm and resigned to their fate. He reminded his listeners of the wars France had lost in the past and he exhorted them to obey Marshal Petain and General Weygand implicitly, as these French leaders have shouldered the responsibility for France's future.

There was no mention of the Polish Government or the Polish Army. The announcer concluded his communique with the statement that the British troops were being evacuated to England. Over the air waves came the strains of the *Marseillaise*. To hear this proud French anthem played under such tragic circumstances seemed so blasphemous that Leniutka, who was sitting nearest the radio, immediately turned it off. Without saying a word, Paderewski rose to his feet and laboriously walked out of the room, supporting himself on his cane. The creaking of the stairs told us he'd gone to his study. We, too, silently dispersed to our appointed tasks.

June 19, 1940. The telephone that woke us up at dawn today brought news of Polish troops crossing the Swiss border. This must be the end of the Polish army's brief but heroic fight on French soil.

We're waiting for the car. The President has instructed Sylwin to proceed to the spot, somewhere in the mountains several hours away by automobile, where the army is crossing into Switzerland, presumably to be interned. We'll be in the line of fire from the French side. Sylwin asks if I'm afraid and I answer that the only thing I'm afraid of is that my nerves will fail me when I see our routed army retreating from the field of battle.

June 20, 1940. We spent all of yesterday far up in the mountains near La Chaux de Fond close to Vervier on the French border. During the long ride through picturesque country my heart was pounding with fear at what we would find at journey's end.

But you never know. Yesterday turned out to be the proudest, most inspiring day in my life.

The last lap of our trip from the town of La Chaux de Fond was up a steep highway. Paderewski's Cadillac took the incline in its stride until it suddenly ground to a halt at the edge of a huge clearing encircled by high flat mountains. Our startled gaze took in a spectacle so unexpected and incredible in the face of the reality of the situation that our feeling of admiring amazement left no room for painful emotions. As far as the eye could see, the clearing was thickly dotted with soldiers, while far away to the left we noticed an unending procession of soldiers leading their horses down a precipitous mountain pass, a gray ribbon winding toward the clearing.

Jumping out of our car, we hastened toward our massed troops. I felt like rubbing my eyes. Was this the routed, disorganized Polish army? It looked exactly like a gigantic camp ready for a dress parade or maneuvers! Rifles neatly stacked in a row, trucks loaded sky high, ambulances, field kitchens, even horses, gleaming with a freshly groomed look, all stood in crisp military formation. Groups of soldiers were sitting in the abundant Swiss grass. Here and there someone was playing a harmonica. Others were dozing, obviously tired and heavy lidded. As we passed, they raised their eyes with interest.

Making our way through the throng, I looked in every direction on the chance I might spot a familiar face. It wasn't long before I heard my name called. I turned around in time to see Stanislaw Skarzynski running toward me. There were tears in his eyes, but he recovered quickly. His first words were: "I suppose I could write a letter from Switzerland. My wife and children have been evicted from their estate. They're in Warsaw in great poverty. Will you help me send them something?"

Stefan Sztukowski turned up next. Greeting me with emotion he asked if we had heard from the Regulskis. All around us the soldiers looked up, eyeing us and listening to our conversation. I couldn't get over their appearance.

Shaved, in clean uniforms and polished boots, if it weren't for their frightfully blood-shot eyes, one might think they had indeed returned from a military parade instead of from heavy fighting. We asked how an army could look so presentable after so many battles and after such a long forced march over formidable mountains. The officers told us that in the last eight days of fighting the Germans under horribly adverse conditions at Maiche-St. Hippolyte, Trevilliers, and Damperichaud, all they'd eaten was one tomato per person a day. Once they got into the mountainous country all officers and men dismounted and continued their journey on foot to spare their horses. Having arrived at a clearing, their first concern was to water and groom the horses and to set up the field kitchens. Then they apparently shaved.

Gradually soldiers started coming up to us and bombarding us with questions: "Where's Geneva?" "Just exactly where are we?" "Is it far to Geneva?" We were nonplussed by the repetition of this question. Our officers explained the men didn't know they were going to be interned in Switzerland. They asked about Geneva under the misapprehension that this was merely a march across Swiss territory and that they'd reenter France by way of Geneva to give the Germans hell.

We moved from group to group to talk with as many soldiers as we could. One would have liked to chat with them all. But there were some twelve thousand men in that clearing. The soldiers and officers with whom we spoke were touched by the reception accorded them by the Swiss. When the local women saw them grimy with sweat and smoke, these men related, they appeared with washbasins and soap, scrubbing the legs and washing the backs of those too exhausted to do so themselves. The Swiss angels of mercy even took the soldiers' dirty linen and promised to bring it back washed in the evening.

The Swiss authorities offered to feed the troops, but the Polish quartermaster thanked them for their generosity and set up field kitchens which are preparing a square meal for the whole division. We learned from the officers that the division brought along more stores of ammunition, weapons, and food than it had in France. It seems that the Poles picked up everything the French army, retreating in disorder, had cast aside. They had no intention of leaving anything to the Germans. It was a gigantic scavenger hunt all right: cannon, arms, bicycles, coffee, tea, and other foodstuffs which they claim can last them for two years. They've brought into Switzerland over a thousand trucks piled high with these supplies.

Sylwin inquired about General Prugar-Ketling, the commander of the division. We headed for the little house in which the General and his staff were quartered.

We greeted General Prugar-Ketling without words, too moved to speak. He warmly shook our hands and asked us to sit down. Trying to take up as little of his time as possible, we asked about points of greatest interest. We learned that our Polish troops made such a strong impression on the Swiss by crossing the border with full battle equipment and in excellent order while they were at the same time repulsing the attacking Germans, that the Swiss high command, in recognition of their military bearing and discipline, ordered the artillery regiments to deliver their cannon themselves to a special artillery park where the equipment is to be stored for the duration of the internment. Thanks to this decision the Polish army will march over a large part of Switzerland in full military dress before it is disarmed. This is the highest tribute the Swiss could have paid to the valor of the Poles.

At the conclusion of our visit the General assured us that should he receive permission from the Swiss authorities, he will not fail "to report to the President."

Returning to our car, we found a round loaf of bread with the carved inscription "POLAND 1939." I took the loaf in my hand; it was hard as a rock. Our chauffeur said some soldiers had come up and asked whose car this was. When he told them it was President Paderewski's automobile, they went away and returned with the bread and said, "Please deliver

this loaf of bread to President Paderewski as a remembrance
from Polish soldiers. Tell him it comes from Poland and has
survived all our battles with us."

The World Needs Such a Man

June 26, 1940. This past week has been so eventful I don't
know where to begin. One of us was always listening to the
radio, later relaying to the others the contradictory crumbs
of information coming out of France. The first report of
direct interest to us was that the Polish Government had
moved from Angers to Bordeaux. Then came an announce-
ment that General Sikorski had flown to England. A load fell
from our chests because we'd been very worried about him.
But why had Sikorski gone to England when the Polish Government is in Bordeaux? Paderewski resolved our doubts at
once. The General of course flew to London to prepare the
evacuation of the Polish Army to England. President Raczkiewicz and the Polish Government would probably also go
to England. Paderewski's prediction was confirmed in a
subsequent radio report, but almost simultaneously it was
announced that Sikorski had returned to France. What could
this mean, we wondered uneasily. And again, thanks either
to his intuition or to his ability to reason logically, Paderewski allayed our fears with his contention that Sikorski's return
could only mean the success of his mission in London: he
must have come back to France in order personally to supervise the evacuation of our troops. Poor Mrs. Wilkonska in-
curred the President's displeasure by remarking that it might
be so and then again it might not be. The English could have
decided that dispatching their fleet to French ports at a time
when France is in German hands would involve too great a
risk and Sikorski could have returned to his soldiers to fight
with them until the end. "You're an incurable pessimist,"

Paderewski retorted to his sister, which reproach effectively barred further discussion.

The news from France is very bad. Not only has the population accepted the capitulation, but it actually manifests joy that the war is finally over for France, without showing much concern for the way in which that war has ended. The one consolation Paderewski finds in all this mess is that the fate of France rests in the hands of Marshal Petain and General Weygand, who are oldtime friends of his. The President believes something can still be salvaged and that Petain and Weygand are the only people who might be able to do it.

What torments Paderewski most is the possible effect in Poland of the news of the German victory in France and of the liquidation of the front on the continent. Even discounting the capital made of their success by German propaganda, the fact alone that the Germans have become masters of Europe and that therefore the war will drag on for years, while the Poles will be condemned to a prolonged taste of the German yoke, must have depressed those who had never surrendered to the Germans in Poland. Their hope for a speedy liberation could have easily changed into bleak despair and discouragement. That's what the President fears most. Nevertheless, he hasn't lost his faith in the moral vigor of his nation and doesn't suppose for an instant that the Poles could have permitted even these heart-breaking developments to sway them from their fight for freedom to collaboration with the enemy.

The French defeat has not caused Paderewski's confidence in the ultimate victory of the good cause to waver. Nor has his faith been shaken by the pessimistic reaction of the press. Some newspapers are forecasting an immediate invasion of Britain and do not estimate English possibilities of defense at more than a few weeks. But Paderewski told a few Swiss friends yesterday that he was certain Hitler would lose the war because the United States simply could not afford to stand by and watch England go down. In his opinion we shall see a repetition of the history of the first world war when the

United States wished to remain neutral but was forced to enter the war by the course of events. "You'll see," the President added, "it'll be the same this time."

June 27, 1940. Today at last the tension at Riond Bosson, provoked by recent swiftly moving events, has been eased. We finally know that the Polish Government has landed in England and that President Raczkiewicz was met at the station in London by King George and the Cabinet. Paderewski is very pleased about that because he says it proves our ally, Great Britain, is treating the exiled President of Poland with the courtesy due the head of a sovereign state. When it was further reported that the evacuation of the Polish Army had been carried out successfully and that all units which had managed to fight their way through to the French ports had been shipped to England, Paderewski beamed with happiness and pride for the first time in many, many days.

His good mood could not be dispelled by a garbled report from London about the alleged resignation of General Sikorski's Cabinet and about negotiations regarding the selection of his successor. At the first news of this, Paderewski dispatched a long cablegram to President Raczkiewicz, warning him of the danger of giving the enemy even a hint of any misunderstanding between him and General Sikorski. He also sent a similar cable to Sikorski.

Discord between Raczkiewicz and Sikorski had been in evidence as early as Paris and later at Angers. But Paderewski had been the third deciding factor in the Polish political configuration at the time and had on many occasions used his influence to restore harmony. Judging by his past successes, he may again be able to heal the breach, even though it has now come out into the open.

June 29, 1940. Paderewski received a cable from Sikorski thanking him for his help in the mild government crisis and informing him that all differences between himself and President Raczkiewicz have been ironed out. Simultaneously, a cable came for Sylwin as well, instructing him to leave at once for Vichy, the new headquarters of Marshal Petain and the French Government. The Polish Embassy along with its head, Minister Feliks Frankowski, was evacuated to Spain and has hitherto been unable to get back. Pending Minister Frankowski's return, Sylwin has been temporarily appointed in charge of the Polish Embassy in Vichy.

Sylwin can't go by train because all transportation facilities are under the control of the Gestapo. Fortunately, Mr. Kollupajlo is in France, having contacted us from Toulouse and subsequently from Saint Raphael, whither the events of the military campaign brought him. Inasmuch as Mr. Kollupajlo has a car, Sylwin wired him to pick him up at the Franco-Swiss border, at Saint Gingolph in Haute Savoie. I'm supposed to take Sylwin up to the border in the Riond Bosson automobile.

Paderewski's face clouded when Sylwin showed him the telegram. It's a risky business for a Pole to travel across German-infested territory. We've heard that there is a German garrison in Lyons, a city through which Sylwin will have to pass. But the President realizes Sylwin must go to see Petain. Sikorski's wire emphasizes the importance of settling the burning question of what is to be done with Polish military units which could not be evacuated to England because they were too far away from the ports or because they were otherwise engaged at the front. The Germans are clamoring to have these men turned over to them by France. Another equally pressing problem is the fate of the Polish civilian population in France, including the former government employees who weren't able to get out in time. So Paderewski embraced Sylwin, told him to avoid unnecessary risks and to turn back if there was any danger of falling into the clutches of the Gestapo, and sat down to write a letter to Marshal Petain in which he asked the Marshal to lend his support to Sylwin in the latter's fulfillment of his mission.

July 1, 1940. I've just returned from Saint Gingolph. Before we left Riond Bosson, the President, Mrs. Wilkonska,

Leniutka, and the rest of our household came outside to see Sylwin off. When the car started, Paderewski made the sign of the cross after us.

Thanks to the courtesy of the officials on both sides of the border, the frontier-crossing formalities were over in less than five minutes. I was very glad to see Mr. Kollupajlo and asked him to stay with Sylwin all the time. I feel better after having talked with him. He laughed off my fears about Lyons, telling me the German army had occupied only the airfield. The sole difficulty may be trouble in getting gasoline which is strictly rationed in France. But the official nature of Sylwin's trip and Paderewski's letter to Marshal Petain may help procure it. They'll spend the night at Saint Gingolph and leave early in the morning, arriving in Vichy the same day.

July 7, 1940. Yesterday was quite a day. Sylwin had wired me to pick him up at Saint Gingolph at 4 P.M. I waited three hours at the border before they finally showed up. Mr. Kollupajlo remained in Saint Gingolph because he has no Swiss visa. He will wait for Sylwin, who has to return to Vichy Tuesday or Wednesday.

Sylwin's general impression of Hitler-defeated France is none too favorable. The French press, especially that published under the German occupation in Paris, outdoes itself in flattering the Germans, praising their "chivalry," their friendly attitude toward the population, the iron discipline of their army. The Germans are even credited with having started a wave of prosperity, for they invade Parisian stores and buy presents to send back home, paying the fancy prices without protest. No mention is made that France pays the Germans four hundred million francs daily as "re-imbursement for the cost of occupation" and that the Germans are spending this French money to denude the country of its products. The Germans must be laughing at the naïveté of the French, but the population, impressed by propaganda and the fact that money is flowing into its coffers in a broad stream, doesn't realize it is giving up irreplaceable goods in exchange for worthless paper.

One redeeming feature of the French catastrophe is the stand of the young people. Sylwin talked with a group of young Frenchmen he happened to meet in a restaurant; they weren't afraid to express their vociferous disapproval of what had happened, even though Vichy is teeming with Gestapo agents. These young people assured him French youth would soon declare war on the invader. They named General de Gaulle as the man who would save the honor of France and restore her freedom.

Marshal Petain received Sylwin on the third day after his arrival in Vichy and conversed with him for an hour and a half. The Marshal already knew Sylwin, having met him in Paderewski's company on a number of occasions. In spite of his advanced age, Petain has retained his alertness of mind and even his soldierly bearing, which his civilian clothing cannot disguise.

At the outset, the Marshal inquired very solicitously about Paderewski's health, emphasizing repeatedly that "in times like these not only Poland, but the world needs such a man." He told Sylwin he would leave his reply to Paderewski's letter with his secretary, and he promised to lend his support to Sylwin's efforts in behalf of the Polish troops stranded in France as well as in behalf of the civilian population. However, Sylwin was to discuss these matters with the Marshal's military head and with the Ministry of the Interior. The Marshal would issue instructions that both questions be settled as favorably as possible, "Of course, within the limits of France's present possibilities," he added with a melancholy smile of resignation. "I can assure you of one thing," said Petain, "that we shall resist all German demands to hand over the Polish troops, because a betrayal of our comrades at arms would bring dishonor on France. Should you encounter any basic difficulties in your negotiations, please let me know." It looked as if the interview was over,

so Sylwin got up to go, especially as the Marshal's secretary
had asked him not to tire Petain by staying too long.

But the Marshal put out his hand in a restraining gesture.
"Don't go away yet. I'd like to ask you a few questions.
Sylwin sat down again and the Marshal began a monologue.
"Being a trusted friend of President Paderewski, you must
know his view of the present situation. The President writes
me he believes Hitler will be defeated. You see, I, too, delude
myself secretly that something will happen to make Hitler
lose the war. I live in that hope, for that would be France's
only salvation. But a sober analysis of the situation as I, a
soldier, see it, voids this hope. Unfortunately, we have lost
the war. England is still making a desperate attempt to
hold on. But she will be invaded and nothing will keep back
the pressure of the motorized German armies. If the British
organize islands of resistance, they will only destroy their
country and will in the end suffer defeat. A nation does not
disappear after a lost war, but it can be exterminated by
modern methods of warfare if it does not cease a hopeless
fight in time. We were aware of this and were the first to
step out of the war. As the vanquished we accepted all conditions forced upon us. I refused to accept only those which
would have violated France's honor or threatened the
existence of our nation. We had to do this to forestall a
further senseless shedding of French blood. Besides, our
soldiers no longer wanted to fight when they saw the enemy's
overwhelming technical superiority.

"The British betrayed us. They promised to help us and
they didn't. German airplanes had a field day over France
while the English, notwithstanding their promises, spared
their air force. Had they kept their word, the situation at the
front might have been different. The morale of our soldiers
would not have been broken. Britain paid for her breach of
faith with Dunkirk, and God alone knows how much she will
yet have to pay, but France has paid with her blood and a lost
war. Today, in the face of the inevitable, I am trying to save

France. I do not have long to live and I don't care how posterity will judge me. I know I have fulfilled my duty as a Frenchman, that I am serving my country in the darkest hour of its history, and I expect no approbation, much less gratitude for it.

"Every human life is precious to decimated, war-ravished France. I have taken upon myself a heavy cross, I am carrying it to my Golgotha, with faith in God and in His help. I have sacrificed myself for the good of my country, I have saved hundreds of thousands, perhaps millions of human lives, I have saved from destruction cities which have been built by the toil of unnumbered generations through the ages, this gives me a clear conscience.

"I shall see to it that France carries out all the victor's terms to which we have agreed and I hope Hitler will carry out his. There will be no further concessions on my part. My task is to enable the French nation to weather with a minimum of losses the interval until the world returns to a state of peace."

Marshal Petain spoke excitedly for almost half an hour. It was clear to Sylwin that he had to make this statement for his own peace of mind. For all his brave words, he was not so sure of himself. Filled with great respect for Paderewski, placing a high premium on the President's friendship, he wished to explain and justify his stand through a trusted intermediary. Deeply touched by this unexpected confession of the Marshal, who had opened his tormented soul to him, Sylwin made a second attempt at leaving. Again the Marshal held him back. "You haven't replied to my question," he said in a calmer, controlled voice. Sylwin was so taken aback by the dramatic scene he had just witnessed that for a moment he didn't know what the Marshal had in mind.

"On what does President Paderewski base his hope that Hitler will be defeated?" Marshal Petain repeated his question.

It was Sylwin's turn to make a speech, of which this is the

gist: "Before I left for Vichy, the President and I had a long talk on this very subject. I believe I can tell you, Monsieur le Maréchal, almost word for word, what President Paderewski told me: 'I believe steadfastly that Divine Justice will not desert us while we are fighting for a good, honest cause. England has lost many battles, but she has won every war. Her leader is a tenacious British bulldog, Winston Churchill, who will not capitulate. It's true that Hitler may ultimately invade the British Isles, but it will be a dearly bought victory. We know how long it took the Germans to get over their losses after the relatively brief campaign in Poland. Now, though they try to hide it, they've lost their momentum after the French campaign. Are they capable of the immediate new effort of invading England? Let Hitler and his staff worry about that. But even if they should conquer the British Isles, what of it? That's not the end of the war, it's only the beginning. The British Empire remains untouched, and the Germans will again have lost something of the dynamic quality of their blitz. However, the deciding factor will be the United States. America cannot stand by idly while the rest of the world falls under Hitler and Stalin domination. Even if considerations of the deep and natural sympathy entertained by the American people for the English-speaking commonwealth of nations should not prevail, a realization of the threat to their own security and a healthy sense of self-preservation must in the end carry weight. The events of the first world war will be repeated and Hitler will follow in the footsteps of Kaiser Wilhelm to an ignominious defeat.' "

Petain was all ears. He drank in every word. As if anxious to make sure his hearing had not deceived him, he said again: "So Paderewski thinks Hitler will lose this war? That America will enter the war? God grant it, God grant it," he repeated.

Sylwin then told the Marshal that the President intends to leave for America. "Good," responded Petain, "let him go there. They need him there. I'll do everything to facilitate his transit across France. Tell the President he should go. Providence itself directs him thither. God will take care of him."

Taking leave of Sylwin, Marshal Petain added half-jokingly: "You know something? The Germans would give a lot to know the subject of our conversation and our feelings."

"If they don't know what they are, Monsieur le Maréchal, they have every reason to guess them," Sylwin replied in the same vein. The audience was at an end.

Sylwin's talks with the French army and government officials to whom he'd been referred by Petain were a far cry from the frankness and trust characterizing his interview with Petain. To be sure, the military had high praise for the heroism of the Polish soldiers and asked questions about General Sikorski and the troops that had been transported to England, but they explained they were under such heavy German pressure that they'd be able to ease the lot of the Polish soldiers and officers only in secret, wherever possible. In principle, they've agreed to intern the Poles. "All we can do," they said, "is to look the other way when Polish soldiers smuggle their way into Spain. Or refrain from hounding those who manage to get civilian clothing and go into hiding in France. Polish troops must be interned in camps, which, however, we are endeavoring to set up as far as possible from the demarcation line of the German occupation. We shall do everything to make life in the camps tolerable. Polish understanding of our forced situation will largely determine how that camp life will shape up. There can be no question of a mass evacuation of the remnants of the Polish Army to North Africa at this time. Such an evacuation would constitute a violation by France of the German armistice terms she has accepted."

The outcome of Sylwin's negotiations with the Ministry of the Interior regarding the civilian population was even less encouraging. Refugee Poles can expect no privileges deriving from their status as former allies. They come under the jurisdiction of the prefecture in each department. Should there be any substantiated cases of ill treatment of Poles by the local authorities, the Ministry will make an investigation and will remove the injustice. However, the Ministry cannot issue a special circular letter on this matter to the prefects because the seizure of such a letter by the Germans would jeopardize French relations with the occupants. The Poles must apply individually at the proper prefecture for the right to work and for the right of residence.

When he picked up Marshal Petain's letter to Paderewski, Sylwin had a long talk with M. Menetrel, the Marshal's private secretary, who is a son of the Marshal's physician and lifelong friend. Sylwin complained about how little he'd been able to accomplish during his conferences with the French higher-ups. M. Menetrel attributed their hesitation to the as yet unsettled Franco-German relations, but he promised to use his influence with the Marshal if the need ever arose and assured Sylwin that Petain would do his utmost to help the Poles.

July 18, 1940. Minister Frankowski is already in Vichy, so our Embassy is now functioning normally. Nevertheless, the situation continues to be complicated because the Germans are insisting that the French government liquidate the diplomatic representation of Poland, a country which, in their view, has ceased to exist as an independent state.

The President listened attentively to Sylwin's report. It has turned out that more Polish soldiers are stranded in occupied France than was at first believed. Thanks to the help of the civilian population, which shelters them during the day and from which they have received civilian clothing, they trudge southward under cover of night, trying to get as near as possible to some French port or the Spanish border. The knowledge that many of their comrades ended up in Gestapo prison does not deter the others from attempting to rejoin the Polish Army in England.

While in Vichy, Sylwin met a few high-ranking officers, among them, Colonel Wlodzimierz Onacewicz and General Szyszko-Bohusz. As a rule, they try to make a detour around Vichy, where the French police are extra vigilant and where there are so many Gestapo agents. It doesn't require any great skill to recognize a Polish officer or soldier even in disguise. Their clothes seldom fit them, being either too big or too small, and thus conspicuous. General Kleeberg, our Embassy's military attaché, has been placed in charge of the evacuation of our military personnel. But enterprising individuals like General Szyszko-Bohusz and Colonel Onacewicz prefer to rely on their own instinct and luck, and set out on their long journey by themselves.

Escaping Soldiers

Switzerland — July 28, 1940. I'm afraid to write this even for my own benefit. Nobody knows about it and nobody must know. Sylwin and the President especially have to be kept in the dark or they would be guilty of disloyalty because of their official connection with the government. I help interned Polish soldiers to flee from Switzerland. This is in violation of the strict injunction of the Swiss authorities against internees leaving the area and in violation of the order of the Polish Commander-in-Chief that all internees loyally adhere to Swiss military regulations. General Sikorski has particularly forbidden individual soldiers and officers to escape.

It's a waste of time to try to talk them into staying in the camps until the war ends. Impelled by a sense of duty, I make every effort to persuade them not to break their word and not to expose the others to unpleasant consequences, but I know I'm wasting my breath. Once a Pole decides to make a break, you just can't make him stay put.

Our trips to the camps are always in a car piled high with packages. The minute we tell the President about the need for something in a camp he instructs us to make the necessary purchases and sends us to the camps to make delivery. Neither soldiers nor officers make any requests, however. We have to find out about their needs from the camp commandant. In one of the camps, where the decimated Reconnaissance Unit was interned, there was a shortage of virtually everything. They were above all handicapped by their lack of mess kits. The President told us to buy mess kits but there were none to be found in all Switzerland. To save the situation we went from town to town and bought up all the aluminum baking molds we could lay our hands on. They doubled very nicely as regulation mess kits and the fact that they were a present from Paderewski made them extra precious to the interned Poles.

I wrote that the boys did not make any requests. That's not strictly true. They did ask for two things: Polish books and maps of Switzerland. I know why they're so anxious to get hold of a map.

The President has placed his entire library at the disposal of Leniutka and myself, giving us a free hand in the selection of Polish books. We've organized a circulating library, that is, each camp sends back to Riond Bosson for forwarding to another camp the books that have been read. It's a constant source of wonder to us that these books are returned in perfect condition. Never is a copy missing, nor is a book soiled or torn. Each volume comes back in a paper cover inscribed: FROM THE LIBRARY OF PADEREWSKI — RESPECT POLISH BOOKS. When we showed these books in their new military dress to the President, he said, "That's very touching," and fell into a reverie.

Notwithstanding Sikorski's stringent order forbidding flight, more and more of our interned enlisted men and officers are disappearing from the camps. The successful escape of their predecessors across the "green frontier" has apparently spurred others to try their luck. Morges is the first stop in their itinerary. They tramp across the Swiss countryside hungry but drunk with their newly found freedom.

My first encounter with one of these escaped internees caused me an uncomfortable moment or two. He telephoned me from Morges asking if he could see me somewhere in town on a matter of the utmost importance. Naïvely I told him I'd ride down on my bicycle in a jiffy, described what I was wearing so that he might know me (the fellow was a stranger to me), and said I'd meet him at the station. As no train was due, the tiny station was deserted except for the two of us. We greeted each other in the presence of guards marching up and down the platform. I froze in my tracks when the young man, clad in the most fantastic assortment of clothing, drew himself up to attention in army fashion, clicked his heels, and bent over my hand. "Have you gone mad to greet me like that? Anyone can see you're a soldier," I whispered furiously. Meanwhile the guards, who'd begun to observe me curiously, recognized my jewel of a shining bicycle — which I'd lifted up into the air to cover up our confusion — as belonging to the lady from Riond Bosson; they saluted and discreetly turned their backs on us.

My knees grew weak from relief. I took the lad with me to the park in Riond Bosson and it was not until we had secreted ourselves in the densest part of the shrubbery that we began to talk freely.

Going into the bushes the following day, I found the young man gone. However, I'd outfitted him with a small valise filled with food and some money. Aside from a holy picture from Poland given him by his mother, our young warrior had been completely stripped of his worldly possessions.

When similar scenes grew increasingly frequent, I let Leniutka in on the secret and the two of us set up a sort of relief station for the daring runaways who report under Paderewski's protective wings individually or in twos or threes. As soon as they make a successful break from their camp, they head for Riond Bosson, feeling perfectly safe here. Paderewski would be the most surprised person in the world if he knew what was going on in his own house. Leniutka and I unconcernedly feed and equip the boys for the remaining and most difficult part of their journey. We have our difficulties too. It's not easy to keep our activities secret with so many members of the household and servants around all the time. We have to wait until the President retires (often not till well after 2 A.M.), until the servants disperse, and until Mrs. Wilkonska and the other ladies go up to their rooms. When Sylwin is away, I can manage to slip out by about 3 A.M., but when he's home, I have to wait until he, too, falls asleep. Fortunately, Sylwin is not a victim of insomnia. The few times he did awaken, or on those occasions when Mrs. Wilkonska, who keeps her door open all night, heard me walking down the corridor and wanted to know why I was up, I told them to go back to sleep, that I was merely suffering from a slight stomach-ache.

Having safely negotiated the descent, I meet Leniutka downstairs. Guided by our flashlight we steal out toward the bushes, where our soldiers have been waiting for us as agreed. Then we let them into the kitchen by an unused side entrance, stuff them with food — whatever happens to be left over from supper — ply them with wine, and present them with a bundle of provisions, a watch, a flashlight and some money. At 5 A.M. they leave the park and entrain at Morges for the green frontier and the Polish army.

Mrs. Wilkonska has begun to notice a chronic discrepancy in the number of meatballs she always puts away for the next day. The poor woman can never figure out why the supply dwindles overnight. We have made Franciszek the chief culprit, maintaining with a straight face that, because he has to stay up until the President goes to bed, he fortifies himself with an inordinate quantity of meatballs in lieu of sleep. We loyally add that we consume our share while waiting for the President to finish his prayers, in which he is engrossed nightly after the bridge game, amid the photographs and mementoes of his past. Franciszek's first reaction was indignation at being accused of secretly eating meatballs, but he soon caught on without a word being exchanged between us (no wonder the President calls Franciszek "Professor") and is now our silent accomplice. The rest of the company, headed by the President, suspects nothing.

The other evening the President and Franciszek went upstairs exceptionally early. Taking advantage of this rare opportunity, we went out into the park at midnight. We advanced to the strategic bushes and called out the password "Sylwin." No answer. We called again in a louder voice. Silence.

Two hours later, we tried a second time. The boys emerged from hiding at the first summons. We asked where they had been at twelve o'clock. "Oh, we heard you calling but we were afraid to come out because you said you wouldn't be here before two o'clock."

"But how did you know it wasn't two o'clock on such a moonless, starless night?"

"Well, you see, we've been without watches for so long, we finally got to tell what time it was just by the feel of it."

I could go on writing forever about the camps and their inmates. But before I get writer's cramp, here's a final vignette:

One Polish internee escaped from a camp through the good offices of a friendly Swiss peasant who provided him with civilian clothes, bought two railroad tickets, and took him on a trip around Switzerland just to show him the country before he left it. His Swiss benefactor climaxed the conducted tour by personally escorting the Polish boy from the Morges station to Riond Bosson, insisting he couldn't be in Switzerland and not see Paderewski. "Now that he's here, I leave him in good hands," and after a brief but cordial farewell of his protegé, he rapidly disappeared.

How fine, good, and cultured the Swiss are! What a magnificent nation!

Heartening News

July 31, 1940. There were plenty of guests on the President's name day. Outwardly the occasion bore all the earmarks of a family celebration. But we could not really shake off our awareness of the chaos into which Europe is steadily sinking nor our depression at the impunity with which the forces of evil and destruction are riding roughshod over the world. The President received many congratulatory telegrams. He was particularly pleased by the messages from President Raczkiewicz and General Sikorski, which gave evidence of an abiding conviction that the spirit of the Polish nation would not break in this battle, that it would not even flag, that the Polish army, air force, and navy are prepared to make the greatest sacrifices to insure victory and then rebuild a Free Poland.

During the reception, attended by some of his Swiss friends, the President had his moment of personal triumph when he reminded them that, all the gloomy predictions of the press to the contrary, he had been right in maintaining that Hitler would not conquer England within the next few weeks and effectively end the war. Six weeks have elapsed since the capitulation of France and Hitler hasn't even tried an invasion. The recent conclusion of the Anglo-Soviet twenty-year mutual assistance pact is the best indication of the change in the situation.

"This doesn't mean," Paderewski went on, "that the Soviets will honor the pact if it should suit them to tear it up the way they did at the time of their joint action with Hitler against Poland, but Russia has a good intelligence service. The Russians are not blinded by Hitler's temporary successes. They must have arrived at the conclusion that if the victorious impetus of Germany has not yet been checked, it has at any rate been quite weakened. They see that the most dangerous phase of the blitzkrieg has come to an end without achieving its goal. By the same token, Russia is no longer so sure of a German victory. Her pact with England is her insurance against Hitler's defeat. That such conclusions have been reached not by our wishful thinking friends, but by our realistic enemies, is a particularly valuable and heartening piece of news to us."

The Unwelcome Guest

August, 1940. The President hardly ever receives guests at lunch or dinner any more. We have company only on Sunday. But some time ago Mrs. Simonne Girond de Pourtales began to be a constant visitor at Riond Bosson, trying to crash the President's "inner circle." The first time Simonne invited herself over, both Mrs. Wilkonska and Paderewski were only too glad to entertain her at lunch because they've known her since she was a little girl. She's the daughter of a very respectable Swiss couple. The next few luncheons made it so clear that Simonne's convictions are definitely pro-Nazi that Mrs. Wilkonska decided to stop inviting her. Easier said than done. Simonne always managed to maneuver her way in, especially when Sylwin was away. Finally, at her last luncheon, this strange woman in all earnestness launched into a defense of Hitler. She brazenly declared that we Poles don't understand and don't appreciate the greatness of the Führer, that Hitler's victory will make Poland great and mighty, and that if Paderewski met Hitler and had a heart-to-heart talk with him, he'd change his mind about the Führer's worth· We were all struck speechless. The President threw her an oblique look of ironic pity and said not a single work in reply. Not till after lunch, when we'd gotten rid of her, did the President comment: "Simonne is completely crazy."

I forgot to mention that she also told us about having seen Hitler at close range from a darkened room where an SS friend of hers had concealed her at the risk of his and her life. And she recounted how she'd once been standing so close to Hitler during some mysterious goings-on in the courtyard of the German Chancellery that she could have shot him if she'd had a gun. She cited these incidents as proof of how the Nazis trust her.

After that famous luncheon, Simonne drove Sylwin to distraction by her repeated telephone demands for an invitation. She met with no success because the President had emphatically stated that he did not wish to see her again. Undaunted, Simonne came *without* an invitation on one of Mrs. Wilkonska's open-house Sundays. She took advantage of the President's being alone in the card room and slipped in without asking permission. We later learned she had attempted to persuade the President to make some sort of gesture of reconciliation toward Hitler, as this was in her opinion the only means of preserving Poland's independence. Assuring Paderewski his gesture would be wholly reciprocated, she insisted he would thereby go down in history as his country's savior.

Mrs. Wilkonska's eagle eye noticed Simonne's disappearance and she forthwith dispatched Sylwin to relieve the President of his unwelcome guest. Paderewski then accompanied Simonne into the dining room. Taking leave of him in the foyer, she asked: "Master, when can I see you again?"

The President replied in a calm but definite voice within the hearing of us all: "I'm very sorry, but it is no longer possible for me to receive you at Riond Bosson. You have pleaded the cause of the enemy of my country, you must therefore understand that we have nothing further to say to each other. This in no way diminishes the affection I feel for your dear mother, who will always be welcome here. As for you, I hope you will revise your ideas, which are unfortunate not only for Poland, but also for Switzerland and for the future of the world itself. Perhaps we shall see each other again some day under more favorable circumstances, but for the time being I can only bid you adieu."

"Is it possible, Master?" Simonne cried out with tears in her eyes. Paderewski silently bowed to her and walked away. Such was Simonne's last visit in Riond Bosson.

But Simonne did not give up that easily. She changed her tactics, trying to browbeat Sylwin into patching up her ruptured relations with Riond Bosson. Sylwin's adamant stand has driven her wild with fury. She has embarked on a vilification campaign against Sylwin. Luckily, her methods are so obvious that they have only boomeranged against her.

Thwarted in Swiss social circles, Simonne commenced to call on the editors of the Swiss newspapers in an effort to sell them the idea that Sylwin is a criminal, holding the President as a virtual prisoner in Riond Bosson, and should be publicly exposed in the press. Her story was so fantastic that these editors, who've known Sylwin for many years, have been calling up to inquire why Simonne Girond is waging such a consistent slanderous campaign against him.

That crazy woman—I don't think she's clever enough to be a real Hitler agent—has been making life miserable for us. She's a real menace. Sylwin pooh-poohed the whole affair, relying on his reputation and the friendliness always shown him by official and unofficial Swiss circles.

However, when our journey to America was definitely decided upon, Colonel Valloton, a prominent Lausanne lawyer, former president of the Conseil National [the Swiss Parliament], and a good friend of Paderewski's, came to Riond Bosson and advised both the President and Sylwin to sue Mrs. Simonne Girond de Pourtales for slander. The Colonel agreed that the lady's campaign cannot harm Sylwin at the moment inasmuch as nobody takes anything she says seriously, but suggested that in view of our imminent departure, it would be better to settle the matter in court to prevent unpleasantness at some future date, when the facts of the case are no longer fresh in people's minds. Sylwin expressed his appreciation but was reluctant to bring the case to court. However the President insisted that Sylwin sign the necessary documents, stressing that he felt indirectly responsible for the whole trouble.

We're only sorry that the President will have to appear in court when the case comes up for trial. I don't suppose he's ever been in court in his life before. But the President wasn't in the least flustered. He laughed heartily and declared gaily that it would be a pleasure "to testify for Sylwin."

Trouble in Spain

August 7, 1940. This was our wedding anniversary but only Leniutka remembered it. Sylwin is in Vichy. The President's decision to leave for the United States has made Mrs. Wilkonska frightfully excited and restive. Though she says nothing, it is obvious she is afraid. I can understand her fears. After so many years in Switzerland, where her friends and all her memories are, she is bound to feel strange elsewhere.

The President quietly explained to her why he has decided to leave. In the first place, he believes it is his duty to serve Poland without let-up, but at the same time he realizes that he cannot violate Swiss neutrality by his anti-Hitler political activity when he is enjoying the hospitality of Swiss soil. The Swiss treat the President with cordial respect and give him as free a hand as their neutrality permits, but he himself has marked off the limits of his freedom and feels hampered within them. The President has already had to cancel a radio speech from Switzerland because the military censorship eliminated portions of his address which he considered of basic importance to the Polish cause. Furthermore, the President feels that sooner or later, when it suits their purpose, the Germans will quarrel with Petain or they will occupy the rest of France without a pretext. In either case, the President would be completely cut off from the rest of the world. America also appeals to him because of his affection for Polish Americans and his appreciation of their concern for the fate of the land of their fathers.

"The American Poles will try to help Poland by every means at their disposal. It is my duty to be among them and work with them," Paderewski said with deep conviction. "Besides," he added, "I know for a certainty, or rather I'm profoundly convinced, that America will enter the war. We must see to it that the American nation includes among its war aims a reparation of the crime perpetrated against Poland—expulsion of its enemies and restoration of freedom. President Roosevelt has always been my friend. He helped me in the days of Wilson, he won't deny me his help now."

Mrs. Wilkonska capitulated. "When do we leave?" she asked. "I don't know myself," Paderewski replied. "We don't have our visas yet. Sylwin is trying to arrange for our transit through France. Anyhow, I still have many things to take care of before we go. I should say in a month."

September 10, 1940. There is currently deep anxiety in Switzerland—probably fanned by German propaganda to sow panic—that this country's neutrality will be violated by Italy and Germany. Though patriotic feeling is running high, and everybody—the military as well as civilians—is convinced Switzerland will resist any aggression, Riond Bosson is in danger. We keep hearing that in the event of an attack, the Swiss would abandon Geneva and the lowlands to the Germans, saving their resistance for the mountainous areas. Be that as it may, it is entirely possible that we might wake up one beautiful morning and find ourselves under German occupation. When rumors of this sort grow more persistent, our well-meaning "friends" rail at us for not taking the President to America. When the tension abates a little and there is less talk of an invasion of Switzerland, these same "friends" of Paderewski want to know how we dare subject him and Mrs. Wilkonska to such a risky and dangerous trip. To listen to them, we should neither stay nor leave. It would indeed be an impossible decision for Sylwin and myself to make, were it not for the fact that the President declared a long time ago that he wants to go to America. Sylwin applied for the passports and visas several weeks ago.

Our departure is set for Wednesday, September 25th. Leniutka is bravely accepting the tragedy of parting with us. Since her mother is too weak to stand the journey, Leniutka has elected to remain with her in Switzerland. The rest of the "entourage" is making Sylwin's life miserable importuning him to remind the President to provide for everybody left behind, at least for as long as they live and unto the third generation.

We're all busy making preparations for our trip. The President frequently goes to see his lawyers, Mr. Valloton and Mr. Gonvers, to wind up his affairs. But sometimes I have the feeling we won't go to America after all. It's too dangerous. Paderewski is anathema to the Germans. Although we shall be going through the unoccupied part of France, the frontiers are guarded by the Gestapo. Besides, there are plenty of German spies everywhere and Simonne is liable to turn informer just to get even.

Meanwhile, Mr. Kullupajlo telephones us daily from Annemasse on the French side of the Swiss frontier to urge us to hasten our departure. He says that the situation is unsettled and the sooner the President leaves, the safer he will be.

September 20, 1940. We're advancing our departure from Switzerland by two days. It was really my doing. Whenever I think of the possibility of Simonne's reporting us and of our arrest in France, I feel a cold hand clutching at my heart. The Germans would certainly do everything in their power to keep Paderewski from reaching America.

So I said to Sylwin today: "Let's go before the twenty-fifth. Let's go as soon as we can. Every day counts. If they close the frontier, it'll be too late."

At first Sylwin raised objections. We'd never be ready. There was still so much to take care of.

Well, I said, I know there's never any end of things to

take care of as far as the President is concerned, but his life is more important than all his affairs. I wouldn't give in, and Sylwin had to submit my suggestion to the President. As soon as the President gave his consent, I made sure Sylwin telephoned Annemasse to have Mr. Kollupajlo meet us with his car at the frontier on Monday, September 23rd, at 7 P.M.

September 22, 1940. We leave tomorrow, but how will we ever get to America? Neither Sylwin, Anetka, nor I have visas, because the United States Legation in Berne so far has not received a reply from the State Department in Washington. They tell us, however, that by the time we get to Lisbon, the Legation there will be notified to grant us visas.

On the way out of Switzerland—September 23, 1940. I'm writing this in the car to have at least a brief record of this fateful day. Our departure from Riond Bosson should have been filmed! Whenever Paderewski goes on a trip there is bedlam, but today topped all previous departures for disorganization and pointless running around. Even Leniutka and Sylwin lost their heads. Only the President, surrounded by a swarm of well-wishers, maintained his imperturbable dignity.

Two cars, their tanks brimming over with gasoline, stood in the driveway, but it didn't occur to anyone to put our luggage inside them because the multitude of guests who had come to see the President off were saying "hello" and a tearful "good-bye" to everybody else. No one even seemed to know which bags were going into which car and which were to be left behind. Everything in Riond Bosson had been packed, but Sylwin and I are taking only one suitcase apiece, Mrs. Wilkonska two, and the President five. The rest, along with the papers and documents, will be left in charge of Leniutka and Mr. Valloton.

As Sylwin and Leniutka were constantly buttonholed by people with "important messages for the President," I got Franciszek to load the bags where I thought they should go.

A few minutes after 5 P.M. the President, Mrs. Wilkonska, and Franciszek got into the Cadillac; Anetka and I
are in the other car, which Sylwin is driving until we pick up
Mr. Kollupajlo at the border.

Before the President took his seat, he shook hands with
each servant and with all the guests. He was grave and sad
but perfectly calm and at ease.

I feel heart-broken at leaving Leniutka behind. Though
the poor girl smiled bravely, I know how unhappy she is
about not coming with us. At parting I said to her: "You
must come to America too."

Grenoble, France—September 23, 1940. At the Franco-Swiss
border in Annemasse—where a crowd of onlookers gaped
with curiosity at our overloaded cars, in one of which two
very old people, Paderewski and his sister, presented a truly
touching picture by their calm and dignified demeanor—
Sylwin transferred to Paderewski's Cadillac. Mr. Kollupajlo
took the wheel of the other car and we acquired another
passenger, Monsieur Roger Garric, an agent of the *Sûreté
Générale* (the political police) who has been assigned to
Paderewski by the French Government to facilitate our
journey over unoccupied France.

We arrived in Grenoble at 11:15. Although there is a
compulsory blackout in France and we didn't see a single
light in any window, the Hotel des Trois Dauphins was ablaze
in honor of the President. Despite the lateness of the hour, a
table was beautifully set in the brilliantly lighted dining
room and the maître d'hôtel and waiters were ready with
supper for us. Monday is a meatless day in France, but we
were served roast chicken.

We won't leave Grenoble until 3 P.M. tomorrow, so as to
give the President a chance to get a good rest.

Nimes—September 24, 1940. We drove into Nimes at 9:30
this evening. There is such a shortage of hotel space that
only two rooms could be rounded up for the President in the

first-rate Hotel Imperator. To secure even these, the management had to ask one of its guests to check out.

Perpignan, France, Grand Hotel—September 26, 1940. Arriving here at 1:30 P.M. we stopped for lunch and a bit of rest. We left Nimes at 10 A.M.—on the dot for once!

Barcelona, Hotel Ritz—September 27, 1940. At two o'clock this morning we finally got into Barcelona. What a lovely city! I'd like to do at least a little sightseeing in it with Anetka, but first I want to describe our trip from Perpignan.

Quitting Perpignan at 3 P.M., we were at Le Perthus on the Franco-Spanish border an hour and a half later. Our entire journey over unoccupied France proceeded remarkably smoothly, because whenever we were halted or questioned by the authorities or the police, M. Garric simply flipped his lapel and revealed his badge. Our would-be interrogator instantly saluted and we were on our way. Mr. Garric proved he was a perfect gentleman because instead of taking leave of us at the border, where his duties were officially at an end, he crossed the border with us and requested his "colleagues" on the Spanish side to extend their protection over Paderewski.

I certainly had the jitters during our crossing of the Spanish border. I was positive that because of the war and because it was Spain, we would be subjected to customs inspection. Once they saw so much manuscript, my diary would be confiscated or at best retained for censorship.

On the Spanish side of Le Perthus, the customs authorities were completing inspection and passport formalities for passengers entering Spain in a bus. A second crowded vehicle stood near-by. As soon as the Spanish border authorities learned of Paderewski's arrival, instead of making us wait our turn, they decided to expedite our clearance. When Sylwin began to talk with the head customs official, the latter didn't even inquire how many persons were accompanying Paderewski. He only asked us to take our passports to the customs building, adding that Paderewski and his sister need not present their documents in person, but could remain in the car.

My interview with the customs department was rather unorthodox. While he was stamping my passport, the official cordially remarked in French: "You are with Paderewski? How happy you must feel!" Then he suddenly started humming the *Minuet*. "You certainly know this, the Paderewski *Minuet?*" and he resumed his warbling, at the same time brandishing his stamp in the air.

Mr. Kollupajlo tells another story, which has made him so happy he's wearing an ear-to-ear grin. The official told him during the passport inspection: "You're lucky you're with Paderewski. You still have three months to go to your fortieth birthday. We send men of your age to a concentration camp, which is near here, while you'll be traveling freely all over Spain."

But it was Sylwin who outdid the rest of us by his absent-mindedness. When he presented the passports of Paderewski and Mrs. Wilkonska for stamping, he forgot to submit his own, so that he entered Spain without a stamped visa. We had to turn back from the road to Barcelona to take care of this ultra-important matter.

Leaving Le Perthus, we felt light-hearted and gay. The magnificent wide highway to Barcelona, lined with hoary spreading trees, invited speeding. Mr. Kollupajlo's car led the way and I kept turning around to make sure we did not lose the President in this strange country. Mr. Kollupajlo drove with the aplomb of a lifetime resident of Spain.

Unfortunately, we didn't enjoy the startlingly beautiful highway very long. Suddenly it grew cloudy and lightning flashed on the horizon. Twenty minutes later, we were in the midst of a terrifying storm. Darkness settled over the world, completely obscuring the road, a hurricane wind tore off huge boughs, hurling them in the path of our car. We moved only when a fantastic flash of lightning zigzagged through the heavens and revealed a road strewn with thick branches.

A furiously relentless downpour added to our woes. Time and again Mr. Kollupajlo had to get out in the cloudburst and remove the tremendous branches blocking the road. Ear-splitting thunderclaps alternated with the crashing noise of trees rent asunder that we thought would topple on us and crush our car.

Gradually the ripping sound of splitting timber was replaced by the ominous roar of water. A painfully brilliant flash of lightning told us we were crawling along a serpentine road high above the sea. The strong wind and the heavy rain had washed out sections of the road, while the torrents which rushed across the highway from the mountain on our right threatened to sweep our automobile into the sea. Frightened though we were, our imaginations were stirred by this amazing show put on for us by the elements. Mr. Kollupajlo kept remarking that this tempest was something out of Shakespeare, and blithely got the Studebaker to jump over the mountain streams just as I used to make my horse leap over hurdles. I must say, though, that I could not take such a purely romantic view of the tempest. I was terribly afraid the water rushing down the mountainside would carry us seaward. In spite of the terrific wind, I held the car door ajar so that I could jump out and not drown inside the automobile if we were pushed into the sea. I was thankful that Paderewski's Cadillac was a heavier car and could take more buffeting than ours.

We negotiated five streams safely enough. In front of the sixth, Mr. Kollupajlo hesitated and stopped. A regular river was hurtling down the mountain, across the road, and down the cliffs to swirl into the Mediterranean. To proceed or not to proceed? We had no idea how deep the water was. But our mood was one of desperate courage. With Paderewski behind us, we had to determine how dangerous the crossing would be. Accordingly, neither Anetka nor I attempted to curb Mr. Kollupajlo's dare-deviltry. He stepped on the gas and we forded the river without mishap. Behind us the Cadillac slowly but confidently repeated our performance.

We breathed a collective sigh of relief. A few dozen feet later, our car sputtered and then stopped altogether. Water had seeped into the gasoline tank and we were stalled only six kilometers from Barcelona in a storm which showed no sign of abating. When the Cadillac passed us we knew the President would be at the Hotel Ritz in a little while, so, oblivious to the fury of the elements, we nibbled on cookies and chocolate bars and relaxed. In an hour the Cadillac came back and hauled us into Barcelona.

Saragossa, Gran Hotel—September 28, 1940. We're imprisoned! The President is under arrest and so are we! It sounds incredible, but it's true. To be sure, we're not in a prison cell, but in a first-class hotel. Nevertheless, we have been forbidden to leave the premises, which are surrounded by the police, while our automobiles together with our belongings have been sealed and taken to police headquarters. What luck that I always carry my jewelry and my diary with me!

We've been in this hotel since 7 P.M. It's now well past midnight but neither Sylwin nor I feel like sleeping. Gnawed by awful anxiety, we're waiting for the dawn. Sylwin is reading the Spanish newspapers and I'm writing everything down from the beginning, for who knows what tomorrow will bring us?

We left Barcelona at ten o'clock this morning, and around five o'clock in the afternoon, we drove into the outskirts of Saragossa. Upon entering the city proper, our cars were halted by militiamen who insisted on seeing our documents. When they made sure it was Paderewski, they instructed us to wait while they telephoned headquarters. At first we thought the Spanish wished to honor Paderewski by giving us a police escort. However, their behavior soon made it clear something else was afoot. One soldier with a rifle brutally shoved over Anetka and sat down beside her. Another climbed into the back seat and I graciously made room for him before I realized what was up! But I noticed that Sylwin was unceremoniously trying to oust an armed soldier from the Cadillac. The rifleman insolently seated himself next to Franciszek. These soldiers in addition to two police cars, were the escort that brought us to the police station.

At police headquarters they kept us waiting from 5:30 to 7 P.M. All that time the President, Mrs. Wilkonska, and Franciszek sat in the car, parked in front of the main police gate. Kollupajlo, Anetka, and I walked back and forth beside the two automobiles, worriedly trying to figure out why Sylwin was talking with the Spanish authorities such a long time. When at long last Sylwin came out of the building accompanied by policemen, he was deathly pale and so furious he could barely choke out a few words of explanation: "They wanted to force us to return to Barcelona right away, but I wouldn't give in. We're going to the Gran Hotel, but we're under arrest."

We got back into our cars and were escorted to the hotel by the police. Militiamen and secret agents roam all over the place.

Having installed Paderewski and Mrs. Wilkonska in their quarters, Sylwin went downstairs to put through a telephone call to our Legation in Madrid, only to be refused a connection. However, he did manage to send telegrams to Minister Szumlakowski, to American Ambassador Weddell in Madrid, and to Sir Samuel Hoare, the British Ambassador. We wonder whether the Spaniards will permit the messages to be delivered.

Sylwin has just read in the local paper that the city of Saragossa is proud to be playing host to the famous statesman and great artist, Paderewski! That item, with an impressive headline to boot, was enough to make Sylwin launch into a description of his tempestuous ninety-minute session at police headquarters.

Even though they spoke in Spanish, Sylwin had understood that the Police Commissioner was demanding our immediate return to Barcelona. Failing to understand Sylwin's reply in French, they had summoned an interpreter through whom Sylwin declared we had no intention of going back. He had met their insistent threats with a question: Why? The reply was "concern for Paderewski's safety." Besides, they said, we had no right to leave Barcelona without reporting our intention to the police. To which Sylwin had responded that there had been no secrecy shrouding our departure from Barcelona, that the Ritz Hotel was opposite the police station and that when Paderewski had left at ten in the morning, Barcelona police had been on hand to prevent the eager crowds gathered around his car from disrupting traffic. Anyway, he concluded, we hadn't traveled 320 kilometers along a mountainous, precipice-studded route to expose the President to a return trip through such difficult country and at night into the bargain.

Sylwin's arguments to the contrary, they had made every effort to extort an agreement from him to go back at once. That made Sylwin good and mad. He retorted he'd never agree, let them arrest us if they wished, but Spain would suffer the consequences of such treatment of Paderewski. He was sure there must be some misunderstanding, and he insisted the Commissioner get in touch with the person in Barcelona who had ordered our return to that city. The Commissioner then told Sylwin to go into another room, apparently suspecting him of understanding Spanish and not wishing him to hear any conversation. Having cooled his heels twenty minutes, Sylwin reentered the room. But they said *conferencia* and made him leave. Sylwin thought the person wanted on the other end was in conference and couldn't be reached. Finally it dawned on him that *conferencia* in Spanish meant the line was busy. After more waiting, he gained the impression that nobody had any intention of getting Barcelona on the wire at all. The Commissioner called him in to inform him that Paderewski would be permitted to spend the night in Saragossa, but that tomorrow morning at eight the police would come and force us to return to Barcelona. Sylwin then demanded he be allowed to telephone our

Legation in Madrid. When this met with a refusal, Sylwin boiled over. He shouted so loudly that the walls of the police station trembled. From down in the street, we were not able to make out the words, but we distinctly heard him and were at a loss to understand why he was yelling so. Now I know that when Sylwin asked the Commissioner whether we were under arrest, and the Commissioner replied we were merely under police protection and for our own safety would have to depart for Barcelona tomorrow morning, Sylwin announced in stentorian tones: "Arrest us, but remember, if a single hair falls from Paderewski's head, Spain will be covered with shame for having harmed that old man whom the world reveres and adores. And we will not leave tomorrow at eight because in all his life Paderewski never left for anywhere at eight in the morning. Besides, if we do leave, it will be in the direction in which we wish to go and not to Barcelona!"

Saragossa — Sunday, September 29, 1940. Just as they'd promised, two secret service agents in civilian dress arrived promptly at eight and announced meaningfully that they'd come to accompany us to Barcelona. They of course left empty-handed, because Sylwin informed them that Paderewski was fast asleep and we were definitely not going to Barcelona. But the absence of any reaction to Sylwin's three telegrams over Paderewski's signature had us worried until, at 9 a.m., the phone rang in our room. At last! Minister Szumlakowski called to tell us he had received our wire. He was surprised to hear of our detention in Saragossa and had already communicated with the American and English Ambassadors, who have likewise received Paderewski's telegrams. Ambassador Sir Samuel Hoare stated immediately that as an Englishman he is so unpopular in Hitler-scared Spain that any demarche on his part could only harm Paderewski. The United States Ambassador alone can help Paderewski. In fact Ambassador Weddell has already promised to intervene. Minister Szumlakowski also told us that the Counsellor of the Legation, Mieczyslaw Skolimowski, would arrive in the afternoon to take charge.

Later. Shortly after his arrival and a brief chat with the President, Skolimowski went to the Governor of Saragossa Province to find out why Paderewski and his party had been detained. He came back without accomplishing anything because it's Sunday and the Governor is away for the week end.

Saragossa — Monday, September 30, 1940. Three different times today Mr. Skolimowski has tried to see the Governor, but that august official is still week-ending. Meanwhile we "prisoners" are free to move about the hotel.

To kill time we play cards all day; we also joke and laugh a lot to maintain a cheerful atmosphere around the President, who is as calm and unconcerned as if he weren't the center of the controversy. Poor Mrs. Wilkonska, on the other hand, cannot refrain from making her dire prediction: "You'll see, the Germans will throw us all into a concentration camp and they'll keep us there until the end of the war." We greet her grim prognostication with peals of laughter, although secretly we're inclined to agree. Personally, I'm convinced they won't dare to imprison Paderewski or his sister, four years his senior. I'm terribly afraid, though, that they will arrest Sylwin and Mr. Kollupajlo.

Saragossa — Tuesday, October 1, 1940. An appointment with the Governor today seems completely out of question: the whole town is celebrating General Franco's name day, so the Governor will be busy all day. "And tomorrow the Governor won't see you," says Mrs. Wilkonska to Skolimowski, "because the Governor will be tired after the holidays." She's not far off at that. For four days now we've been held up, and we still can't learn anything from the authorities because they're perpetually on a spree.

This afternoon Minister Szumlakowski telephoned from Madrid that Ambassador Weddell had wired President Roosevelt and that he, Szumlakowski, had intervened with the Papal Nuncio in Madrid, who has promised to do everything in his power to help.

Saragossa—Wednesday, October 2, 1940. A break came this afternoon when Minister Szumlakowski called again to tell us that at President Roosevelt's telegraphed request to General Franco to permit his personal friend Paderewski to proceed, we were free and could go on to Madrid. The same good news was personally telephoned to the hotel by the Governor of Saragossa. Mr. Skolimowski claims the Governor was really delighted at this turn of events.

The Governor's call was followed by our receipt of a telegram:

[WE WOULD BE SO HAPPY IF YOU WOULD BE OUR GUEST AT THE EMBASSY ON YOUR WAY TO PORTUGAL STOP PROMISE YOU REST AND QUIET.

WEDDELL AMERICAN AMBASSADOR]

The President replied:

[DEEPLY TOUCHED BY YOUR MOST KIND INVITATION TO BE YOUR GUEST AT THE EMBASSY STOP I REGRET BEING DEPRIVED OF THE HONOR OF ACCEPTING YOUR GENEROUS HOSPITALITY STOP MY SISTER AND SEVERAL FRIENDS ARE TRAVELLING WITH ME AND WE HAVE ALREADY MADE RESERVATION IN MADRID STOP I WISH TO EXPRESS TO YOU MY WARMEST THANKS FOR THE KIND INTEREST YOU HAVE TAKEN IN MY EXTRAORDINARY ADVENTURE WITH THE SPANISH POLICE AND AM EXTREMELY GRATEFUL FOR YOUR MOST VALUABLE ASSISTANCE AND SYMPATHY STOP SINCERELY HOPE TO BE ABLE TO OFFER YOU PERSONALLY MY RESPECTFUL REGARDS ONCE PERMITTED TO LEAVE SARAGOSSA FOR MADRID.

PADEREWSKI.]

We're free and under the protection of the American Embassy. The Lord be praised! Tomorrow we leave for Madrid.

Madrid—October 3, 1940. A few kilometers before Madrid the Szumlakowskis met us with their car. All the way from Saragossa we were escorted by a car from the American Embassy and by Mr. Skolimowski. We're stopping at what must be the finest hotel in Madrid. If I didn't know we're in Spain, I'd think we're in Berlin. All the other residents here are German officers in uniform, who arrogantly parade all over the hotel and ride about the city in open cars, the better to be seen.

Just as soon as we got in, Paderewski changed and went with Sylwin and Franciszek to the American Embassy. When they came back, Sylwin told me that the Spanish authorities are no longer stopping us but are even anxious to see us leave Spain as quickly as possible before Serano Suner (the Minister of Internal Affairs and a brother-in-law of Franco) returns from Germany. They're afraid of a new dispute if Suner should have made too many commitments to Hitler. They even hinted at our leaving Madrid today, but as we feel quite safe under the protection of the United States Embassy, Sylwin replied that Paderewski is too tired and must rest.

Madrid—October 4, 1940. We had a very pleasant lunch at the Legation attended by Ambassadors Weddell and Sir Samuel Hoare. My enjoyment of it was dampened by a calamity that has befallen me: to do justice to the occasion I decided to change from my crumpled and soiled suit to a fresh one. When I went to get my only suitcase, I discovered it wasn't there. I don't see how it could have been lost and I find it hard to believe that it was stolen by the Spanish police in Saragossa. At one blow I've lost all my things. All I own is what I have on right now.

Estoril, Hotel do Parque—October 5, 1940. We're in Portugal in the story-book coastal resort of Estoril, near Lisbon. Our journey from Madrid was uneventful. At the Spanish frontier they settled our exit formalities with feverish haste to be rid of Paderewski and the responsibility for him. In general, the

Spaniards were rather sympathetic toward us, except, of course, for those who were charged with the execution of the German Gestapo's orders.

Once in Portugal, we felt as if we'd been admitted to heaven. What a wonderful feeling it is to be free. At the border we were glad to see our Minister to Portugal, Mr. Dubicz-Penther, and his wife. An unexpected surprise was finding our dear Monsignor Kaczynski. The prelate joined Paderewski in the Cadillac and I rode with the Penthers. Anetka and Kollupajlo traveled behind us and got lost on the way.

Estoril, Portugal—October 15, 1940. Portugal appeals to us very much. We like the country, the people, the wonderful climate. Every day the President goes for a long drive along the seacoast. Mrs. Wilkonska and Franciszek are his constant companions while the rest of us take turns. We have no idea how much longer we shall stay in Portugal. Everything depends on how soon Sylwin, Anetka, and I get our American visas.

Another problem is getting space on the boat. We want to travel on the neutral American Export Line, but we are seven people! The President and Mrs. Wilkonska refuse to make the trip on separate ships. Sylwin suggested we fly to New York on the Clipper. Thank heavens the President won't even hear of it.

Before Monsignor Kaczynski flew to England a few days ago he promised to visit us in America.

To Reach the Hearts of People

October 25, 1940. We're supposed to sail from Lisbon to New York on the American Export Line's *Excambion* on the twenty-seventh. Sylwin and I went to see whether the cabins and accommodations are suitable for the President and his sister. The ship struck me as awfully small. All his life the President has traveled on huge ocean liners. But we must take this boat or none at all.

Bermuda, On Board the Excambion — November 4, 1940. We've stopped at Bermuda for a few hours. What we can see from the deck is quite lovely, but we can't inspect the island at closer range for no one is allowed to leave the ship.

We sailed out of Lisbon on October 27th. Before our departure the Dubicz-Penthers entertained us royally at a dinner in the Legation. Mrs. Penther was surprised to see me swallowing tears along with the wine. "Aren't you glad to be going to America?" she finally asked. To which I replied that I was very glad, but that I felt terribly sad to be leaving Europe and to be going so far away from Warsaw.

The usual crowds were there to see Paderewski off and many came personally to wish him bon voyage. When Mrs. Wilkonska saw the stairs we'd have to mount to board the ship, she drew back perplexed. How *would* Ignace ever get up? That was exactly what I was thinking myself. The staircase was narrow and steep, almost ladder-like, and I wasn't sure there was room for Sylwin to take one arm and Franciszek the other to help the President. We didn't have to wait long for a solution. With a decided gesture, the President grasped the railing and without hesitation easily negotiated all the stairs. Mrs. Wilkonska commented loudly: "How that Ignace wants to go to America!"

The President is extraordinary. He takes ocean trips like a seasoned mariner. One day he really put us to shame. A violent storm had sent Mrs. Wilkonska, Anetka, and me to bed as a precaution against seasickness. Suddenly there was a knock on the door and the President walked in to visit us. "How are Antosia and my dear children?"

Antosia and the "children" felt rather foolish, so just as soon as the President left, Mrs. Wilkonska jumped out of bed and said: "If Ignace can walk around, we can too. Let's go and visit Ignace now." Half an hour later, we were dressed and "officially returning the President's call," which duly impressed him.

Another incident might also be worth recording: One afternoon a fire alarm sounded. Mr. Kollupajlo, who is familiar with nautical procedure, told us it was only a practice alarm, strictly observed in wartime. This reassured us, but when we saw the seamen playing streams of water on the decks and ordering us to don life preservers, I came to the conclusion that there was a real fire, and that Mr. Kollupajlo had wished to keep us from getting excited. Just then, Franciszek emerged from the President's stateroom in a life preserver which didn't even go halfway around his person, and asked in his thundering voice whether the President should also be dressed in a preserver. Anetka appeared in a life belt which could have gone around her four times, and Mrs. Wilkonska's had slid up under her armpits. They all struck us so funny that we doubled over with laughter and I was convinced that the alarm was only a practice one. In his cabin Paderewski, seated in a chair, was very clumsily trying to adjust his life preserver by himself. "Surely *you* don't have to put it on," I said to the President.

"Everybody means everybody," he replied. Whereupon Anetka and I helped the President don the cumbersome belt. He was pleased as punch to conform to regulations.

We had one genuine scare, though, when a German submarine stopped the *Excambion* in the dead of night. Our first thought was that the Germans who'd failed to stop Paderewski in Spain might now take him off the ship. After twenty minutes, which seemed an eternity, the U-boat permitted us to proceed and we thanked our lucky stars for the narrow escape. We never did find out why we were stopped.

It's now 11:30 A.M. We shall weigh anchor in a few minutes and proceed to New York.

New York, Hotel Ritz Tower — November 6, 1940. Thank God! We are in America at last, out of the Gestapo's reach.

Paderewski is safe. We sailed into New York harbor this morning on his eightieth birthday.

There was considerable excitement on board the *Excambion*, for yesterday the American people were electing a President. The returns indicate a Roosevelt victory and Paderewski is pleased; he is counting on his good relations with the White House to advance the Polish cause.

A large crowd turned out at the pier to welcome Paderewski to America, but it was a long time before the President emerged from his stateroom, where he was holding an impromptu press conference. To the representatives of the Polish press he issued a statement for Americans of Polish descent which he had written during the crossing. Here is the full text of the statement:

"Fellow countrymen! In these brief words of greeting I wish to express my joy that again—as a quarter of a century ago—it has been given me to be among you, the greatest concentration of free Poles.

"I do not come to rest, though I might perhaps be entitled to it. But who is capable of thinking of himself at a time when our oppressed Motherland drips with the blood of her finest sons? I wish to serve her until my last breath, so long as my strength holds out, and if God wills it, to live to see her liberation.

"You who have already once before offered such a generous sacrifice of blood and money at her altar, you who have now at the first report that she is suffering again and is again soliciting your help, responded so magnanimously and so readily to that call, will understand me best.

"Unable to shoulder arms, I shall endeavor to reach the hearts of people by means of the good word and shall try at least in this way to stay in the ranks of those who are fighting for their Motherland, for justice, for freedom, for human dignity, for the rights of nations to an independent existence.

"At the very outset, I strongly appeal to you, beloved Brethren, to co-operate with me, to lend unanimous support to my efforts. Every Polish home in America should become a center radiating Polish thought. Take advantage of every opportunity to tell others about Poland, about her beautiful and glorious past, about her thousand-year-old culture, about her right to independence, about her present misfortune, about the outrages and looting to which she has fallen prey, about the sufferings of a nation of thirty-five million whom a barbarous enemy wishes to destroy and obliterate from the face of the earth.

"Speak to them of the heroism of our army and our civilian population; tell them about the defense of ruined and gutted Warsaw, about the defense of Westerplatte, Modlin, and Hel; tell them about our troops in France who battled to the end as befits Polish soldiers and who are continuing the fight under banners bearing the historic device HONOR and COUNTRY at the side of our powerful ally, Great Britain.

"The Polish land army, the Polish navy, the Polish air force — how much heroism, how much sacrifice, how much character and endurance are contained in these words! Each of them is a new leaf in the laurel wreath of the immortal fame of Polish valor and we owe to each the deepest homage and the warmest gratitude.

"Finally, tell them that you are Poles, that you are proud of the ties of blood that unite you with our great, albeit at the moment, unhappy nation. Tell them you believe steadfastly in victory, in divine justice, that you believe in Poland just as I believe in her, just as believe thirty-five million Poles among whom neither force, nor trickery, nor terror could find a single traitor who would collaborate with the enemy.

"We have the right to look every free nation squarely in the eye: Poland's honor has not been sullied. No one can accuse the Poles of cowardice on the field of battle or submissiveness under the barbarous rule of the invaders. The sound moral foundation of the nation has not been damaged, and the present generation has proved that it is worthy of its ancestors who died on the field of glory or at Siberian hard labor in the name of Her who has not perished and never will perish. At such a very difficult, although glorious moment in our history, we must thank God for having at last sent us the grace of harmony and unity. Our eyes have opened to our errors, misfortune not only has failed to break us, but on the contrary, it has tempered and strengthened our spirit.

"The President of the Republic, Mr. Wladyslaw Raczkiewicz, as well as General Wladyslaw Sikorski, the Prime Minister and Commander-in-Chief, command universal respect. They enjoy the full confidence not only of our Government and our army but of our entire nation, which has submitted to their leadership unhesitatingly and unreservedly.

"I come to you in close agreement with the President of the Republic, with General Sikorski and with the government. I address to you, Reverend Clergy, to you Worthy Leaders of our deserving Organizations, Alliances, and Societies, to all of you, my very dear compatriots — these words of the warmest appreciation and heartfelt gratitude, and I direct to you my appeal for help and support in my work. I know that you will not withhold it from me, that within the limits of the laws in force here on hospitable and free American soil I can count on you exactly as was the case during the previous war and as will be the case during the present war, which has long ago dimmed the earlier conflict by its savage cruelty and destruction. We shall all, as one man, plunge into this holy work with redoubled energy because the strength of the enemy already is ebbing, because the day of retribution is drawing near.

"Long live the United States!

"Long live Poland!

"Long live the Poles in America!"

After the interview, they got the President on the upper deck, where a battery of newsreel cameras were all set to grind away. In the great press of people I lost Mrs. Wilkonska, whom I was supposed to produce for the picture-taking. The poor woman, bewildered and frightened by the milling throng, had retreated into the cabin and was quietly sitting there with Mrs. Sigismond Stojowski and her son.

Every few minutes someone smilingly greeted us. Many of the faces were familiar from visits to Paderewski at Riond Bosson or Paris, but in all the confusion I didn't know which names to pin on whom. I felt relieved when I caught sight of Mr. Michal Kwapiszewski, and when Roman and Tomasz Majewski kissed me with joyous whoops, like the dear friends they are. The three gentlemen took Mrs. Wilkonska and Anetka under their wing.

To the accompaniment of shouts of welcome we were escorted down the gangway to the waiting cars. Paderewski's car moved slowly to give the crowds lining the streets a chance to get a good look at him. Mrs. Wilkonska was in the second car with Mrs. Stojowska, Anetka, and myself.

In addition to the multitude along the unfamiliar streets from the pier to the Ritz Tower, hundreds of school children holding Polish and American flags stood on the curb. Truly it was a soul-stirring sight. No wonder Mrs. Wilkonska was completely stunned. I couldn't resist asking her with a triumphant note in my voice: "Wasn't it worth coming here to see how America welcomes and loves our President?"

November 9, 1940. We have a real housing problem on our hands. The President and Franciszek are on the twenty-seventh floor, Mrs. Wilkonska and I are on the seventh, while Sylwin and Kollupajlo are elsewhere. This is most inconvenient as Paderewski likes to have us all together.

Although the Ritz Tower is a very beautiful hotel and would be fine if the President and Franciszek were staying here alone, it simply won't work out for our sizable flock. The expense is also something to be reckoned with.

In view of this trying arrangement, Sylwin and I have asked all those who consider themselves friends of the President to scout around for a suitable hotel.

To make matters worse, Paderewski isn't feeling well and has lost his zest for food. We don't even have a doctor. Someone recommended Dr. Jachimowicz from Warsaw. We're glad the President consented to have a new doctor and allowed us to summon him.

November 10, 1940. For the first time today I unexpectedly spent Sunday out of town. The Edward Witkowskis persuaded me to accompany them to Father Antoni Tralka in Bayonne, New Jersey. Dinner at the parish house was to be followed by a special program of tribute to President Paderewski. I didn't know how to get out of the invitation and there was no one to ask advice of. Sylwin is away and Mrs. Wilkonska is disoriented and fatigued. The Witkowskis were insistent, so I went upstairs to consult Paderewski. Franciszek did not hide his displeasure that someone dared annoy the President this early.

Briefly, I explained my dilemma to the President. "Oh, Father Tralka! Why, he's a nice, dear priest. He could serve as an example of a good Shepherd and Citizen. Too bad Sylwin can't go. Father Tralka deserves it. Please, will you go."

I could have sworn I didn't know Father Tralka, but one glimpse of him as he came to the door and I recognized him as the priest I'd seen at Riond Bosson!

It's a pity Mrs. Wilkonska and Anetka missed the program celebrating Paderewski's eightieth birthday, which was both moving and inspiring. I tried to fix the details in my mind to report them back to the President. The Roman Catholic and Greek Catholic choirs sang beautifully. A real treat as far as I was concerned was the playing of Chopin compositions by Aleksander Brachocki.

November 17, 1940. Today Sylwin told me that since he wouldn't be in this afternoon, I should be downstairs in the lobby to receive John Rhodes and Charles Smith, the two Negro porters who had for many years waited on the President during his American concert tours in his private railroad car, and who had now made an appointment to call on him. Paderewski said he wished to see them as well as Augusta, the maid who used to travel with the Paderewskis. Though I'd never met John and Charles, I'd heard a good deal about them from Sylwin. Seeing them was like meeting old friends. Augusta, on the other hand, threw her arms about my neck and burst into tears.

The President received his colored servants from by-gone days with his usual cordiality and he chatted with them a long time.

November 30, 1940. This afternoon we moved to the Hotel Buckingham. At last we're all living near one another, and on the second floor. The funny thing is that with Paderewski's

legion of friends promising to find us new lodgings, it was I
who, without any knowledge of the city, found the new place,
though by sheer accident, I must admit. Coming out of the
Ritz Tower, I started walking down Park Avenue. Before I
had taken a hundred steps, I ran into Mr. and Mrs. Piotr
Bagniewski, old friends from Warsaw. Meeting them was a
godsend because they immediately suggested I try their
hotel, the Buckingham. Inexpensive, quiet, and with a fine
cuisine, it sounded like the answer to our prayers. Promising
to visit them in the near future, I hastened to the Hotel
Buckingham. A Mr. Donegan, the hotel's handsome and
dapper manager, patiently listened to my speech. As it was
in English, I wonder how much of it he really understood.
But he did show interest when I concluded by telling him I
needed a suite of rooms for Paderewski and his household.
Mr. Donegan said he had only a single apartment vacant and
took me up to look at it. The hotel had received a number of
offers for the suite, but of course *Paderewski* would get
priority. So, to make up for my limited English vocabulary,
I folded my hands in supplication and entreated Mr. Donegan:
"Please wait two days. My husband will be back from
Chicago and will decide."

Well, no sooner did Sylwin return from his trip than I
dragged him over to the Buckingham before he even had a
chance to wash and change. He liked it at once and was especially pleased because it was newly decorated and all new
furniture had been brought into the suite. The President, too,
readily agreed to move.

December 10, 1940. Our new hotel brought me luck. Walking
down the corridor I came upon a tall woman carrying what
was obviously a heavy suitcase. I didn't remember the lady,
but I did recognize my lost suitcase! I grew speechless with
disbelief and joy. Mrs. Ceresol, whom I had met in Switzerland, smiled at me in a friendly fashion and handed me the
key to the bag. I asked her with embarrassment why on earth
she'd lugged such a heavy bag herself. She laughed merrily

and said: "I wanted to deliver it to you in person to see your pleasure. Your joy and surprise are my reward."

Collecting myself, I asked Mrs. Ceresol into our sitting room, and everything was cleared up. It seems that after we left, Leniutka recognized my suitcase with the key hanging from it. Making sure it really held my things, she commenced to look for someone bound for America who might take my bag along. She turned to the Ceresols. Mrs. Ceresol refused, explaining that her husband had especially warned her not to accept any parcels, not even letters. The following day Mrs. Ceresol called back to say she'd be glad to take Mrs. Strakacz's bag. When her husband had learned what it was all about, he'd said everything connected with the person of Paderewski was sacred as far as he was concerned!

New York—Christmas Eve, 1940. With our country in mourning, we had no intention of celebrating Christmas Eve this year. We were merely going to eat supper together in the President's sitting room. Miss Crafts was to be our only guest. Meanwhile, a touching surprise was in store for us. Mr. Antoni Gordon, the manager of the Polish Restaurant, sent over a full-course traditional Christmas Eve supper, along with three Polish waiters. Knowing that the President has a Steinway in his suite, the Restaurant's orchestra came over toward the end of the supper and played Polish Christmas carols for us. We were all moved to tears.

Never in my entire life have I seen so many presents, letters, and telegrams as poured in on the President from every part of the United States. The sitting room was jammed literally ceiling high with gift packages, making it impossible for anybody even to turn around in it. When Anetka and I unwrapped this mountain of presents to show them to the President, half of the room was littered with colored tissues and ribbons. The poor chambermaid retreated in awed wonder at sight of the fantastic pile of boxes and paper.

It was no joke for me either. For five solid days and nights I had to be signing for messages and packages. No chance of getting dressed, bathed, or going down for some nourishment, because the bell kept ringing every minute to announce a new messenger and a new gift.

Terribly depressed and sad though the President is, he remembered each of us with a present. Nor did he forget fettered Poland—witness the beautiful speech he broadcast on Leon Cieciuch's Polish Hour over radio station WHOM. The President's address impressed me so deeply that I'm copying its most striking passages into my diary:

"My dearly beloved fellow countrymen: I turn to you with a heart seized with pain at the thought of the sufferings of our nation, but full of trust and faith that God is with us, to break the Christmas Eve wafer with you in the spirit of brotherliness.

"When the Star of Bethlehem appeared in the firmament, the simple shepherds followed it until they arrived at the lowly stable to pay humble tribute to the Divine Infant. To us that Star of Bethlehem today is faith in our beloved Poland. . . . Her majesty, which our enemies are vainly attempting to desecrate, shines in all its glory amidst the ruins and misery, radiates in a heavenly brightness from the pale faces of those who are of their own free will giving up their lives in a sacred sacrifice so that She, that beloved Poland of ours, might not perish!

"Poland shall not perish because she is immortal! Poland shall not perish because millions of her true sons shield her buckler-like with their heroic bosoms. She shall not perish because she is needed by the world, by civilization, by the freedom of peoples. She shall not perish because she will live in our hearts for all eternity.

"On this Christmas our grieved thoughts and our painfilled hearts hasten into space across the broad ocean to those who have seated themselves around the Christmas Eve table. That table does not tempt the eye by an abundance of courses; perhaps even a loaf of dry bread did not find its way to each to appease hunger at least on this one day, but over every Polish home, in the village and in the city, in our motherland or in exile, hovers the flaming crown of martyrdom. Its hues are those of the Polish flag; in it glitter the diamonds of the tears of innocent mothers and children and the rubies of the generous blood of fallen heroes.

"That is why we approach this Christmas Eve table with profound humility, with a feeling of admiration and warmest gratitude, to assure all Poles in the world who have sat down to this table that we give them our hearts as a gift and that we vow to bring them help in accordance with our power and means."

Then follows a vibrant appeal for contributions to the Polish National Council for relief in occupied Poland. And here again the President's concluding words:

"The time of my earthly pilgrimage is running out, but I am grateful to the Supreme Deity that He permitted me to come here, to this free soil of the United States, that He granted me the strength still to serve Poland, still to say these few words to you. If these words have reached your hearts, give expression to it by speeding your contributions to help Polish children!

"Forgive me, if on this day of celebration I have not conveyed to you until the end of my speech my warmest wishes for your happiness, if I have perhaps abused your patience, if I again appeal not only to your hearts, soliciting new donations. . . .

"But forgive me in the name of that holy love of Poland, the country of your fathers and forefathers, whom I shall serve faithfully until the end of my days, as long as my strength lasts, as long as God on high wills it!"

January, 1941. Sylwin and I began the year 1941 with a trip. We've been on the go all month. I'm snatching a few free minutes to get at least a bare outline of what we experienced down on paper because this American tempo leaves me very little time for writing.

Our first stop was in Chicago where we attended the deliberations of the Polish National Council, headed by Censor Swietlik. I was greatly impressed by the speeches and proposals of the members of the Council, every word of which betrayed a deep concern over the need of bringing help to the Polish Nation. Taking advantage of my stay in the windy city I visited the magnificent museum of the Polish Roman Catholic Union which is being maintained with such piety by its worthy custodian, Mr. Haiman. I paid a visit to the biggest Polish women's organization in the United States—The Polish Women's Alliance of America, whose president, Mrs. Honorata Wolowska, received me very cordially and took me around her entire realm. I was dazzled by the Alliance's set-up, the outstanding organization of its offices and warehouses. How sumptuous it all is in comparison with Europe. It seems incredible that one woman should be able to cope with all the problems of an organization numbering sixty-five thousand. I can only marvel at Mrs. Wolowska's inexhaustible energy and will power.

Wherever we went, we were welcomed very warmly, because Sylwin came to represent Paderewski who unfortunately no longer has the strength to participate as he used to in Polish-American conventions and deliberations.

This has been a busy month. Four days in Chicago, two days in Detroit, a trip to Pittsburgh where we attended the exercises commemorating Paderewski's eightieth birthday and the golden anniversary of his artistic activity in the United States, a mass at Father Nowicki's Saint Pankracy Church in Chicago, a mass at Father Sonenfeld's Church in Pittsburgh, a visit to the Academy of the Sisters of Nazareth at Bellevue, a meeting of all the women's committees of Pittsburgh held at the Falcons' Building—all this will remain inscribed in golden letters in my heart as one of the richest memories of my life. When I go back to a free Poland, I should like to tell my compatriots what a reservoir of good will and concrete help they have on this side of the Atlantic.

Now that I have gotten to know the "Polonia" of both East and West, now that I have had a chance to observe the respect, love, and devotion it feels for its "Spiritual Leader," as Paderewski is generally called, I can appreciate how fully Americans of Polish descent reciprocate his faith and trust in them.

Between trips we stopped in New York on January 7th to attend a luncheon at the Lotos Club for Paderewski, represented by his sister. Among the speakers were Mayor La Guardia, Mr. Frederick Steinway, Miss Dorothy Thompson.

Mrs. Anne O'Hare McCormick. Sylwin read a letter from the President thanking the gathering for the honor. Poor Mrs. Wilkonska didn't enjoy the meal one bit because she knew she would have to make a speech of appreciation in reply to all the addresses. When one stops to think that she's eighty-four years old and had never in her life made a speech in public, one must marvel at how she scored a big hit with the Americans. They were enchanted with her sense of humor, which is something highly prized in this country.

The President's absence is the only shadow over the enjoyment we derived from these tributes to him. He's so weak that he delegates Sylwin to attend every function in his name. Nevertheless, the President doesn't rest at all. As a matter of fact, he continues to lead a very exhausting life. Not a day passes that he doesn't receive several delegations in addition to personal friends. Furthermore, he is constantly writing all sorts of appeals and personally attends to his large correspondence. It's really too much even for a young man and the pace is beginning to tell on him. What worries me particularly is that he chokes on his food increasingly often. Dr. Jachimowicz is very insistent on his leaving for Florida at once. However, it's hard to talk the President into going, for he has no desire to vacation in Florida. He likes his old habits and would rather go to Paso Robles in California. But a trip to the West Coast would be both tiresome and costly.

Florida Sojourn

Palm Beach, Florida—February 11, 1941. The President, his sister, Sylwin, and Franciszek arrived by train on February 4th. Anetka, Dr. Jachimowicz, and myself were driven down by Kollupajlo several days earlier to prepare everything and make the President's stay as comfortable as possible.

Our villa has been leased from Mrs. Stecker who went to a great deal of trouble to take care of every detail making for comfort. Cheerful and fairly glistening with cleanliness, the house has several porches, a huge glass enclosed veranda, two gardens profusely abloom, and a beautiful view of the lake from the dining room window that reminds us of Riond Bosson. Just a few steps away is the sea. In spite of all this, the President is dissatisfied and Mrs. Wilkonska doesn't like Florida. Neither of them says anything because their innate tact does not permit them to hurt anyone, but they clearly do not approve of this Florida sojourn.

February 15, 1941. I am in an awful quandary. The President asked Mr. Kollupajlo today when Sylwin, who's in New York, is to return. He then instructed Mr. Kollupajlo to get tickets for a return trip to New York! It's impossible to defy the President, but we did prevail upon him not to decide the date of our departure until Sylwin's return.

February 17, 1941. Sylwin managed to persuade the President to remain here at least another week. He's trying a strategy of delay, because the President would never consent to stay if he thought it was for a longer period. The President doesn't know it but Dr. Jachimowicz is very emphatic about his staying here until May for a prolonged rest cure.

Good news! Sylwin got a letter from Colonel Valloton from Switzerland informing him that Simonne Girond de Pourtales's sentence of September 12, 1940, for defamation of Sylwin's character had been upheld by the appellate court on January 30, 1941. The President was very pleased when we passed on to him this bit of information.

February 20, 1941. We feel all the time as if we were about to leave; the President keeps talking about going back to New York. I try to do everything I can to get him to relax and regain his health. Mr. Kollupajlo takes him and Mrs. Wilkonska for long drives, inevitably climaxed by a halt at an orange grove where they both drink quantities of fresh orange juice. Visitors drop in by the dozen, but the President absolutely refuses to receive anyone. The only exception was Mrs. Edward T. Stotesbury, who is the first lady of Palm Beach. Not only did he see her one afternoon, but he even accepted her invitation to a "Testimonial Concert to Honor Ignace Jan Paderewski on the Golden Anniversary of His American Debut" at her residence "El Mirasol" on March 8th.

Fortunately, Miss Crafts has come down and enlivens our luncheons by her frequent presence. Tade Styka is also down at Palm Beach for a few days. The President likes him a lot and told us to invite him to all our luncheons and dinners during his stay. But our prize guest is a baby alligator which Anetka received from Mrs. Albert Sidney and which it would be difficult not to mention. Anetka is delighted with it and carries it around with her, but I have such an aversion for the creature I feel like running out of the room whenever I see it. Today Anetka had the bright idea of letting it loose on the dining table as we sat drinking our demi tasse. The alligator commenced its journey among the cups, pausing to look around every so often. Naturally, I ran away from the table and sought refuge on a window seat. The President, whose habit it is to keep his hands on the table, drumming out something or other with all five fingers, held them motionless at sight of the approaching 'gator. I appealed to the President to remove his hands from the table, but he left them there, inspecting the reptile the while. My heart almost stopped beating for fear the alligator might bite the President's hand, but a few moments later we were all staring in incredulous amazement. The alligator had moved right up to the President's hand, which didn't even quiver, pulled out a webbed foot and unmistakably had begun to stroke the President's fingers. Then it drew even closer, rested its tiny head against Paderewski's hand and remained motionless. That wasn't the first time I'd seen the President reveal such a strange attraction for animals.

March 9, 1941. Yesterday's reception at "El Mirasol" was spectacular. Unhappily the President has become unaccustomed to such well-attended gatherings at which he has to say a few pleasant words to each guest introduced to him. Although Mrs. Stotesbury had him ensconced in a special armchair from which he didn't budge all evening, he's tired and worn out today. He really shouldn't participate in such functions any more.

Nevertheless, he has announced today that he is definitely going back to New York, that he will not stay here any longer, not even until Sylwin returns. Mr. Kollupajlo and I are in a fine pickle—we wired Sylwin an S.O.S.

March 20, 1941. At last the President is a little more animated. He went calling on Mrs. Eleanor Roosevelt, who is also in Florida just now, and returned pleased with the hourlong chat he had with her. He said she is as charming as ever and a great lady. Franciszek, who accompanied Paderewski, is of the same opinion. What met with his favor is the fact that she was waiting in front of the house, without servants, to welcome Paderewski.

For once there is no longer any talk of going back to New York. God alone knows how many subterfuges were required to prolong the President's stay here. He could not get used to Florida and he is displeased about Sylwin's absence. He's always sending Sylwin out somewhere to represent him and then he keeps asking when Sylwin will be back.

General Sikorski is in America to confer with Roosevelt, and Paderewski has assigned Sylwin to the General for the duration of his visit. In a few days now Sikorski will come down here to spend Easter with the President. Mr. Stanislaw Mikolajczyk is coming, too, to give the President an official report on the activity of the National Council in his capacity as Executive Vice President of that body. Paderewski is still President of the National Council in London.

Tom Majewski and Jurek Kwasniewski are also around. The latter is a young seaman who took advantage of a brief leave from the Polish merchant marine to fly down to Palm Beach.

Easter—April 13, 1941. I had quite a siege of anxiety before
the arrival of General Sikorski, his aide, Capt. Zamoyski, and
Mr. Mikolajczyk, whom I hadn't known before. They are
staying at "El Mirasol." On leaving Palm Beach, Mrs:
Stotesbury placed her entire house at Paderewski's disposal
for the period of General Sikorski's visit. What worried me
most was feeding our guests in a manner the President would
consider proper. How was I to prepare the traditional Polish
Easter hallowfare with a colored cook, without access to any
stores—for everything is ordered by telephone here—and
last but not least, with my culinary aptitude, which doesn't
even include scrambling eggs?

Obviously, no one was happier than I to see the huge
crate which arrived from New York by mail simultaneously
with General Sikorski and which bore the telltale return address of the Polish Restaurant.

Headed by the President, our entire household turned out
to greet our visitors at the station on Friday. There was
nothing official about the meeting and as soon as the introductions were over, the gathering was like a family reunion.
Arriving at the President's villa, we sat down without further
ado to lunch in the dining room. Franciszek opened the crate
and lo and behold! there was a complete Easter repast sent
by that nice Mr. Gordon.

When I commenced pulling the delicacies out of the crate,
and the General noticed the painted eggs, the multicolored
mazurki, the coils of sausage, and the luscious ham I was
placing on the sideboard, he jumped up and lent a hand in
bringing all these gifts into the dining room, so that in no
time we had set a truly Polish traditional Easter table. The
President was deeply moved and said, "What a good man
Mr. Gordon is."

All day yesterday the President, Sikorski, and Mikolajczyk conferred on matters of vital importance. In the afternoon newsreel pictures were taken at El Mirasol by Paramount.

This morning General Sikorski attended Easter church

services and at 1:30 arrived with Capt. Zamoyski and Mikolajczyk for our joint Easter dinner. In the course of the meal, the President lifted his wine glass for a toast, rose from his chair and addressed the General as follows:

"Dear and beloved General, Commander-in-Chief of our Armed Forces, and Leader of our Heroic Nation! My emotion does not permit me to deliver a speech. Therefore, I wish to express in a few heartfelt words my deepest joy and gratitude not only for your coming to me, but above all and especially because you have taken into your strong and firm grasp the helm of the government of the Republic and because you have assumed the entire burden of responsibility for the fate of Poland.

"In this difficult historic task of yours, may you derive support and comfort from the consciousness that the whole nation back home and we, all scattered by fate in foreign lands, and our beloved army, stand humbly and loyally by you, ready at every moment for the sacrifices which Poland or you in her holy name may demand of us.

"May god bless you and may He help you bear this burden of our trust and our faith in you and further guide the destiny of Poland which we have confidently placed in your worthy hands."

In a voice quivering with emotion the General replied in these words:

"Most revered, dear, beloved Mr. President! In the name of the government, which is not an Emigré Government but a sovereign legal government of the Republic, enjoying the full political and moral support of the nation, in the name of the Polish Army, not only of the soldiers fighting abroad but also of those who fight unarmed in every phase of daily life, and also of that soldier who, though he be temporarily physically disabled, is nonetheless spiritually with us—in a word, in the name of Fighting Poland, together with the President of the Republic who has empowered me to do so, I express to you, most venerable and beloved Mr. President, in this, for me, historic moment, my deepest joy that I have found you in good health, in even better health than you were on the occasion of the solemn inauguration of the National Council.

"Your moral authority is tremendous and recognized by the entire world.

"With all my heart I hope you will see very soon the triumph of our holy cause in the ceaseless service of which you have spent your industrious meritorious life.

"Always and steadfastly you have fought for a Great and Just Poland, for such a Poland we too are ready to sacrifice all.

"I extend these wishes not only as Head of the Government and as Commander-in-Chief, I extend them likewise as your old friend, wholeheartedly loyal to you these two decades, who has always regarded you as the highest symbol of those lofty principles of justice and democratic freedom on which we are rebuilding the greatness of our country."

Then the President proposed a toast to Mr. Mikolajczyk, thanking him for the way in which he had presided over the National Council in Paderewski's absence. He requested Mikolajczyk to take back to the National Council and to all its members his best wishes for continued fruitful work. To which Mikolajczyk replied: "I came to you deliberately, Mr. President, to express to you in the name of the National Council the tribute of our profoundest respect, and to report to you about our labors. I am happy that I can assure you that the National Council is co-operating in complete harmony with the President of the Republic and the Government in the spirit of the program of work and aims outlined by you in your address before the inaugural session of the National Council. Even though you do not at present participate personally in our work, we are proud and happy that you preside over us, knowing that in an emergency we can always turn to you for your enlightened advice."

Before we had finished eating, radio engineers started setting up equipment in the drawing room in preparation for the broadcast which Paderewski was to make at 6:15 over the National Broadcasting Company's coast-to-coast hook-up.

Our villa is on the main road and not a day passes that a number of cars do not slow down or make a full stop in the hope they might catch a glimpse of Paderewski. It's Riond Bosson all over again, just like the days when strangers parked their cars in front of the "Villa Paderewski," photo-

graphing the house and patiently waiting for the President
to put in an appearance. And now, the appearance of a radio
truck has created a mild sensation around here.

To make my record of our first American Easter complete, here is the text of the President's broadcast:

"I consider it a personal privilege to participate in this broadcast under the auspices of the Council of Democracy. It is a great
honor to represent Poland on such an occasion. Poland was the
first nation, the first state to resist the Nazi aggression by force of
arms. We have set the example. It is an example of patriotism, of
national pride and honor, of attachment to liberty and to democratic
principles.

"My country has endured and is enduring the burden of enemy
occupation, but Poland is striking back by means of her armed
forces and will strike back until the day of a common victory. The
heroic resistance of Greece and the brave reply of the Yugoslavs
to the barbarous aggressor provide further evidence of the sanctity
of these immortal principles. All the nations which have become
the victims of German aggression are at present forming a united
front under the leadership of the British Empire.

"In this capacity we solemnly proclaim our solidarity and
unshaken determination to continue this war effort, to endure its
barbarous cruelty, to make any sacrifice in order to save the world
from moral destruction, from shame and slavery.

"We are also taking this opportunity to denounce the lies
of German propaganda which cynically pretends that the so-called
new order in Europe, based upon German domination, is capable of
satisfying the invaded countries, of meeting with their approval or
of finding them resigned to its acceptance.

"The only way to assure the democratic system to nations in
Europe is that which has already been chosen by Poland and again
set by that country as an example for others to follow: Through
their respective governments in London, Poland and Czechoslovakia
made a solemn declaration on November 11th, 1940, proclaiming
the federation of free, peace-loving nations as the only way to safeguard democracy in Europe and to assure mutual protection against
any aggression.

"May I be permitted to express my ardent wish and sincere
hope that this example may be followed by other nations in order

thus to establish a real democratic basis for a new, happy, and prosperous Europe."

General Sikorski's arrival in Palm Beach evoked considerable social interest. Invitations poured in. Of course, because the General is here for such a brief spell — he's leaving tomorrow — acceptance of them is out of the question. The one invitation he did accept was that of the Albert Sidneys. The General met Mrs. Sidney, who is a Pole, years ago in Paris when she was a youngster. Her mother, Countess Jodko-Narkiewicz, a typical Polish matriarch from the eastern borderland has become friendly with Mrs. Wilkonska here at Palm Beach. Throughout our entire stay the Sidney family has given us countless sincere and tactful proofs of friendship.

This flying visit of General Sikorski and his colleagues was a pleasant interlude for us all, but it especially impressed the President in that it emphasized how very much the Polish Government in London and the General himself reckoned with his person. Furthermore, the picture of the current political situation which the General painted for the President while obtaining his advice with regard to the government's future policy has again thrown Paderewski into the very center of political activity, which has had a beneficial effect upon his morale.

God Will Not Deny His Blessing

New York — May 9, 1941. We are all glad to be back at the Buckingham at last. Although Florida is a lovely state and the climate is surely better than that of New York (which Mrs. Wilkonska definitely denies), the President felt out of things in Florida and the light carefree mood so characteristic of that place did not suit him one whit.

This time we all returned by train. Passing through

Washington the poor President, who is always conscientious, was up and dressed by 11 A.M. because he was being met at the station by Ambassador Ciechanowski and our dear Minister Michal Kwapiszewski.

May, 1941. After the quiet and relatively orderly life we led in Florida we've returned to feverish activity. I'm back at my welfare work to which I can't devote as much time as I should. I work only from nine till noon at the Social Welfare Bureau in the building of the Polish Consulate. The Bureau is headed by Aleksander Znamiecki, who worked with Paderewski during the last war.

We have two regular daily guests. One is Countess Helena Morsztyn (a Polish pianist of international fame), to whom Mrs. Wilkonska has transferred all the friendship she once had for Helena's brother Paul, who died at sea of a heart attack during the evacuation of the Polish Government from France to England. The other is Roman de Majewski. A director of Steinway and Sons, he had a piano placed in Mrs. Wilkonska's bedroom and thereby earned her undying gratitude. Roman is an ideal friend—ever cordial and considerate. He's the only one who has access to the President at all times.

Maurice Pate has been received by the President several times. He has completely won Mrs. Wilkonska's heart by his sincerity and friendliness. He touched me too—kissing me with disarming simplicity and calling me Aniela with the accent of a Pole, after so many years of not seeing me. Whenever Maurice calls, all of us, even the President, make a special effort to show our friendship and gratitude for his endeavors on behalf of Poland as director of the Commission for Polish Relief. How often have I heard it remarked that the man deserves to have a statue erected in his honor in Poland in appreciation of his loving and self-sacrificing labor for Poland.

Another person singled out by the President who has captivated Mrs. Wilkonska and myself is Mrs. Vernon

Kellogg, head of the Paderewski Testimonial Fund. Mrs. Kellogg speaks of Poland with such affection you'd swear she had been born there. She thinks the world of Paderewski and is the founder and the guiding spirit of the American committee which has been formed to commemorate in his eightieth year the golden jubilee of Paderewski's artistic activity in America. Local committees have been formed in all the big cities of the United States and have organized or are organizing thousands of musical tributes to the President, the proceeds of which are to be earmarked for Polish relief according to the President's wishes. The membership of these committees reads like a miniature edition of *Who's Who* and the *Social Register*. Our own Elizabeth Crafts is secretary of the national committee, whose honorary chairmen are Ambassador Robert Woods Bliss and Walter Damrosch, and whose first vice-chairman is none other than Hugh Gibson.

In addition to everything else, Mrs. Kellogg is beautiful. It gives me pleasure just to look at her, and I was quite thrilled when this very distinguished lady, who is older than I, asked me to call her Charlotte.

Every evening we go down to eat at the Automat across the street. The food is good and Mrs. Wilkonska enjoys the self-service, which is something new to us Europeans. The President's dinner (as well as his lunch) is brought in to him from the restaurant downstairs and he eats it alone in his sitting room. After dinner, Sylwin and Kollupajlo drop in for a little while to report to the President how they have carried out his instructions. Neither of them is around in the evenings. The traditional rubber of bridge is also a thing of the past. The President is too tired. But he is very fond of solitaire, which Mrs. Wilkonska and myself take turns laying out before him countless times. He frequently dozes off in the process and we patiently wait until he awakens before going on with the game. But once the President wakes up, he moves the cards around with such lightning speed, I can't possibly keep up with him. When the President is more animated, I regale him with gossip culled during the day, carefully observing his reactions to make sure I'm not boring him. Never up to now have I dared to engage him in such conversation, but I want to do what I can to cheer him up. When Sylwin is away he feels neglected and is forever asking me whether he will be back soon. At sight of Sylwin he perks up and is contented when after their conversation and before he retires for the night, Sylwin lays out a game of solitaire for him.

Once I asked the President jokingly whether he had ever in his life been angry with Sylwin. Paderewski reflected for some time, then answered: "No, never—only once with your brother."

May 27, 1941. Today the President tendered a reception to representatives of the clergy so that they might meet Mikolajczyk, who has remained in the United States on an extended visit to make a tour of the large Polish communities and to become acquainted with the "Polonia" and its organizations.

The clergymen were headed by Monsignor B. Puchalski. Among the lay guests were Mikolajczyk and Dr. Teofil Starzynski, President of the Polish Falcons. Mrs. Wilkonska, Sylwin, and I did the honors for the President who did not feel well enough to attend. Following the dinner, a group of older priests who had worked with Paderewski during the last war and had maintained friendly relations with him through the years, went up to his suite. The President was delighted to see them and made the following little speech to them!

"Very Reverend Fathers who are my dear and faithful friends! I am exceedingly happy that I am able to receive you here today, that you have deigned to come here to me. Today's well-attended gathering is the best proof that when it is a question of the national cause, the Polish clergy is always ready for generous and productive work.

"Missing among you is your beloved leader, the Most Reverend Meritorious Bishop Paul Rhode. As in my case, age has limited his strength and the possibilities of his active participation in the work to be done. So I appeal to you, his worthy successors, to take upon your shoulders, to grasp in your vigorous hands the leadership of Polish priesthood in their godly labors so that you might bring back to life and action the well-deserving Alliance of Roman Catholic Priests. We have no time to lose. So work hard for our great cause; work with faith and God will not deny you His blessing."

We were very sorry we could not invite all the priests up, but the President's small sitting room could never have accommodated the hundred and some guests. Although Paderewski radiated happiness after the visit of the clergy, he was extremely tired.

May 31, 1941. This is Anetka's and my name day. Everybody has forgotten the occasion and we haven't reminded anyone of it. I'm especially concerned about the President, the state of whose health has long been a source of deep anxiety to me. Sylwin doesn't see anything wrong. He attributes it all to Paderewski's advanced age. Sylwin believes the President must be all right if despite his weakness he works as intensely as he does. It is still around Paderewski that all our political and welfare activities revolve. Not a day passes that the President does not issue some sort of appeal or dictate letters. Sylwin is away half the time, representing Paderewski. Only Mrs. Wilkonska and myself see this tremendous difference in the President's health and although we don't talk about it, I'm sure we feel the same way.

Several times a day Mrs. Wilkonska says to me, "Aniela, don't leave Ignace alone." It's difficult to explain to her that the President is not alone, that Franciszek is always at hand in the next room and that when he goes out to eat, I sit in his room, because I know by now when the President wishes company and when he prefers to be by himself. But Mrs. Wilkonska will not understand this and insists we both stay with him all day, which I'm positive the President does not like.

What disturbs me most is the President's lack of appetite. I sometimes try to coax him into eating, but I see he feels an aversion for food. As soon as he eats or drinks something, he starts choking. Meanwhile, I can see the President is losing weight and is growing weaker from day to day. It seems to me he needs a thorough cure of some kind. But there is no one to talk to in New York. Everybody's in a hurry, everybody's busy with something or other, engrossed in world events, the war, politics, and gossip.

June 22, 1941. Nobody slept last night. At two in the morning we received the news that Germany had attacked Russia. The President's reaction was: "Whom the gods would destroy they first make mad." All night we fiddled with the radio, too excited to go to bed.

Today the President is going to Oak Ridge, New Jersey, to address a rally of Polish war veterans on the occasion of the twentieth anniversary of the founding of their organization. Last night's news has furnished him with plenty of subject matter for his speech.

However, I don't see how the President will be able to go through with such a tiring public appearance. Franciszek summed up the situation when he said: "There is no sense to the President's going, but you can't oppose the President."

We Have Lost the Heart of Poland

(*Letter from Aniela Strakacz to Helena Liibke.*)
1396 Park Lane
Pelham Manor, New York
July 15, 1941.

Dearest Leniutka:

I learned so very late of this opportunity to send you a letter to Switzerland that I don't know whether I can manage to write you as fully as I'd like to about the President's last days. Besides, it won't be easy for me to turn my mind back to those difficult and painful moments we experienced.

On Sunday, June 22nd, special exercises were held at the Polish National Alliance Summer Camp in Oak Ridge, N. J. to commemorate the twentieth anniversary of the Association of Polish War Veterans (members of General Haller's American-recruited army). The President made the trip from New York to Oak Ridge to address the Veterans and the many thousands of Polish-Americans who, following the field mass, awaited his arrival at the camp. The heat that day was unbearable, which made me afraid the trip would be too much for the President. I was all the more uneasy because Franciszek had told me two days earlier with real horror in his voice—you know yourself the President never confided in anyone—that for the first time in his life he heard the President say when mention was made of the trip to Oak Ridge: "Franciszek, I no longer have the strength." These words cut right into my heart and filled me with misgiving.

The President rode with Sylwin and Franciszek in a convertible automobile so that he could speak without getting out. Mrs. Wilkonska, Helena Morsztyn, Anetka, and myself followed in Mrs. Albert Sidney's car. We rode for more than an hour and a half through slightly rolling, pleasantly wooded country. The first glimpse of the President provoked such enthusiasm in the camp that I thought the crowd would crush his car. Women with small children in their arms tried to force their way through the throng to get as close as possible to the President. People kissed his hands. Those who couldn't get that close tried at least to touch a piece of his sleeve or clothing and kiss that. None of us suspected that it was the President's last public appearance, that the triumphant greeting was at the same time a parting.

As the President spoke, the audience of many thousands stood motionless in the broiling sun, their reverence for him plainly marked on their faces. His speech over, both cars drove out of the thickest part of the crowd. The heat continued terrific and we were all dripping with perspiration. Suddenly the President stopped in front of a small house. At first I didn't know what had happened. It developed that the President wanted a drink of water. Anticipating his thirst, I had brought with me a thermos filled with red wine and water. When some kind people brought out a glass of iced water, I jumped out of our car, ran up to the President with my thermos and delicately suggested he drink some of the wine and water instead. He refused, downing the iced water in one gulp. In view of the crowd that had again started gathering, I didn't dare insist and hastily withdrew.

The President returned from Oak Ridge pleased but very tired. That evening he didn't feel well. Dr. Jachimowicz came and diagnosed his indisposition as indigestion.

The following Friday (June 27th) at noon the President was taken ill. He didn't tell anyone he was sick but we noticed he was feverish and very flushed. Dr. Jachimowicz was away in Washington. As soon as Sylwin telephoned him, he flew back to New York, and from that moment until the end did not leave the President, snatching some sleep in the sitting room of the President's suite. Two American physicians called in by Dr. Jachimowicz for consultation (Dr. Lincoln, a lung specialist, and Dr. Murphy, an internist) agreed on a diagnosis of pneumonia. The President's temperature was now over 104°. The doctor gave him several of Dr. Jaworski's injections, a supply of which we had brought to America. Two male nurses took turns at the President's bedside night and day, while Franciszek never left his room next to the President's, ready for every call. The President received the best care available. Everybody did his utmost to save the President's life. Both nurses, although they had known the President only these three days, wept when he died.

On Saturday there was a marked improvement in the President's condition. His temperature came down to 99.6°. Dr. Jachimowicz was hopeful the President would weather the crisis because his heart and pulse were good and his constitution rugged. But the President had a terribly poor appetite and whenever he tried to swallow something, he'd choke and return the food. He seemed to have lost a lot of weight.

Sunday the 29th the President felt still better. He seemed to be out of danger. The state of his health was so satisfactory that at ten in the morning Sylwin left for the dedicatory exercises marking the opening of Paderewski Park, founded in New Britain, Connecticut, by Monsignor L. Bojnowski. In the face of such an improvement in the President's condition, Sylwin suggested I accompany him, but somehow I didn't feel that confident, and as Mrs. Wilkonska was also uneasy and nervous, I decided to stay. In spite of the best medical and nursing care obtainable, I didn't want to leave him alone. My Lord, how fortunate that I didn't go! I would not have seen him alive again.

That morning Franciszek was in a good mood because the President had jokingly rubbed his chin to indicate the need of a shave. "So I shaved the President!" Franciszek boomed jovially.

Around noon I went into his bedroom: he was sitting in bed, propped up by several pillows. He greeted me with his radiant smile and kept on smiling, his glance following my head. I finally realized I had forgotten to remove a lavendar kerchief and four curlers from my hair, which must have presented an interesting sight. You have no idea, Leniutka dear, how my heart contracted as I looked at our haggard President. I kept thinking, if only there was something I could do to help him.

The Doctor told me that now the President would absolutely have to be fed forcibly, that he was on the right road if only he would eat and not lose his strength. I cooked some farina, the President even began to eat it with relish, but he suddenly started to choke, the farina boiled over in his throat and came back with a terrific quantity of black phlegm. Never in my life have I seen anything like it. It must have relieved him, because he began to breathe more easily. Not till after two did Mrs. Wilkonska, Anetka, Mr. Kollupajlo, and I go downstairs for lunch. We hadn't finished eating when Franciszek came down after us. He was self-controlled as usual, and said quietly, "The Doctor asks you to come right away because there's something wrong with the President." But the expression on his face made my blood chill. To avoid frightening Mrs. Wilkonska, Anetka and Mr. Kollupajlo rose slowly to escort her up, while I dashed out with Franciszek for the elevator.

Entering the sickroom promptly at three, I saw the President lying inert in the arms of deathly pale Dr. Jachimowicz. The President's face was blue, his tongue protruded, his hands and feet had turned black. The way both men looked, I didn't know which one would expire first. "Is he dying?" I asked the Doctor in a low voice. The Doctor nodded and his white lips whispered desperately that Paderewski was dying because he was choking with phlegm, he might choke to death any minute. And he continued, "Just look how his heart is beating evenly, his pulse is good, but he's being killed by the phlegm in his chest and throat."

A cold fear gripped me: Mother of God, the President is so pious, so religious and he's dying without a priest. And Sylwin is away. "Doctor," I whispered, "I have some holy water from Jasna Gora."

"Yes," he replied, "that's about the only thing that could help him now."

I ran to my room to fetch the miraculous Czestochowa water which I'd gotten from Granny in Warsaw and which was the only thing I'd taken from my home when I left Poland before the war. On the way to my room I recalled that the top was on so tight Franciszek had been unable to open the bottle once when Mrs. Wilkonska asked for some of the water to relieve her aching eyes. I grabbed the bottle, tried to open it, and wonder of wonders, the metal top worked loose at the very first twist. The Doctor took the bottle from me and with a sure hand poured a draught of holy water down the President's throat. I made a sign of the cross and prayed on my knees that he might live at least until the priest and Sylwin arrived. The doctor propped the President up in bed and I sprinkled his bluish fingers with the holy water. In a moment the President started choking and again got rid of an unimaginable quantity of black phlegm. Gradually the blue color receded from his face, hands, and legs and his nails took on a more natural hue. We breathed easy — saved by the holy water of Czestochowa!

Mr. Kollupajlo ordered oxygen, which was brought in ten minutes. Simultaneously, the radio announced the President was already receiving oxygen. We learned about it from Mrs. Schelling and Tom Majewski, who hurried over to the hotel as soon as they heard the report and stayed with Mrs. Wilkonska and Anetka in the next room. Mrs. Wilkonska did not enter the sickroom at all.

At long last the priest came, summoned by Mr. Kollupajlo. As he administered the last rites to the President I knelt on the threshold. Having annointed the President, the priest made a hurried departure, leaving me his address. The President fell asleep. Anetka and I knelt at either side of his bed, waiting for him to awaken. Around 5 P.M. he opened his eyes and seeing us both next to him, took my hand and kissed it, and then took Anetka's hand with his other hand. Holding us both, he kissed each alternately. When Anetka tried to stop him, I made a sign to her not to oppose the President. Then we kissed his cheeks and forehead and the

President kissed us on both cheeks. He couldn't move his own head because he had the oxygen tubes inserted in his nose. So he held on to our hands, smiling without words (he could no longer talk). I don't know whether he was bidding us farewell or whether he was merely thanking us the way he always did, as you well know, whenever anyone showed him the slightest kindness or courtesy. Then Franciszek came up and asked if the President would care for some champagne. "Please." That was the last word the President uttered. He drank some champagne with appetite and fell asleep again. The doctor told us not to delude ourselves, that he expected another attack in a few hours, that there would be three altogether, that if he survived them, he'd come through, that this night would be decisive.

I was anxiously awaiting Sylwin's return, because there had been no means of letting him know about the President's relapse. We had called the parish house in New Britain but there was no answer as everyone had left for the dedicatory ceremonies in the park. Around eight o'clock Sylwin came back. The President was still asleep, breathing in the oxygen, but there was an ugly gurgling sound in his chest. No sooner did Sylwin enter the President's room than a second attack started, much lighter. But this time the poisonous phlegm blocking the respiratory passages was not thrown off. The President failed to open his eyes again. I kept my hand on his pulse, the doctor listened to his heart—and so we stayed at his bedside. The pulse grew weaker and when the heart stopped beating, we looked at each other and bowed our heads. It was one minute to eleven, Sunday night, June 29th.

There was no change in the color of the President's face because it had been deathly pale already for several hours. I folded his arms, Anetka gave him her rosary and a picture of Our Lady of Czestochowa with the White Eagle (I'm sending you a duplicate of the one the President's holy hands held in the coffin). A few moments after death, the President's tired face smoothed out completely. Not a single furrow showed, he seemed like an ivory sculpture—as calm as if he'd just fallen asleep. And at five o'clock he had had such strangely beautiful blue eyes when he looked at us, smiled at us, kissed us. I don't know whether the President had realized he was dying. He said something to me, but the whisper that came out of his constricted throat was so muffled that although I pressed my ear to his very lips, I could no longer make out anything.

The hotel, the strangeness of the place, made us feel horribly empty and desolate. Franciszek was in despair that there were no tapers to be lighted. I pulled out some candles I had brought from Riond Bosson and we lit them and placed them at the President's head. Franciszek blessed the President all over with holy water. Because it was Sunday night, everybody was away for the week-end. Our steadfast companions were Tom Majewski and that angel Peggy Schelling.

At two in the morning a coffin was delivered by Mr. Smolenski, a Pole who is the owner of a funeral establishment and a leader in his community in Brooklyn. We took the President's body down to Brooklyn to be embalmed so that he would remain as he is forever in a glass-covered casket to be seen by everyone when he goes back to Poland. But what next? We were frantic. You can't keep a body in a church in America. Just before the funeral Archbishop Spellman did make an exception for the President, but a churchman who had forty years service behind him had also just died and was occupying St. Patrick's Cathedral until his burial. Meanwhile they proposed a chapel in Brooklyn, terribly far away. We didn't want to leave the President any old place, alone and abandoned.

In our complete helplessness, the kind-hearted manager of our Hotel Buckingham, Mr. Donegan, came to us with a suggestion that we return the President to his suite in the hotel, to remain there as long as we wish, and placed the entire hotel at our disposal. A load fell from our minds: the President would return, he'd be with us. All day and night long the populace of New York—regardless of nationality, social class, or religion—streamed through the narrow corridors of the Buckingham to pay a last tribute to the President.

At five o'clock on Monday we brought the President back to the Buckingham. His sitting room was transformed into a beautiful chapel. The President lay in a casket that was covered only up to the knees. His hands, folded in prayer, held a rosary, a picture of St. Anthony which he always carried in his vest pocket and a picture of Our Lady of Czestochowa.

Wreath after wreath was brought into the hotel, all white and red flowers with white and red ribbons; their fragrance was so heavy in the unbearable heat that the Polish Army veterans mounting continuous guard kept fainting away. But our wonderful Mr. Donegan had thought about everything. He removed the hotel guests from our floor and placed all the rooms on it at our disposal. The elevators groaned under unaccustomed loads while the crowd flowed and flowed day and night. People stood in line, signed their names in the book, the police maintained order. Priests in one room, Sisters of Nazareth in another, police in a third, reporters in the fourth, Polish veterans in the fifth, and miscellaneous visitors in all the others, waited to pay their respects to Mrs. Wilkonska. Fearful of another death, we literally locked Mrs. Wilkonska in her room under the watchful eye of Helena Morsztyn, who flew in from Minneapolis. Elizabeth Crafts also cut short her vacation to return to New York. On the go twenty-four hours a day, in this inhuman heat, I wondered desperately whether Sylwin could stand the pace. It was to him everyone came with innumerable questions and problems. His face was a sickly gray-green.

Then the news came from our Embassy that President Roosevelt had decreed Paderewski was to be buried at Arlington Cemetery in Washington. In our hour of sorrow we felt a touch of pride that this supreme honor had befallen our President. The honors bestowed upon him cover our nation with glory! This is realized not only by the "Polonia" — they've always known here who Paderewski is — but also by all those Poles from Poland who hadn't appreciated his

greatness. Now at last they saw what Paderewski represented, not only for Poland, not only for the United States,
but, as Archbishop Spellman said in his eulogy in the cathedral, his death steeps the entire civilized world in mourning.

Although the transfer of the President to St. Patrick's
Cathedral was done privately, crowds lined the streets to
witness it, and new throngs entered the cathedral to pass by
his bier.

We returned from St. Patrick's Cathedral to the empty
sitting room. All that remained in it were the masses of
flowers which may not be kept in church. It's a funny thing,
we all noticed that the flowers had borne up wonderfully
under the heat all these days, but as soon as the President left,
they wilted in the twinkling of an eye. Nevertheless, American girls came in to spray each flower individually.

The rooms in the Buckingham felt horribly empty. We'd
slip out one by one and go to the cathedral, where we'd come
upon the others. Then we'd return together to the hotel, and
in a little while the scene of reunion at the cathedral would be
repeated.

The solemn mass in the cathedral was most impressive.
All the Polish clergy were there, presided over by Archbishop
Spellman, and the huge temple was overflowing with wor-
shippers. I shall never forget the exit from the cathedral,
with American soldiers presenting arms and holding the
Polish flag while an orchestra played Chopin's *Funeral March*.
I can't describe the funeral to you. There were too many
impressions. I can't remember the sequence of events. We
all walked to the railroad station directly in back of the car
in which only Mrs. Wilkonska rode with Helena Morsztyn.
Then we accompanied the President to Washington in the
private car, the one in which he had traveled during his last
concert tour. In the drawing room in which the piano used to
stand, they placed the President's casket draped in a Polish
flag with the white eagle, and banked with flowers. In the
next car were additional members of the funeral cortege.
Franciszek took me around the car to show me everything,

because I'd never seen the President's concert car before. They even gave us the same porters to take care of us, old John and Charles.

When the coffin was being removed from the funeral train in Washington, a storm was raging in all its fury.

Because of the great distance to the Polish Embassy, we all rode in cars. The veterans carried the President's body to the first floor where they placed it in the center of the huge reception room.

The following day we buried the President in Arlington Cemetery. The United States Army gave nineteen salvoes, the highest anyone other than a Chief of State can receive.

I've written you everything I could, Leniutka dearest. It was difficult for me to touch upon these painful memories. I've done it for you, and only for you.

There is such emptiness in our hearts. To Sylwin and myself, Paderewski's death is even more than the death of our own father.

"You will be close to the Heart of Poland," a fortune teller once told me. We have lost forever the Heart of Poland.

Your,
Aniela

Index

This index does not list references to Ignacy Jan Paderewski, the author, the author's husband, or her daughter. Nor does it, in general, list those persons about whom only casual mention is made in the text.

337